Gods in the Making

and Other Writings

by W.H. Church

A.R.E.® PRESS • VIRGINIA BEACH • VIRGINIA

Note to the reader:

Most of the selections from the Edgar Cayce readings appear in boldface type. The number following each reading is the file number assigned to the person or group for whom the reading was given. For example, 317-6 identifies the sixth reading given for the person who was assigned number 317.

All Cayce readings (over 14,000) are available for public inspection at the A.R.E. Library in Virginia Beach, Virginia.

ISBN 87604-148-9

The decorative motifs used throughout *Gods in the Making* are from original artwork by Nena von Leyden, for *Gautama, The Story of Lord Buddha,* as told by Shakuntala Masani, and published in America by The MacMillan Company, New York, in 1956. The author gratefully acknowledges permission from Blackie & Son Limited, Glasgow, Scotland, the original publishers, for their use.

Printed in the U.S.A.

Table of Contents

To all of the Tirados,
present and departed—and others yet to come!

Foreword

This little volume of essays represents a selection of the more popular pieces I have published in the pages of *The A.R.E. Journal* during the past twelve years or so. And for added measure, I have included an as-yet-unpublished essay, *The Music of the Spheres,* in which I have pulled together some philosophical observations on the ever-popular subject of astrology, as presented in the psychic readings of the late Edgar Cayce.

My unswerving aim, as a journalist and researcher who has glimpsed in the Cayce legacy its extraordinary significance for our times, has been to validate and interpret some of my findings for others. The many profound truths I have discovered at that source have changed my life around. (This transforming element, in fact, is the true "test" of the readings' validity.)

Although a very humble figure, and one who was regarded by many as a freak during his lifetime, Edgar Cayce was undoubtedly a psychic genius. In half a century of service to God and man, he left us with a compelling body of psychic data (the transcripts of more than 14,000 psychic readings) touching on virtually every phase of the human dilemma and providing answers to life's deepest mysteries. There is no doubt, really, that the world has been immeasurably enriched by Edgar Cayce's passage through our midst.

This anthology owes its appearance to a number of people, over the years, who have suggested that a collection of my writings in the *Journal* would represent a useful contribution, however slight, to those who seek a clearer understanding of the multi-faceted Cayce phenomenon. To those who have asked for this book, let me express my appreciation. The joy of service is all that really counts.   —*W.H. Church*

God has planted many marvellous secrets in man, so that they lie in him like seeds in the earth.
Let man consider who he is and what he should and must become. —Paracelsus

Ah, my God, I see all gods within your body.
Great in soul are they who become what is godlike. . . —Bhagavad-Gita

I have said, Ye are gods; and all of you are children of the most High. —Psalm 82:6

Before Abraham Was

"Before Abraham was, I AM."[1]

When Jesus spoke those words of Light to the scribes and Pharisees, they took up stones to cast at Him.

If only they had opened their hearts instead and had asked the Master to interpret that marvellous statement, history might have been changed. But they preferred the comfort of the dark, where sinful conscience rested, and still rests.

Thus, it has taken us almost twenty centuries to reach a full interpretation of that cabbalistic utterance. That interpretation is found in the Edgar Cayce readings, which trace the origins of man through the aeons of time and numerous incarnations, to his divine estate as a Son of God, unfallen, at One with the Father, the Great I AM.

And there, in his spiritual reality, man still *is:*

Ye *are* in eternity. 281-27

You are there—but self must be eliminated. 5392-1

Some will consider it a curious coincidence, while others will see in the event a higher law at work, but confirmation of the Edgar Cayce readings on this important subject now comes from an unexpected source: the words of Jesus Himself.

In 1945, the year of Edgar Cayce's death, thirteen papyrus volumes were unearthed in a ruined tomb near Nag Hammadi, Upper Egypt. One of the volumes was found to contain what purports to be *The Gospel According to Thomas,* consisting of one hundred and fourteen sayings attributed to Jesus.[2]

Before we examine some of these *logia* in relation to the Cayce readings, it may be important to ask ourselves why this newly revealed gospel should contain spiritual truths and

---

[1]John 8:58. See pages 209-216 for footnotes.

esoteric information not included in the four known gospels in the New Testament. The answer becomes clear enough when we consider the numerous translations and revisions to which the entire New Testament has been subjected, down through the ages. This includes the notorious censorship by the Fifth Ecumenical Council of Constantinople, in A.D. 553, as reported in detail by Noel Langley in his informative book, *Edgar Cayce on Reincarnation.*[3]

The lately discovered gospel, attributed to the apostle Didymos Judas Thomas, appears to be based upon an original text produced in Greek about A.D. 140. Because the Coptic manuscript has lain concealed from the ravages of time and the censors since the fourth century, we have good reason to believe that the sayings of Jesus contained in this unique volume may indeed represent His original utterances in unaltered form.

In the passages that follow, the sayings of Jesus appear side by side with correlative comments from the Cayce readings, so that the reader may compare them more readily and reach his own conclusions:

From the Logia	*From the Readings*
Jesus said: If they say to you, 'From where have you originated?', say to them, 'We have come from the Light, where the Light has originated through itself. It stood and it revealed itself in their image.' If they say to you, 'Who are you?', say: 'We are His sons and we are the elect of the Living Father.' (L. 50)	For, as is given in the beginning: God moved and said, 'Let there be light,' and there was light; not the light of the sun, but rather that of which, through which, in which, every soul had, has, and ever has its being. For in truth ye live and move and have thy being in Him. (5246-1)
Jesus said: Blessed is he who was before he came into being. (L. 19)	He will bring that to thee that will give thee the more perfect understanding of that estate He had with the Father before the world was, before those experiences in the earth. (281-27)
Jesus said: When you see your likeness, you rejoice. But when you see your images which came into existence before you, which neither die nor are manifested, how much will you bear! (L. 84)	...that we see manifested in the material plane is but a shadow of that in the spiritual plane. (5749-3) In the beginning, celestial beings. (262-52)

From the Logia	From the Readings

From the Logia

Jesus said: On the day when you were one, you became two. (L. 11)

When you make the male and the female into a single one, so that the male will not be male and the female not be female. . . then shall you enter the Kingdom. (L. 22)

Jesus said: Whoever finds himself, of him the world is not worthy. (L. 111)

Jesus said: If the flesh has come into existence because of the spirit, it is a marvel; but if the spirit has come into existence because of the body, it is a marvel of marvels. But I marvel at how this great wealth has made its home in this poverty. (L. 29)

From the Readings

As flesh is the activity of the mental being (or the spiritual self and mental being) pushing itself into matter, and as spirit— as He gave—is neither male nor female, they are then both, or one.

And when man had reached that period of the full separation from the Creative Forces in the spirit, then flesh as man knows it today became a reality in [the] material plane. (5749-7)

. . .in that land known as the Atlantean when there were the separation of bodies as male and female. (2121-2)

In the beginning, as was outlined, there was presented that that became as the Sons of God, in that male and female were as in one. . .(364-7)

The soul is an individual, individuality, that may grow to be one with, or separate from, the whole. (5749-3)

Ye, then, are not aliens, [but] rather the Sons of the Holy One. (262-24)

Adam. . .first discerned. . .that which made for the propagation of beings in the flesh. . .(364-5)

In. . .the experience of. . .Adam and Eve, the knowledge of their position, or that as is known in the material world today as. . . sex relationships, came into the experience. (364-6)

In the Atlantean land, during

3

From the Logia	*From the Readings*

<table>
<tr>
<td></td>
<td>those periods when there were the encasements and indulgencies of many that had put on matter or material bodies. (618-3)</td>
</tr>
<tr>
<td>Simon Peter said to them: Let Mary go out from among us, because women are not worthy of the Life. Jesus said: See, I shall lead her, so that I will make her male, that she too may become a living spirit. . . (L. 114)</td>
<td>To be sure, man and woman alike; for, as given from the beginning, they are one. Not as man counts oneness from the material viewpoint. (364-8)</td>
</tr>
<tr>
<td>The disciples said to Jesus: Tell us how our end will be. Jesus said: Have you then discovered the beginning so that you inquire about the end? For where the beginning is, there shall be the end. Blessed is he who shall stand at the beginning, and he shall know the end and he shall not taste death.</td>
<td>. . .the coming into the earth has been, and is, for the evolution or the evolving of the soul unto its awareness. . .(5749-5)

In the beginning, Mary was the twin soul of the Master in the entrance into the earth! (5749-3)

And this was the entity Adam. And this was the spirit of light. (5023-2)</td>
</tr>
</table>

There are still other texts from *The Gospel According to Thomas* that could be cited in confirmation of the Cayce readings; but in this brief essay it has been our purpose to present only those sayings of Jesus that are pertinent to our subject, namely, the antecedents of Abraham. The interested reader will want to explore the *logia* for himself and seek out further references, such as the following:

The man old in days will not hesitate to ask a little child about the place of Life. . .(L. 4)

And what said Cayce of the newborn infant's wisdom? This:

Oft has it been said, and rightly, with a babe's smile 'Dreaming of angels' and close in touch with them—but what has *produced* that dream? The contact with that upon which *it* has fed!
364-10

In our search for Truth, we find that the process of unfoldment is a continual spiritual activity. Thus, it should not be surprising to us, really, when the earth literally opens up and reveals to us her hidden wisdom. This occurs as our advancing age is ready to accept and use such sacred records for His purposes. And we can expect the future to reveal further confirmation of our heritage, out of the buried archives of the past, and also in our own awakening consciousness, even as Edgar Cayce foretold. But we have a responsibility to fulfill, if such unfoldment—whether from without or from within—is to continue. We must apply in our daily lives the wisdom gained from each advancing step,

Knowing, as ye *use* that as is *known,* there is given the more and more light to know from whence ye came and whither ye go!
364-4

Science and the Future

"The time has come to realize that an interpretation of the universe—even a positivist one—remains unsatisfying unless it covers the interior as well as the exterior of things; mind as well as matter."
—*Pierre Teilhard de Chardin*[1]

"A nexus of ideas exists of which nothing is known—a vast system of ideas—a cosmos of thought. There is an entity, a Soul-Entity, as yet unrecognized."
—*Richard Jefferies*[2]

The age of scientific materialism is dead. It has gone into permanent eclipse, along with the dodo bird and the mastodon. Extinct images, all of them! Now we see the shape of a bold and imaginative new science emerging.

Science today is offering us some startling new theories about the nature of man and the universe. We are told, for example, that every thing in the universe, from a man to a mountain or a swirling galaxy, is no more than a mass of vibrating waves. What we see, therefore, is only the outward appearance, or the "wave form," of the underlying reality.[3] We are also told, in a quite dramatic illustration of the point, that we might one day be able to drive our car out of the garage without troubling to open the garage doors, because matter is composed mostly of space; and since this "space" is constantly shifting, the moving object might conceivably meet the stationary one in such a unique juxtaposition of atoms as to pass right through it, unobstructed and unchanged![4] In another direction, modern biologists claim to have found evidence of *mind* in plant life; and Dr. C.G. Jung is reported to have expressed his belief that it exists even in so-called *inorganic* substance, such as stone.[5] But the famous astronomer, Fred Hoyle, offers perhaps one of the most startling theories of all: that the stuff of which stars are made is engendered from clouds of intergalactic hydrogen, which, in turn, *comes from nowhere. It is created out of nothing.*[6] And another astronomer, Dr. Gustaf Stromberg, has concluded that the underlying source of all life in the projected universe must be traced to "a realm beyond space and time," in the domain of mind, which he identifies as the Soul of the Universe.[7]

This new language of science makes us marvel, for it so closely approximates the language of the mystic. Can we not recall, for example, a statement by Johannes Eckhart, the 14th century mystic, which parallels the statement of our modern scientist about the garage door? Thus spoke Meister Eckhart: "I am certain that a man who wanted to do so, might one day be able to walk through a wall of steel."[8]

What is happening here? Let us analyze it briefly. Our modern scientist approaches the potential miracle of one seemingly solid object passing through another from the level of a newly discovered principle of physics; while Eckhart probably discerned the operation of a spiritual law that might, under certain favorable conditions, create within a man the necessary vibratory rate to translate him to a higher dimension, where he could negate and overcome a material limitation—say, a steel wall. But both the scientist and the mystic have relied, at least initially, upon the intuitive process to reach their parallel conclusions. Similarly, we might compare the intuitive-deductive supposition of Dr. Jung, the psychologist, concerning the existence of a mind-force in what is termed inorganic matter, with the purely intuitive comment of the New England Transcendentalist, Henry David Thoreau, that "There is *nothing* inorganic."[9] Here, again, the mystic and the scientist are, in effect, saying the same thing.

Science and religion, so long regarded as irreconcilable antagonists, are at last reaching out together from a common base—the base of intuition, or call it "inspiration" if you will!—to discover and interpret our common destiny. In the past, the mainstream of science, materially oriented, has concentrated on the spatial universe of material form and substance—the visible macrocosm; religion, on the other hand, has just as energetically examined the mind and soul of individual man—the intangible microcosm. Now science has finally recognized its need to probe *both* universes—the inner, as well as the outer; microcosm and macrocosm, together—as it becomes increasingly clear that they have a unitary relationship, and may indeed be one.

Thus, the inward search has begun in earnest.

It began officially, perhaps, some decades ago, when Albert Einstein sounded the death knell for scientific materialism. His Theory of Relativity, along with the Quantum Theory, destroyed the existing scientific concept of a mechanistic universe, and physicists could no longer avoid asking metaphysical questions of one another. The long search outward was turning around at last, and bringing man back, to look within himself.

Always an intuitive thinker, Einstein openly declared his reliance upon the intuitive process (the path within), before proceeding to "prove" his inspirations by the empirical scientific method used as a starting-point by most of his less imaginative colleagues. In some published notes "On Science,"[10] Einstein voiced his heretical views unequivocally: "I believe in intuition and inspiration," he wrote. And once he went even further: "The most beautiful and most profound emotion we can experience is the sensation of the mystical," he said. *"It is the sower of all true science."*[11] *(italics ours)*

A profoundly religious man, in the cosmic sense, Einstein was obviously responsible for breaking down some of the traditional barriers between science and religion, so that a gradual synthesis of the two conflicting catechisms could be brought about in later decades by imaginative leaders in both groups, without fear of derision or loss of respect.

He spoke of a level of religious experience that he termed the "cosmic religious sense," wherein the individual rose above the level of personal desire or the sense of individual destiny, and, glimpsing "the nobility and marvellous order which are revealed in nature and in the world of thought," sought to "experience the totality of existence."[12] (In such remarkable words, which undoubtedly reflected Einstein's own intensely personal revelation, one is reminded of the interesting theory on cosmic consciousness propounded at the turn of the century by a medical doctor, Richard Maurice Bucke, who was one of the forerunners in the now-respectable field of parapsychology. Bucke's treatise, published under the full title, *Cosmic Consciousness; A Study in the Evolution of the Human Mind*,[13] was first published in 1901 and is today an acknowledged classic on psychical research.)

Of the cosmic religious experience, Einstein dared to assert that it was "the strongest and the noblest driving force" behind any great scientific research. He saw it, for example, as the force inspiring the tireless efforts of Kepler and Newton in their lonely work to unravel the secrets of the exterior universe. And who but Einstein himself would have known so well what he was talking about!

Undoubtedly his enlightened views inspired and simplified the contemporary efforts of a whole host of spiritually directed scientists, such as Sir James Jeans and Sir Julian Huxley and Pierre Teilhard de Chardin, in the present-day task of building connecting bridges between science and religion, so that future generations will be able to cross over with ease, recognizing the two worlds as one.

An articulate and imaginative spokesman for the new order of scientists, Willis W. Harman, has now extended this theme of a religio-scientific synthesis (although he would perhaps eschew that term!) in a recently published paper, entitled "The New Copernican Revolution."[14]

It is Dr. Harman's contention that the current, unprecedented wave of scientific interest in hypnosis, telepathy, psychedelic drugs, and various other aspects of psychic phenomenology marks the emergence of a new science, which he has dubbed "the science of man's subjective experience." In outlining the pattern for a systematic exploration of man's inner being, Dr. Harman clearly recognizes some of the potential hazards. And he has emphasized the responsibility of the New Science to be guided by an overarching vision of the future that is at once constructive and spiritually oriented. He tells us that the cure for our present ills will lie in building a nobler self-image for future generations to set their sights upon. Only as we become aware of our higher self, he seems to be saying, can we lift ourselves and others up to a nobler, more purposeful level of accomplishment, where man can reach and utilize "states of consciousness transcending the usual conscious awareness."

It becomes evident, in any case, that the New Science will furnish the key to unlock the enormous reservoir of man's untapped potential for good or evil. Whether this New Copernican Revolution, opening the flood-gates inward as Copernicus opened them outward, will produce an unprecedented flow of enlightenment to float us up to God, or will drown us like the legendary Atlantean culture in a sea of untempered self-indulgence, is a decision that rests largely in the hands of this generation. As the initiators of the New Science, it is up to us to set the pattern and formulate the objectives. What will they be? Where will they take us?

They can take us into serious trouble if we let science operate solely for science's sake, or in response to political pressure, or to serve the selfish interests of any group. We can see how hypnosis or telepathy, perhaps developed to a stage of mechanical application under scientific auspices, might become the means of violating our very souls if not carefully controlled. Similar dangers exist already in the field of hallucinatory drugs. In medical science, revolutionary genetic and surgical techniques are being prematurely introduced, without first investigating their psychological consequences. A biologist on the faculty of Stanford University, Paul R. Ehrlich, points to the future potential for "genetic engineering," but he reminds us that we have not yet considered "what kinds of human beings we want to engineer, and to what purpose."[15] We would go a step further than that. We would remind science that the whole concept of genetic engineering may be morally unsound, because of its implied interference with the soul of man, whose existence science cannot deny and whose peculiar needs for development are not scientifically known.

While Ehrlich cites the computer as "the most revolutionary of all man's prosthetic devices," and actually to be regarded as an extension of the human mind itself, he also reminds us that the Computer Age has altered the power structures of larger institutions and has to some extent deprived human beings of the decision-making function. Yet this function, it can be effectively argued, is crucial to the survival of any free and moral society.

We express concern.

But let us take hope. There stirs within us something that refuses to be extinguished. Our faith is not blind. What is faith but knowledge transcended? And if we have come this far, something tells us it is to fulfill an evolutionary event of high significance. The next step will reveal itself. We can trust to the higher urge that brought us here.

"It is well understood by some that a New Order of conditions is to arise," said Edgar Cayce.[16]

The New Order is already awaiting us, in fact. We have only to wake up.

"There is 'no time, no space, no beginning, no end. . .' "[17]

"We are all *in* His presence, whether we acknowledge it in the present or not."[18]

As humanity evolves toward its awakening, it will be the task of the New Science to confirm our spiritual heritage at the empirical level. But it will not be able to do so without the aid of the religious sense. The task will require inspiration, humility, and—yes, even faith.[19] Science has all of these at its disposal, and we urge it to use them. We urge it to revolutionize itself along spiritual lines. Not until then can science wholly transcend its present barriers. For man's discovery of himself is not essentially an intellectual pursuit. It is a spiritual one. And the empirical method of investigation will have to be applied at the level of prayer and meditation, first, to demonstrate and prove the Ultimate Science.

The Chronicles of Issa

"One day, in the course of my visit to the Buddhist convent situated on my route, I learnt from the chief Lama that there existed in the archives of Lhasa very ancient memoirs treating of the life of Jesus Christ. . .and that certain great monasteries possessed copies and translations of those chronicles."

—from *The Unknown Life of Jesus Christ*[1]

Contrary to common belief, Tibet has always welcomed strangers. It is the land itself that is forbidding, not the people. The people are singularly hospitable.

The truth of this statement could be warmly attested to by those members of an A.R.E. tour group who were recent guests of the Dalai Lama and his fellow Tibetans-in-exile at their temporary home in a remote but friendly outpost in Northern India, near the Tibetan border. We are told that they were greeted in a spirit of genuine brotherhood and good will. It must have been a truly heart-warming experience—one that no member of that group is likely to forget.

In his book, *Tibet,*[2] Thubten Jigme Norbu—the elder brother of the Dalai Lama—tells of another stranger who once came to his remote country and was graciously received. It is an ancient tale that is related to an old manuscript that was formerly in the Buddhist monastery at Hemis, in Ladakh. This document, we are told by Norbu, contained an extraordinary account of the travels of a humble foreigner who had visited India in his youth, and who finally came to Tibet, where he is said to have resided for a period with the monks at Hemis before returning to his homeland to preach a new religion.

The name of that earlier traveler, we are told by Norbu, was Jesus of Judea, later known as the Christ.

And what happened to those precious chronicles?

In giving us the answer, Norbu demonstrates the tolerant

attitude of the Tibetans toward strangers in their midst. He writes: "A Russian traveler named Notwitch took away the manuscript, and later sent a translation to the monastery, but this in turn was taken away by some foreign traveler."

And now we come to the incredible sequel, which is an even stranger story, in its way.

An alert reader in Canada wrote to the editor of the *Journal*, after reading the March, 1970 issue. He had been struck by the similarity between Norbu's account of the Hemis manuscript, as originally related in Janet Jones's article, "The Dalai Lama Speaks," and an old, typewritten manuscript in his own possession, dated 1907. This manuscript was an English translation of an obscure French publication (circa 1890), entitled: *The Unknown Life of Jesus Christ; from an Ancient Manuscript Recently Discovered in a Buddhist Monastery in Thibet,* by Nicholas Notovitch. Another reader also responded, and both very obligingly sent the editor copies of this obscure publication. The two English translations, although the work of different translators, appeared to coincide, except that one of them omitted certain details in Notovitch's personal commentary, unrelated to the main work itself, which was of course the translated fragments of the chronicles of Issa (Jesus).

It was a quite obvious speculation, by now, that Norbu's Russian traveler, named "Notwitch," was none other than Nicholas Notovitch. (The "v" in this Russian name would, of course, commonly be pronounced with a "w" sound, so that the phonetic spelling—to Tibetan ears—would be "Notwitch," or "Notowitch.")

A crucial question, however, remained: did these chronicles indeed come from the monastery at Hemis, as mentioned by Norbu? They did. Here was proof, in the author's own words, taken from his prefatory comments: "During my stay at Leh, the capital of Ladakh, I visited the great monastery of Hemis, situated near the city. I had the honor of obtaining the consent of their chief (Lama) to have brought from the library the manuscript relating to Jesus Christ, and, aided by my interpreter, who translated for me from the Thibetan language, I wrote down carefully the verses as they were read by the Lama."

If Notovitch purloined the sacred manuscript (which he defined as two bound volumes yellowed with age—not scrolls, apparently, but books), he did not appear willing to admit the theft to his readers. And it is a point we shall not pursue here,

13

because it is not relevant to our purpose.

Our purpose is to examine the chronicles of Issa.

The chronicles have been assembled by Notovitch into fourteen related sections, containing a total of 244 verses. We are told, however, that the original arrangement of the verses, or fragments, was not representative of any particular chronology or order. It was as if the fragments had been hastily gathered at random from a variety of monastic records throughout India and Tibet, at about the time that merchant caravans from the Mediterranean first brought to the Orient the fateful news concerning the martyrdom of Jesus at the hands of the Roman governor, Pilate. Apparently there was a felt desire on the part of the monks to assemble some historic notes on their recent and illustrious visitor, which could be preserved in the major monasteries as a memoriam; but in rather typical Oriental fashion, no one sensed any need to "organize" the assembled fragments. That is a strictly Western compulsion.

Most of these loose, episodic notes had been written in the Pali language, we are informed. It was only later that they were translated into Tibetan by visiting lamas, who brought back their translations to their own monasteries. One can suppose that this may have led, irresistibly, to some modifications in the original texts, here and there, particularly as they related to the role of Issa among the Hindus, or an assessment of his role among the Buddhists. This is a human tendency that is always with us. Notovitch, in fact, may have yielded to the same temptation; he seems, at any rate, to have favored a Buddhistic interpretation of Issa's life, in his lengthy commentary, which would suggest an unwillingness to attach equal significance to the Vedic teachings in the development of Jesus' spiritual knowledge. On the divinity of the Christ, Notovitch was a self-admitted dissenter, preferring to take the Buddhist position that Jesus was a great prophet, and possibly a reincarnation of Buddha, but was not the Son of God; and his commentary on the chronicles also discloses intellectual doubts regarding the role and ancestry of Moses. This means, of course, that we cannot afford to rely entirely upon the textual veracity of his translation of those opening chronicles dealing with the historical aspects of Mossa (Moses) and Judaism, or most of the later chronicles, dealing with Jesus' ministry in Judea and His subsequent martyrdom. If these passages have not been colored by the translator's personal persuasions on the subject,

14

they are at least suspect from the standpoint that they represent secondhand information that Indian and Tibetan scribes had to obtain from traveling scholars, Judaean merchants, or other questionable sources, with the information then to be channeled through the rigid mold of Buddhist traditional thought, before writing it down.

This is not intended as criticism, since it is recognized that different viewpoints are the inevitable and honest result of differing cultures. But since we are unable to study the original Tibetan or Pali manuscripts, we must proceed with some discretion in our interpretation of Mr. Notovitch's translation, which, in turn, has been translated from French into English, with much subsequent editing. (A copy of the original French translation has not yet turned up.)

Our primary interest, in any case, centers upon the period of Issa's life in India and environs, since we are dealing with an unusual manuscript that promises to give us a firsthand account of this particular phase in the earthly development of Jesus Christ.

Do we have any basis for believing that the youthful Jesus may have studied, traveled, and taught in India or elsewhere in the Orient?

We do. Here are some selections from the Cayce readings on the subject:

A portion of the experience the entity [Judy] was the teacher...the entity sent Him [Jesus] to Persia, to Egypt, yea to India, that there might be completed the more perfect knowledge of the material ways in the activities of Him who became the Way, the Truth!   1472-3

[He went] into Egypt for only a short period, and then into India, and then into what is now Persia.
Hence, in all the ways of the teachers...[Jesus] was trained.
From Persia He was called to Judea at the death of Joseph... then into Egypt (again) for the completion of the preparation as a teacher.   5749-7

Q-1. *From what period and how long did He remain in India?*[3]
A-1. From thirteen to sixteen.   5749-2

Q-2. *What part did Jesus play in any of His reincarnations in the development of the basic teachings of the following*

15

religions and philosophies? First, Buddhism.
    A-2. This is just one.

    Q-3. Mohammedanism, Confucianism, Shintoism,
Brahminism, Platonism, Judaism?
    A-3. As has been indicated, the entity—as an entity—
influenced either directly or indirectly all those forms of
philosophy or religious thought that taught God was One. . .
for, as has been given, "Know, O Israel, the Lord thy God is
ONE!" whether this is directing one of the Confucian thought,
Brahmin thought, Buddha thought, Mohammedan thought;
these are as teachers or representatives. . .God calls on man
everywhere to seek His face, through that channel that may be
blessed by the Spirit of the Son—in whatsoever sphere this
may take its form.   364-9

    But let us return to the chronicles of Issa.
    If there had been no concern by the scribes, as Notovitch
reports, for a sense of continuity or unity in the collection, at
least the disorganized fragments appeared to be consistent in
one respect: they all paid homage to Issa as a holy man, who
spoke and taught and moved among them as one of their own
treasured saints, or "incarnations."
    Notovitch relates a conversation with a Tibetan lama at the
convent of Moulbek, who told him that the name of Issa (Jesus)
was much respected among Buddhists as a great prophet, but
that only a handful of lamas were currently acquainted with
the scrolls relating to his life. This was because there were some
84,000 scrolls relating to innumerable holy men in Buddhist
history, of whom Issa was only one—and a passing one, at that,
since he had left the Buddhists and returned to his own country
to preach another religion. But it was the conviction of this
learned lama, according to Notovitch, that Issa had
represented the twenty-second incarnation of Buddha, after
Gautama (the twenty-first incarnation, born circa 500-600
B.C.). Nothing in the translated chronicles of Issa, however,
supports this rather singular opinion.
    What we find is the story of a young Judean who left his
native land at the age of thirteen, and arrived in India,
traveling with a caravan of merchants who brought him as far
as Sindh. Here he dwelt among the Jain sect for a while, and the
"fame of this wonderful youth spread throughout Northern
Sindh." (V:2)
    Then the tale continues:

But he left them and went to Jagannath, in the country of
Orissa, where lie the mortal remains of Vyasa-Krishna. Here the
white priests of Brahma[4] received him joyfully. (V:3)

Those readers who are familiar with yet another account of
the journeyings of Jesus into India and other lands, as told in
The Aquarian Gospel of Jesus the Christ, by Levi[5]—a book that
made its first published appearance in 1908—may note the
reference to Jagannath and Orissa with special interest. For it
was a prince of Orissa, according to Levi's "Gospel," who
petitioned Mary and Joseph to let the thirteen-year-old Jesus
accompany his caravan to India, where He might continue His
spiritual studies with the Brahmins. Levi's account tells us that
the caravan crossed the Sindh, and reached the province of
Orissa, where Jesus was enrolled as a pupil in the temple
Jagannath, where He "learned the Vedas and the Manic laws."

According to Levi, Jesus then traveled and studied in Tibet
and Western India, from whence he proceeded to Persia. This
coincides, in general terms, with the account already quoted
from the Cayce readings, as well as the account in the
chronicles of Issa, which mention the departure of Jesus for
Persia before returning to his native country.

Levi also mentions an Egyptian interlude in Jesus' youthful
training, although the chronicles of Issa omit this phase. But
some of Levi's Egyptian references—notably, those pertaining
to certain details of the "Initiation" at Heliopolis—may appear
questionable, particularly if we attempt to relate them to what
we know, through the readings, of the Essenes and their
customs and teachings. Also, there is a dubious section about
Jesus in Greece, which may suggest to certain readers that Levi
was not always able to rely upon the akashic records from
which he reportedly drew his information. Its "tone" appears
out of harmony with some of the preceding sections in his book.
And we are reminded of a reading in which Cayce was asked,
"Did Jesus study under Greek philosophers?" His unequivocal
reply: "We do not find such." (2067-7)

It is unfortunate that Notovitch's translation of the Issa
chronicles never came to light during Cayce's lifetime, since
this would have provided an opportunity to inquire concerning
their overall validity, at least in the translated form at our
disposal. But we do have this question-and-answer sequence
from the readings, on the subject of Levi's book, which invites
our thoughtful study:

Q-27. We are told [by Levi] that The Aquarian Gospel of Jesus the Christ *is taken directly from the akashic records. Is it historically true, and should I use the facts in my book?*

A-27. It is the experience of an individual, or of Levi, who was in that experience and wrote from his own experience. To him it was an actual fact.   2067-2

An intriguing reply! But let us proceed, once more, with excerpts from the Issa chronicles. We are told of some sharp differences that arose between Jesus and the Brahmins:

He spent six years in Jagannath, Rajagriha, Benares and other holy cities. Everyone loved Issa, for he lived in peace with the Vaishyas and Shudras, to whom he taught the holy scripture. (V:5)

But the Brahmins and Kshatriyas said to him that the great Para-Brahma had forbidden them to approach those whom he had created from his belly and from his feet; (V:6)

But Issa did not heed their words, and went among the Shudras to preach against the Brahmins and the Kshatriyas. (V:10)

He strongly denounced the doctrine that gives to men the power of robbing their fellow men of their human rights; in truth, he said: 'God the Father has established no difference between His children, who are all equally dear to Him.' (V:11)

Issa denied the divine origin of the Vedas and the Puranas, for he taught his followers that one Law had been given to man to guide him in his actions. (V:12)

'Fear thy God, bend thy knee only before Him, and bring to Him alone offerings which come from thy labors.' (V:13)

Issa denied the Trimuti and the incarnation of Para-Brahma in Vishnu, Shiva, and other gods; for he said: (V:14)

'The Eternal Judge, the Eternal Spirit, composes the one individual Soul of the Universe, which alone creates, contains, and vivifies the Whole.' (V:15)

'The Great Creator has shared His power with no one, still less with inanimate objects, as they have taught you, for He alone possesses all power.' (V:17)

'Those who deprive their brothers of the divine gift shall be deprived of it themselves, and the Brahmins and the Kshatriyas will become Shudras (slaves) of the Shudras, with whom the Eternal will dwell forever.' (V:23)

The Vaishyas and Shudras greatly admired these words of Issa, and begged him to teach them how to pray, so that they might secure their happiness. (V:25)

He said to them: 'Do not worship idols, for they do not hear you; do not listen to the Vedas, in which the truth is perverted; do not believe yourselves superior to others everywhere; do not humiliate your neighbor.' (V:26)

'Help the poor, sustain the feeble; do no evil to anyone; do not covet what others possess and you do not.' (V:27)

The white priests (Brahmins) and the warriors (Kshatriyas), having learnt of the discourse which Issa had addressed to the Shudras, determined upon his death, and with this intention sent their servants to search for the young prophet. (VI:1)

But Issa, warned of the danger by the Shudras, left Jagannath by night, reached the mountains, and established himself in the country of the Gautamides, where the great Buddha Shakya-Muni was born,[6] amidst the people who worshipped the one and only sublime Brahma. (VI:2)

Having learned perfectly the Pali language,[7] the just Issa devoted himself to the study of the sacred scrolls of the Sutras. (VI:3)

Six years afterwards, Issa, whom the Buddha had chosen to spread the holy doctrine, was able to explain perfectly the sacred scrolls. (VI:4)

Then he left Nepal and the Himalaya mountains, descending into the valley of Rajputana, and journeyed toward the west, preaching to various peoples the possibility of man's attaining the supreme perfection. (VI:5)

We find in the chronicles no specific reference to Tibet, by name, or to the monastery at Hemis. But it is possible that the passages translated for Notovitch may not have been complete. We probably will never know.

Meanwhile, in his travels westward in India, Issa's teachings once again roused the anger of the local priesthood:

'For man,' he said, 'has not been favored with the power to see the image of God and to construct a host of divinities resembling the Eternal One.' (VI:8)

'The Celestial Law,' said the Creator through the mouth of Issa, 'scorns the immolation of human beings to a statue or to an animal, for I have dedicated to the use of man all animals and all that the world contains.' (VI:12)

'Just as a father would act toward his children, so shall God judge men after their death according to His merciful laws; never will He humiliate His child by making his soul migrate into the body of a beast as in purgatory.' (VI:11)

'Therefore I say unto you, leave your idols, do not perform ceremonies that separate you from your Father and link and bind you to priests against whom Heaven is turned.' (VI:15)

'Perform a miracle,' the priests answered him, 'and let thy God confound ours if they inspire Him with disgust.' (VII:4)

But Issa answered: 'The miracles of our God began with the creation of the universe; they take place now every day, every moment, and whomsoever does not see them is deprived of one of the most beautiful gifts of life.' (VII:5)

'God will expel the contaminated animals from His flocks, but He will take back to Himself those who were misled by having misunderstood the celestial spark which dwelt in them.' (VII:11)

Seeing the powerlessness of their priests, these people believed in the teaching of Issa and adopted his faith, and in fear of the anger of the Divinity, they broke their idols in pieces; seeing this, the priests fled to escape the popular vengeance. (VII:12)

And Issa taught the heathen not to try to see the Eternal Spirit with their own eyes, but rather to feel it with their heart, and by a soul truly pure render themselves worthy of His favors. (VII:13)

The next sequence in the chronicles leads to Persia:

The neighboring countries were filled with renown of the teachings of Issa, and when he entered Persia the priests became alarmed and forbade the people to listen to him. (VIII:1)

The chronicles report that he was arrested and brought before the high priest, who accused Issa of blasphemy for preaching about a new God, contrary to "the laws that were given to Zoroaster in Paradise."

And Issa said unto them: 'I do not speak of a new God, but of our Heavenly Father who existed before the beginning and who will exist after the eternal end.' (VIII:6)

'But,' began the priests, 'how could a people live according to the laws of justice if they had no teachers?' (VIII:12)

Issa answered: 'As long as the people had no priests, they were governed by natural laws and preserved the candor of their souls.' (VIII:13)

'Their souls were in God, and when they wanted to communicate with the Father, they did not have recourse to the mediation of an idol, an animal, or a fire, as you practice here.' (VIII:14)

'You pretend that one must worship the sun, the spirit of good and evil; well, I say to you that your doctrine is detestable. The sun does not act spontaneously, but by the Will of the invisible God who has created it.' (VIII:15)

'The Eternal Spirit is the soul of all that it animates. You commit a great sin in dividing Him into the spirit of evil and that of good, for there is no God except that of good.' (VIII:17)

After having listened to him, the priests resolved to do no evil to him; but during the night, while all in the city slept, they led him outside the walls and there left him to his fate upon the highway in the hope that he would soon become the prey of wild beasts. (VIII:23)

But protected by our God, Saint Issa continued his way unharmed. (VIII:24)

The preceding passage, referring to Issa as a saint, is interesting and unique. It was apparently inserted by a different scribe than the ones who had written those verses dealing with his earlier travels. Further along, we find other references to him as a saint, or as "Holy Issa," but this is the first such reference.

The chronicles indicate that Jesus was twenty-nine years old when he returned to Judea:

Issa, whom the Creator had chosen to bring back the true God to men plunged in sin, was twenty-nine years old when he arrived in the land of Israel. (IX:1)

And although we will leave the chronicles at this point, since they must necessarily be dealing with their subject on a secondhand basis only, there are several significant verses we will include from those final chapters:

The Israelites came in throngs to hear the words of Issa, and asked him where they should praise their Heavenly Father, since the enemy had razed their temples to the ground and lain profane hands on their sacred vessels. (IX:10)

Issa answered them that God had no reference to temples built by the hand of man, but that He meant the hearts of men, which are the true temples of God. (IX:11)

'Enter into your temple, into your heart, enlighten it with good thoughts, with patience and with firm confidence, which you should place in your Father.' (IX:13)

'Earthly power is not of long duration, and it is subject to many changes. It would be of no use for a man to revolt against it, for one power always succeeds another, and it will thus be until the extinction of humanity.' (X:13)

'When you would seek Him, become as little children, for you know neither the past, nor the present, nor the future, and God is master of time.' (XII:15)

The remainder of the chronicles would appear to be of little historical value, and we find some Oriental concepts intermingled with the teachings of Issa that may have been inserted by Buddhist scribes, although they will hold some interest for the scholar. An example:

Meanwhile, an old woman who had approached the crowd to hear Issa better was pushed aside by one of the disguised men who placed himself before her. (XII:8)

Issa then said: 'It is not good for a son to push aside his mother so that he may occupy the front place, which should be hers. Whoever does not respect his mother, the most sacred being after God, is unworthy of the name of son.' (XII:9)

The chronicles conclude with a version of the death and burial of Jesus that denies the Resurrection, and is a version that was commonly promoted at the time by the Jews and Romans alike, for obvious reasons:

> Pilate...feared the throng, and returned the body of the Saint to his relatives, who interred it near the place of execution; the people came to pray at this tomb, filling the air with weeping and wailing. (XIV:5)

> Three days afterward, fearing a general uprising, the Governor sent soldiers to raise secretly the body of Issa and bury it in some other place. (XIV:6)

> The next day the throng found the tomb open and empty; so that the rumor was spread that the Supreme Judge had sent His angels to carry away the mortal remains of the Saint in whom had dwelt on earth a part of the Divine Spirit. (XIV:7)

Such an ending to the Christian tale might also be more in harmony with Buddhist precepts; and we can readily understand the sincere desire of those venerable lamas, who wrote down the history of Issa, to see that it did not contain any revolutionary new doctrine that would be inconsistent with their own cherished beliefs and teachings. Indeed, we are grateful to them for having preserved a record of the early life and works of this Holy Stranger who once dwelt among them; for it has given us, if we accept it, a rare glimpse of a period in His life about which too little has been known or told.

And is it not good to realize that He who came as the Shepherd of all mankind was seen and heard by other flocks, in other lands? For He is not ours alone.

Cycles of Vibration

A Study of Related Forces in Plants and Man

Listen at the birds. Watch the blush of the rose. Listen at the life rising in the tree. These serve their Maker—through what? That psychic force that *is* Life itself, in their respective sphere—that were put for the service of man. Learn thine lesson, O Man, from that about thee!   364-10

Consider for a moment: is there a "Mind-force" in the vegetable kingdom? It is a bold hypothesis. But Cayce never hesitated. He said there was. He referred to it as a "group mind." (262-80) And he spoke of a similar group mind, or commonly shared field of consciousness, in the *mineral* kingdom, as well as in the animal group. Such unorthodox concepts are hard for scientific minds to grasp. They border on the mystical, eluding the nets of positivism. But science is beginning to cope with them.

We quote: *"Plants can learn."*[1]

That conclusion is scientific: it is the positive assertion of a psychology professor at the University of Toledo, who says he can prove it. We will review his evidence later on. It is impressive.

Meanwhile, in a television report on CBS Evening News,[2] it was shown by time-lapse photography that *music can have a stimulating or retarding effect upon the growth of plants*. The results are dependent upon the type of music, or vibration, set in motion. The strains of Debussy and Bach, for instance, were found to inspire lush growth and harmonious plant structure, whereas constant exposure to the discordant vibrations of rock music caused healthy plants to shrivel and die.

And what did Cayce have to say on this subject of music, with its positive or negative effects upon living organisms? Much indeed. We quote a little:

Music. . .is a destructive or a constructive force, dependent upon that to which it appeals in its influence. . .   3509-1

For music is of the soul, and one may become mind and soul-sick for music, or soul and mind-sick from certain kinds of music.   5401-1

The viola tuned to the vibrations of the fires of nature may be destructive or smothering or aflaming same.   275-43

. . .music that is of harmony—as of the "Spring Song," the "Blue Danube," and that character of music, with either the stringed instruments or the organ. These are the vibrations that will set [this entity] again near normalcy. . .   2712-1

There *is* music in jazz, but is there perfect harmony in same? There *is* harmony in a symphony, as in the voices as attuned to the infinite. . .   2072-10

No one mind may conceive all that may be done through the power of the Master Musician [the Christ].   281-8

Prayer can have much the same effect upon plants as music, apparently. In his book, *The Power of Prayer on Plants*,[3] the Reverend Franklin Loehr (who holds a degree in chemistry) has demonstrated conclusively that prayer can favorably affect the growth of plants in carefully controlled laboratory tests. Furthermore, his experiments showed that negative prayer can, in his own words, "repress and even turn back plant growth."

We find this related comment in one of the Cayce readings:

The entity, with the very words or the blessings in planting even a nut, may insure the next generation a nut-bearing tree! The entity with its very abilities of the magnetic forces within self, may circle one with its hands and it'll bear no more fruit, though it may be bearing nuts in the present.   3657-1

But the same reading continued with a cogent warning:

These are indications, then, of how the entity may use the energies or vibrations, even of the body, constructively or destructively. Do not use these for self in either direction. For, as just indicated, if you plant one, be sure it is for the next generation and not for this one. It is others ye must think of, as should every soul. "Others, Lord, others—that I may know Thee the better."   3657-1

In the New Testament, we have an awesome example of negative prayer, or the power of the spoken curse, in this famous anecdote about the Master (Mark 11:13, 14, 20):

"And seeing a fig tree afar off having leaves, He came, if haply He might find any thing thereon: and when He came to it, He found nothing but leaves; for the time of figs was not yet.

"And Jesus answered and said unto it, *No man eat fruit of thee hereafter for ever.* And His disciples heard it.

"And in the morning, as they passed by, they saw the fig tree dried up from the roots."

Was this a misuse by Jesus, then, of His extraordinary vibratory powers? No. Normally, of course, negative prayer of any kind would have to be regarded as an evil, because it calls into play certain destructive forces within self. But in this instance, one has to look for the symbolic significance, which justified the act. The Christ Consciousness was abroad; and the time was at hand, spiritually speaking, for bearing fruit. But the fig tree was not yet ready. It was not responsive to its chosen purpose in that given opportunity in the earth. And therein lay the curse—*within itself.* The lesson is eternal.

It is not clear whether the Loehr experiments with plants involved the use of audible or silent prayer, or both. But the results of audible prayer are apparently more effective, based upon these excerpts from the readings:

. . .the spoken word [in prayer] makes a higher vibration.
                                                                              281-9

. . .speech being even three times greater than the sense of hearing or sight; that is the highest vibration that we have in the body at all.   5681-1

[The body-physical is an atomic structure.] If in the atomic forces there becomes an overbalancing, an injury [or] accident, there are certain atomic forces destroyed or others increased. [The activity of healing, then, is to create or make a balance.] When a body has so attuned. . .or raised its own vibrations sufficiently, it may—by the motion of the spoken word—awaken the activity of the emotions to such an extent as to revivify, resuscitate, or to change the rotary force [of] the atomic forces [in another] in such a way and manner as to set it again in motion.

Thus does spiritual or psychic influence of body upon body bring healing.   281-24

That last quotation shows how the vibrations of one individual, in proper spiritual attunement, act upon the discordant vibrations in another to correct their flow, or rotary motion, much in the manner of a sudden amperage increase in electricity.

Later, we will discuss this concept in further detail, as it relates to plants.

"Plants can learn," we quoted a Toledo professor as saying. In his experiments, Professor H.L. Armus used mimosa plants—a species that is often called the "sensitive plant." The leaves of this plant will fold in the dark, or when shaken or brushed against, but it takes them about ten minutes to do so. However, Armus found that when shaking was preceded by a darkening of the room, the plants came to associate the change in light with the shaking, and they soon folded their leaves without waiting to be shaken. After repeated "lessons," the leaves folded in as little time as four minutes, rather than the normal ten-minute interval. The shaking was presumably an unpleasant sensation; and so the sensitive mimosa leaves had learned to avert the unpleasantness by closing more quickly.

It was an interesting application by Professor Armus of the Pavlovian principle of conditioned reflex, which has been tested successfully on animals and humans, but not, to our knowledge, on plants. The conclusion that plants can learn, by means of a conditioned reflex to certain undesirable sensations, contains the obvious corollary that plants can *feel*. And if they have feelings, they must have emotions of some primitive sort—or of a complex kind beyond our present comprehension.

Indeed, the work of another researcher, Cleve Backster, confirms this conclusion through the unique use of a polygraph (commonly known as a "lie detector"), which is normally used to test emotional stimulation in human beings. By connecting a pair of electrodes to a philodendron leaf, and later applying this sensitive testing mechanism on other house plants, Backster demonstrated that plants can actually register such humanly familiar emotions as apprehension, fear, pleasure, and relief. The evidence showed up in electronic tracings on the monitoring charts. But he also discovered the even more surprising fact that plants are apparently sensitive to the distress signals issued by human or animal members of the immediate community with whom they are closely associated, thus indicating, Backster believes, "the possible existence of some undefined perception" in plants.

Cayce was quite explicit about this matter of emotional sensitivity, or "feelings," extending to the plant world:

"Flowers will love the entity," he told one lady, "as the entity loves flowers! Very few flowers would ever wither while about or on this body." (5122-1)

In the same reading, he offered further indication that flowers have undetected emotional properties, when he said: "Flowers love the places where there is peace and rest."

Their service to mankind, through certain vibratory powers inherent in their colors and odors, was made clear in another reading:

Flowers—no matter whether they be in or out of season—are well to be oft about the body. The beauty, the aroma, the aliveness of same will make for vibrations that are most helpful, most beneficial.
The body becomes quite sensitive to odors, as well as colors.
1877-1

Colors and odors, then, must radiate a vibratory force similar to music and prayer. Thus, it may be said that flowers can affect man, even as man may affect flowers. All elements in the environment are in fact receiving and transmitting vibrations, good or bad, and affecting one another continually.

"All vibrations are part of the Universal Consciousness," said Cayce. (1921-1) And he insisted that "there are radiations from every form of life." (2884-1)

This applies even in the mineral kingdom. The very stones under our feet are vibrant organisms, endowed with certain qualities of mind and spirit beyond our immediate comprehension:

. . .for it [the stone] throws off as well as draws in. . .through the positive-negative vibration.					440-18

As each stone indeed has the spirit—as the spirit of the pearl, the spirit of the diamond—it is the fire that may be in a little different vibration, burned. . . 3657-1

Our subject was plants. We have not forgotten them. But this digression on stones leads us quite purposefully to some interesting speculations about seeds and moon soil.

It was recently reported in *Science Digest*[4] that a group of researchers at the Manned Spacecraft Center, Houston, had set up a miniature farm to test the results of moon soil upon various plants. To their astonishment, minuscule amounts of moon soil fed to vegetable seeds produced remarkable results. The plants were bigger, greener, and healthier-looking than those fed on a diet of earth soil alone.

The researchers have speculated that moon soil, because it is formed in an oxygen-free environment, is in a "reduced state," which may have the effect of neutralizing some growth-limiting hormone in plants. If true, this would allow the plants to grow in an unrestricted fashion.

But we find the explanation inadequate. It can only account for the larger size of the plants, and not for their greener, healthier appearance. We would suggest that the real secret of moon soil may lie in its unique vibratory force. (Certain bacteria cultures exposed to moon soil were destroyed by it, for reasons unknown.)

The following question-and-answer sequence from one of the readings is peculiarly apt, at this point:

Q-1. . . .[900's] experience seemed to be that all vibrations are already in the atmosphere or in space in various degrees of attenuation. That plants get, say, iron, iodine, and other properties, both from vibrations existent in the air, as well as from those existent in the soil. Is this correct. . .?

A-1. . . .vegetation obtains its sustenance from air and soil, correct—but there is seen that each has its effect one upon the other; that is, there must necessarily be the contact with the soil for the plant to obtain sustenance from the air. . .With that vibration set up by the seed itself, in its natural growth, or *life* is sustained in this cycle of vibration. 900-448

Cycles of vibration! Here is the operative phrase. If *life* is sustained in any given organism by a *cycle* of vibratory forces, involving "input" and "output" of current, as it were, then we must consider the cyclic acceleration and general stimulus that would probably occur in plants subjected to an oxygen-free soil, with its vastly different rate of vibration. Its unusual force might destroy bacteria, but it could have an opposite effect on the vibratory cycle of higher organisms, such as seeds and plants, causing them to flourish.

The foregoing would seem to suggest that vibrations are electronic in nature. According to Cayce, that is essentially correct. We quote:

> Just as mind or matter has its part in man's existence, so does vibration, whether electronic or of light only. Both are electronic in action, but the word does *not* indicate the variation.
> A plant treated by a low form of electrical vibration will, if kept from the light but given moisture and air, extenuate itself to a greater extent than when allowed light—*but will not be able to reproduce itself*—see? What's cut off in same?
>
> 900-448

We may conclude that light is the essence of Life itself, and that its creative vibrations are vital to the reproductive forces in our material dimension.

> Life in [all of] its manifestations is vibration. Electricity is vibration. But vibration that is creative is one thing. Vibration that is destructive is another. Yet they may be from the same source. 1861-16

We quote further:

> Electricity or vibration is that same energy, same power, ye call God. Not that God is an electric light or an electric machine, but vibration that is creative is of the same energy as life itself. 2828-4

> Every individual entity is on certain vibrations. 1861-12

> . . .the body is built up by the radiation of vibratory forces from each and every unit of the body functioning in its proper manner. 283-1

> All bodies radiate those vibrations with which it, the body, controls itself in mental, in physical, and such radiation is called the aura. 5756-1

> *Q-1. Where do I vibrate best (that is, in what locality)?*
> A-1. Where thou *art!* For the vibrations should be from *within*, rather than from *without!* 1183-1

Now we seem to be arriving at some interesting conclusions about man, which differentiate him to some degree from the other life-forms on his planet. As a free-will agent, he can *control* his vibrations, setting them in harmony with the Creative Forces or in opposition to them. And he can govern the cycle of his own vibrations from *within,* or submit to inimical vibrations from *without.* He yields nothing when he opens himself to helpful vibratory influences, such as the song of the bird or the blush of the rose, or the harmonies of a sweet symphony, for these are of the Creative Forces and given to him for his development:

One capable of seeing beauty depicted in all expressions in nature, whether the bug about its lowly activity of cleansing the conditions about man, or the beauty of song in music, whether reed or string, or the beauty in the rose, the sunset, the stream, or in the awakening of nature as it illustrates to man the new birth into another experience in the material conditions.   539-2

Meditate, **oft. Separate thyself for a season from the cares of the world. Get close to nature and** *learn* **from the lowliest of that which manifests in nature, in the earth; in the birds, in the trees, in the grass, in the flowers, in the bees; that the life of each is a manifesting, is a song of glory to its Maker. And do thou** *likewise!*   **1089-3**

We are about to conclude. Two closing questions: What is man? And what is the meaning of evolution? From Cayce, these answers:

Man was made in the beginning, as the ruler over those elements as was prepared in the earth plane for his needs. When the plane became that such as man was capable of being sustained by the forces, and conditions, as were upon the face of the earth plane, man appeared not from that already created, but as the Lord over all that was created, and in man there is found that in the living man, all of that, that may be found without in the whole, whole world or earth plane, and *other* **than that, the** *soul of man* **is that making him above all animal, vegetable, mineral kingdom of the earth plane.**

Man *did not* **descend from the monkey, but man has evolved, resuscitation, you see, from time to time, time to time, here a little, there a little, line upon line and line and line upon line.**

All souls were created in the beginning, and are finding their way back, to whence they came.   3744-4

The purpose for each soul's entrance is to complete a cycle, to get closer to the Infinite. . .   3131-1

Life can be viewed, then, as a vast cycle, acted out in a procession of smaller cycles that carry us continually upward, on higher and higher vibrations. And this is surely the very nature of Infinity itself.

The Almond—Symbol of Life

An almond a day is much more in accord with keeping the
doctor away, especially certain types of doctors, than apples.
For the apple was the fall, not the almond—for the almond
blossomed when everything else died. Remember this is life!

3180-3

I

There is a remarkable legend about the almond. It goes back
to the teachings of the Gnostics.

According to Jean Doresse, a noted French scholar and
Egyptologist, the Gnostic sect who originally called themselves
Naassenes (from the Hebrew word *naas,* meaning "serpent")
had borrowed from the Phrygians "the comparison of the
Father of the Universe to an almond kernel, existing before all
things and containing within itself the perfect fruit from which
was to come forth an invisible child, nameless and ineffable."[1]

This allusion, of course, was to the Christ. "The Christ
Consciousness," Cayce once explained, "is a *universal*
consciousness of the *Father Spirit.*" (5749-4, italics ours)

And who were the Naassenes?

We know little about them. But their teachings, Doresse tells
us, had been "passed on by James, brother of the Lord, to
Mariamne."[2] Later on, the Naassenes assumed the name of
"Gnostics." They "claimed to be unique," says Doresse, "in
their knowledge of the deepest things." One of the texts of
which they made use was a *Gospel According to Thomas.* Such
a gospel was among the Coptic scrolls found at Nag Hammadi,
Upper Egypt, in 1945; and the Fall 1968 issue of the *Journal*
contained a comparison of some of the *logia,* or sayings of

Jesus, from that arcane gospel with selections from the Cayce readings.[3]

In another reference to almonds, Doresse reports on some tomb decorations in a Gnostic sepulchre—probably Naassene—unearthed in Rome, circa 1930. We quote: "Among the figures that adorn these vaults we seem to recognize the triad of the Pleroma, and *the Good Shepherd in a frame decorated with almonds*. . ."[4] (italics ours)

Biblical references to the almond are numerous, and a few of them quite clearly suggest an esoteric symbolism.

In the Book of Genesis (43:11), it is interesting to note that almonds are included among the items Israel instructs his sons to take to Joseph, in Egypt, as a ransom for Benjamin. In Exodus (25:33-36), we find that an almond motif was chosen to adorn the golden lampstand of the tabernacle. This choice was unquestionably rooted in mystical symbolism. Finally, there is the beautiful allegory of Aaron's rod, as recounted in Numbers (17:1-8). This is one of the most striking examples of esoteric symbology in the Old Testament, and its reference to almonds undoubtedly holds an underlying significance:

> And the Lord spake unto Moses, saying,
> Speak unto the children of Israel, and take of every one of them a rod according to the house of their fathers. . .
> And thou shalt write Aaron's name upon the rod of Levi. . .
> And it shall come to pass, that the man's rod, whom I shall choose, shall blossom. . .
> And it came to pass, that on the morrow Moses went into the tabernacle of witness; and, behold, the rod of Aaron for the house of Levi was budded, and brought forth buds, and bloomed blossoms, and yielded almonds.

That wondrous effect of the life-giving Creative Forces upon the almond rod for the house of Levi, chosen of God for the priesthood, becomes doubly meaningful when we relate it to the Gnostic legend of the almond kernel. And perhaps we can safely assume that Aaron's presentation of a live almond branch, when offering a rod to represent "the house of his fathers," was the tutored result of his spiritual awareness.

That Biblical account now leads us to speculate upon the meaning of Cayce's words about the almond versus the apple: "For the apple was the fall," said Cayce, "not the almond. The almond blossomed when everything else died. Remember, this is life!" (3180-2)

The apple symbolizes the Fall of Man—his death to God Consciousness—as a result of yielding to a belief in the separation of being, through an illusory power called self-will. This is what happened in the Garden of Eden. The almond, on the other hand, is a symbol of the universal Christ—the Light, the Word—and therefore a symbol of Life itself. It signifies Man's reawakening to the Father Spirit whenever he will heed the call of the Christ Consciousness within, and seek At-onement.

That dark time of which Cayce spoke, "when everything else died," was presumably in the days of the Great Flood, and the breaking up of Atlantis. It was a period when the forces of rebellion against the Law of One had brought self-destruction to much of the Adamic race. We might speculate further that the obedient and God-fearing Noah, whose weary arkload of survivors settled at last upon the upper reaches of Mount Ararat, saw almond trees emerge from the receding tide, and watched in joyous wonder as they burst into flower and, in due season, bore fruit. . .

For, truly, was it not the almond—that sacred symbol of the Cayce said, when everything else died? Remember, O man, *"this is Life!"*

II

The almond tree, identified botanically as *Prunus amygdalus,* is believed to have had its origins in Asia Minor and the Mediterranean Basin. But the resemblance of the tree and its fruit to the peach, which originated in China, has puzzled botanists. The peach, too, is a species of *Prunus.* And in the early stages of its growth, the small, velvety green fruit of the immature peach is identical in appearance to the mature almond husk before it splits open. Moreover, the kernel inside the pit of a peach—or of an apricot, which is closely related— looks and tastes very much like an almond. However, the flavor is apt to be on the bitter side. This bitterness is due to a trace of prussic acid. The same acid is also found in bitter almonds, but not in the commoner, sweet variety.

Rather interestingly, in a book that purports to tell the secrets of the extraordinary longevity and vitality of the Hunzakuts, a people who inhabit the little-known kingdom of Hunza, high in the Himalayan hills of West Pakistan, the oil in the kernel of the apricot seed is emphasized as a contributing factor. The apricot trees in Hunza, however, are specially cultivated for sweet-tasting kernels; any tree that yields notably bitter kernels within the apricot stones, thus indicating the presence of harmful traces of prussic acid in the oil, is destroyed.[5]

In speaking of the almond, Cayce referred to "a form of vitamin" it contains, which is helpful as a preventive of cancer. (659-1) And we have already quoted his comment that "an almond a day is much more in accord with keeping the doctor away...than apples." In the same reading, he also had this to say about almonds:

> ...if an almond is taken each day, and kept up, you'll never have accumulations of tumors or such conditions through the body.   3180-3

Elsewhere, the readings recommend a higher intake:

> And know, if ye would take each day, through thy experience, two almonds, ye will never have skin blemishes, ye will never be tempted even in body toward cancer nor towards those things that make blemishes in the body forces themselves. 1206-13

> Those who would eat two or three almonds each day need never fear cancer...   1158-21

A chemical analysis of the almond, based upon research conducted by the California Almond Growers Exchange, reveals some interesting facts. For one thing, we learn that the almond contains a high percentage of essential amino compounds—fifteen, in all. It is also surprisingly rich in protein (24.5%, in unblanched almonds). This is nearly comparable, on a weight basis, to the protein value in beef or cheese, and substantially more than milk or eggs.[6] And although the 52.4% fat content in almonds is relatively high, it is primarily an unsaturated oil (oleic and linoleic fatty acids) that is readily digested and assimilated. It should also be noted that almonds have an alkaline effect. According to an independent researcher,[7] they are "the most completely alkaline" of all edible nuts.

A study of the mineral constituents in almonds shows generous levels of a number of minerals important to the human body, such as phosphorus, potassium, calcium, magnesium, sodium, sulfur and iron. Other minerals are listed also, but most of them only at trace levels. In the readings, we find an apt comment on two of the significant minerals we have mentioned: "The almond carries more phosphorus *and* iron, in a combination easily assimilated, than any other nut." (1131-2)

And what about carbohydrates? The percentage varies, in the several reports we have examined. It may run as high as 22.3%, apparently, in unblanched California almonds. But the carbohydrates in the peeled almond are quite digestible. We find this confirmed in the Autumn 1969 issue of the *Journal,* which refers to a medical report from the Rothschild Municipal Hospital, at Haifa. It was found that peeled, sweet dried almonds, in a dosage of 30 to 35 gm. twice daily, were helpful in the treatment of heartburn and peptic ulcers. While the oil and protein in the nut, in their interreaction with the gastric juices and acids, were regarded as the beneficial agents in this treatment, the report also mentioned that peeled almonds could even be safely administered to diabetic or obese patients because of the *digestible* carbohydrates, which are present in a relatively low percentage.

Now we come to vitamins, which is the most important aspect of our analysis. Vitamin determinations are as follows:

Carotene	0.0078	mg. per gm.
Vitamin B_1 (Thiamine)	0.0020	mg. per gm.
Vitamin G (Riboflavin)	0.0033	mg. per gm.
Vitamin E (Tocopherol)	2.00	mg. per gm. (0.2%)
Niacin (Nicotinic Acid)	0.07	mg. per gm.
Vitamin B_6 (Pyridoxin)	0.02	mg. per gm.
Biotin	0.00018	mg. per gm.
Choline	0.8	mg. per gm.

Edgar Cayce's reference to "a form of vitamin" in almonds that is helpful as a preventive of cancer—and, presumably, of nonmalignant tumors and skin blemishes, as well—is difficult to interpret or isolate. Are we to look for a scientifically known and established vitamin? If so, we have just listed several. Take your pick. Or is the reference to some unorthodox concept of what a vitamin actually may be? Perhaps we should look for some unsuspected *combination* of elements, which creates an as yet unrecognized vitamin value? To some, a matter of semantics may seem to be involved. In what way, for example, might *"a form of* vitamin" differ from a proper vitamin itself? We can only speculate.

In any case, a substance identified as *Amygdalin* may offer the most promising clue. We find it described in *The*

Encyclopedia Americana (1962 edition) as "a bitter, *relatively non-toxic* substance, one of a group of glycosides found in the kernels. . .of *bitter* almonds, plum, peach and *apricot.*" (italics ours) The crystalline compound, upon hydrolysis, yields benzaldehyde, hydrocyanic (i.e., *prussic*) acid, and a glucose factor identified as gentiobiose.

That doesn't tell us too much, but it tells us enough to rouse our curiosity. (We are reminded of those healthy Hunzakuts and their apricot trees!) Let us speculate for a moment. If bitter almonds are a prime source of Amygdalin, isn't it likely that sweet almonds are a sufficiently good source, too, and perhaps a safer one? Anyhow, sweet almonds are what Cayce seems to have recommended; and the Hunzakuts, of course, are equally cautious in avoiding apricot kernels with too bitter a taste...At this juncture, one is reminded of the homeopathic approach, once highly popular in certain medical circles, which favored drug treatment with attenuated doses. (A little prussic acid may go a long way!)

In a commentary on almonds by Dr. William A. McGarey, we find one of our speculations confirmed. Amygdalin is indeed present in the sweet almond. One catch, however: the bitter almond contains a ferment, emulsin, which is apparently missing from the sweet variety. And it is emulsin, in the presence of water, which acts on the glycoside, Amygdalin, causing it to yield benzaldehyde, hydrocyanic acid, and the glucose factor gentiobiose, previously mentioned. This would appear to be a necessary step, perhaps, in rendering Amygdalin useful within the human system, if it is to play a role as Cayce's mysterious "form of vitamin."

Well, let us speculate once more. Is it not possible that a natural fermenting agent within the human digestive tract may perform the same function as emulsin, when we eat sweet almonds? Thus, we would have our Amygdalin, but without an excess of hydrocyanic acid! And whatever it's good for, ours is not a "kill or cure" technique, but simply a "preventative" one...

But can Amygdalin be considered a vitamin source? Quite surprisingly it *can.* The following reference may be to Amygdalin derived from bitter almonds, rather than sweet ones; it is not made clear; but here is a quite remarkable news release from a Swiss publication, *Vaterland,* which was translated and sent to us by an A.R.E. member in Virginia Beach:

"Medical Science Confirms:

"Almonds contain a curative agent effective in cancer treatment.

"An International Cancer Congress in Baden-Baden, West Germany, with participants from both West and East European countries and the United States, reviewed promising new therapeutics which have been shown to be effective in the treatment of cancer. Several speakers stressed the importance of proper diets, containing *Amygdalin.*

"The effective agent in Amygdalin appears to be a *vitamin* designated B-17. According to the discoverer of Amygdalin, natural sources of it can be found primarily in almonds, apricot kernels, and buckwheat."

Claims of this sort have been vigorously disputed in the past by the conservative majority of the medical profession, as well as the FDA, and we can probably anticipate a similar reaction this time. When a related cancer therapy, Laetrile, was introduced in the United States, its use was subsequently banned, although treatment with Laetrile continues in Tijuana, Mexico, where many cancer patients claim complete cures or remissions. According to *Time* (April 12, 1971), Laetrile is a drug made from apricot pits, and contains "cyanide, among other things." There is no mention of almonds, nor of Amygdalin, by name, although Laetrile and Amygdalin are believed to be virtually synonymous. But the bio-chemist who developed Laetrile, Ernest T. Krebs, Jr., has labeled it *Vitamin B-17*, which coincides with the Swiss article on Amygdalin and almonds. Krebs claims that his drug works against cancer by alleviating nutritional deficiency, which he feels is the causal factor.

According to Dr. McGarey, it was originally hypothesized by the discoverer of Laetrile (described, at the time, as an extract from the apricot kernel) that the hydrocyanic acid released in Amygdalin is destroyed in the body by normal cellular oxidative metabolism, but that cancer cells, functioning *without* oxidative mechanisms, are unable to destroy the acid. They absorb the acid, which, in turn, destroys them. We do not know if that hypothesis still stands. It is an interesting one; but such a mechanism was never described nor mentioned by Cayce. It is not our intention to dispute it, of course; but the "vitamin" theory, which is in harmony with the Cayce readings, would appear to suggest a rather different principle.

In any case, we can feel quite safe in continuing to munch our two or three sweet almonds a day, for "preventative" purposes!

The oil of the almond, incidentally, is a valued ingredient in cosmetics. It is said to have a rejuvenating effect upon the skin. No one knows exactly why. But the compositon of vitamins and other materials in the oil is currently being researched by various workers in this field, we are informed.

What is the best way to eat almonds? Blanching impairs the flavor, and of course cooking or heating of any sort is detrimental to the vitamin content. But when you eat almonds in their raw, natural state, still protected by the thin brown membrane that preserves the volatile oils of the nut, you may be sure you are getting all of the healthful benefits of the almond.

Most of the almonds consumed in the United States are grown in California, where the trees were introduced by Spanish padres in the 1700s. In fact, the California Almond Growers Exchange, in its latest annual report,[8] refers to California as the world's largest producer today (about 180 million pounds annually, at present), and it states that the domestic consumption of almonds has nearly doubled in the last ten years. (We can't help but wonder if that phenomenal growth in the American consumption of almonds may not be due in some measure to Edgar Cayce's well-publicized recommendations!)

But to those who would look to the almond for their health,[9] or to any other material application by itself, it is well to bear in mind these qualifying observations from the readings:

Have ye not read that in Him ye live and move and have thy being? What are those elements in food or in drink that give growth or strength to the body? Vitamins? What are vitamins? The creative forces working with body-energies for the renewing of the body! 3511-1

Urges arise, then, not only from what one eats, but from what one thinks; and from what one does about what one thinks and eats! as well as what one digests mentally and spiritually! 2533-6

For all healing, mental or material, is attuning each atom of the body, each reflex of the brain forces, to the awareness of the Divine that lies within each atom, each cell of the body. 3384-2

Clouds Without Water

An Analysis of Freedom

Be ye not as the winds that blow about, as clouds without water; but be ye steadfast in the word of Truth. **1376-1**

And thus is freedom free indeed, as Truth makes same so. **2021-1**

A troubling question arises today in the hearts of many: *What is the prevailing spirit of the nation?*

Is it freedom, as of yore? Or is it selfishness—rebellion—strife—confusion?

Cayce himself once raised the question, in trance-state, during the parlous days of World War II, when, in mid-1944, we were finally winning our battles abroad but perhaps beginning to lose some of them at home. His answer is as valid now as then—and probably more so, as we draw ever closer to a promised New Order, the beginning of another cycle in the earth:

What is the spirit of America? Most individuals proudly boast "freedom." Freedom of what? When ye bind men's hearts and minds through various ways and manners, does it give them freedom of speech? Freedom of worship? Freedom from want? Not unless those basic principles are applicable throughout the tenets and lines as [have] been set, but with that principle freedom. For God meant man to be free, and thus gave man [free] will, a will even to defy God. **3976-29**

Thus was the warning given, almost four decades ago. Did we fail to heed it then? Then we must meet it now. Now—or surely later. For it is a law: " 'As a man soweth, so shall he reap.' " (451-1)

Today, when fear and violence loom over the land like glowering clouds, there is much confusion. How do the winds blow? Freedom, in her various forms, is loudly talked about, but too little understood or practiced. It is like "clouds without water," which billow with promise, but fail to bless the parched earth in their dry passage.

We spoke of a New Order, a changing cycle:

There is the drawing near to that period of a change again, which is as a cycle... 294-147

It is also understood, comprehended by some, that a new order of conditions is to arise; that there must be many a purging in high places as well as low; that there must be the greater consideration of each individual, each soul being his brother's keeper.

There will then come about those circumstances in the political, the economic and the whole relationships where there will be a leveling—or a greater comprehension of this need.

And then there should be, there *will* be those arising to power that are able to meet the needs. 3976-18

Clearly, then, we need not despair! But, "Rather let the attitude be in that direction of hopefulness for the things to come." (3189-3)

Yet, how does all this relate to the concept of freedom? Let us see:

For hath not God given freedom of choice to every soul? and it is the heritage of every man, every soul—*freedom!* Those that abuse same do so to their undoing. 1129-2

In Him is freedom, and ye shall be free through the more perfect understanding of the application of spiritual and material law, as One. 2734-1

Now, just how do we go about applying that concept to the world or national situation, at present? How do we proceed to make it practical in our daily lives? There is indeed a way:

The ideals, the purposes that called the nation into being are well. It might be answered by saying that there needs to be on the part of each man, each woman, the adhering to those principles that caused the formulating of the American thought. 3976-24

For, as we have given, no country is stronger than its greatest weakness in any section or in any portion of same. For it must be a *cooperative, coordinating* activity as a unit of government in its dictation, its legislation, its administration, and its coordination of *all* of these as a unit.

No *one* may become dictatorial. . .

And the laboring man, the daily laborer that lives by the sweat of the brow, shall have equal consideration before the *law* as those that *direct* the lives of many!

For *all* stand the same before the judgment bar of the Maker; and they that are oppressed, their cry goeth up to Him, ever.

3976-17

The woes besetting us can be traced to a common cause; and all of mankind is involved in the guilt, as well as its expiation:

The world, *as* a world—that makes for the disruption, for the discontent—has lost its ideal.

Man's answer to everything has been *Power*—Power of money, Power of position, Power of wealth, Power of this, that or the other. This has *never* been God's way, will never be God's way.

3976-8

There has arisen and there is arising in the affairs and the experiences of man everywhere the necessity of there being not so much the consideration of a [home-] land as of all lands as a unit. For *mankind* is his brother, and thou *art* thy brother's keeper.

3976-16

As the Spirit of God once moved to bring peace and harmony out of chaos, so *must* the Spirit move over the earth and magnify itself in the hearts, minds and *souls* of men to bring peace, harmony and understanding, that they may dwell together in a way that will bring that peace, that harmony, that can only come with all having the *one Ideal;* not the one *idea,* but "Thou shalt love the Lord thy God with all thine heart, thy neighbor *as* thyself!" This [is] the whole law, this [is] the whole answer to the world, to each and every soul. That is the answer to the world conditions as they exist today.

3976-8

Study to *analyze self* in these directions, and *remember the law.* . . [author's italics]   **2438-1**

As we start analyzing self in these directions, then, let us consider some of the common concepts of freedom and see where we stand. Moreover, let us remember the law, as we proceed. (It has just been defined for us: the law is Love.)

Freedom of speech includes freedom of the press, as well as the visual arts, incorporating the film and television industries, for all of these modes of communication are related. How should we interpret freedom for these various media? We know that we must practice tolerance and love, for these are the law. But does this involve a degree of permissiveness that allows the abuse, by one individual or group, of other individuals or groups, or the incitement to riot and mob rule, or other seditious practices that violate our democratic processes? Does it mean that we shall resign ourselves to the passive acceptance of false or misleading advertising, or to dissemblance and corruption in government or business? Are we to be indifferent to the blatant thrusts of hardcore pornography in films and magazines and books? We can look within and find the answers to all of these questions; and from the readings, we can gain some guidance:

. . .Jesus, the Christ. . .has set the example. . .of freedom of speech, freedom of activity; yet bound within that which is ever constructive. He has not given freedom that is licentious, or freedom that is self-indulgent, or freedom that does not consider the needs, the desires, the positions of others. . .

1352-4

. . .freedom of speech does not privilege any entity, or individual, to speak ill of his neighbor, but rather there is the privilege of thinking, being, a constructive influence in speech, in thought, in activity. 2021-1

. . .do not become an extremist in any sense, whether from the spiritual, mental, physical, social, moral or financial aspect, but knowing that moderation in all gives the clearer understanding. . . 900-88

Anger is correct, provided it is *governed*. . .There is *power* even in anger. He that is angry and sinneth not controls self. He that is angry and allows such to become the expression in the belittling of self, or the self-indulgence of self in any direction, brings to self those things that partake of the spirit of that which is the product or influence of anger itself.

361-4

He, too, showed anger at the house of the Lord being turned into a den of those who took advantage of their fellow man.

602-7

Let that mind be in thee, then, as was in Christ Jesus, who boldly claimed His relationship to God, and so lived among His fellow man. 602-7

Be ye mindful that He of whom ye speak, when ye preach, giveth power to the words, only as ye practice it in thine own life. Ye may not expect to succeed in convincing thy brother that he should be patient or kind, or even hear thee, unless ye are patient and kind thyself. Don't preach one thing and practice another. For this is inconsistent, and inconsistency is sin, and be sure thy sins will find thee out. 5275-1

. . .helpful [i.e., constructive] criticism is helpful to an individual. Criticism that is done in the spirit of criticism is not helpful. Criticism in the spirit of love may always be helpful. 294-204

But what of those disruptive forces that would appear to be eroding the very foundations of our society? Our courts are besieged. The oppressed have become the oppressors. Radical elements of every description are trying to destroy law and order. Our banks and other institutions are being bombed and burned. Crime and violence are increasing in the streets, and a flourishing drug culture shows no signs of abating. America is surely a land in turmoil, with all of its freedoms threatened. How should we meet these chaotic forces?

Know that even as the powers of evil are loosed for the correcting of many, so are the glories of Him made manifest in the hearts and lives of many. 262-30

In an hour of trial, when there are influences abroad that would change or mar, or take away that freedom which is the gift of the Creative Forces. . .there should be the willingness to pattern the life, the emergencies, the exigencies as may arise, much in the way and manner as the Master indicated to each and every soul. 602-7

Ye are to have turmoils. . .
To meet same? Only that each soul turns not to self alone and cry for strength, but that each soul *lives* in such a manner that there may be the awakening to the needs, the purposes, the causes for the nation coming into existence!
. . ."If ye will call, I will hear." 3976-24

So long as ye turn thy thoughts to the manners and means for meeting and overcoming those destructive forces, ye show forth that which may bring to the world that day of the Lord. For the promise is that in the latter days there shall be the purposes in the *hearts* of men, everywhere!   3976-23

Know in self that in giving a helpful influence, the magnifying of virtues in others and the minimizing of faults is the beginning of wisdom in dealing with others. *Not that the evil influence is denied,* but rather that force within self is stressed which when called upon is so powerful that those influences about self *may never hinder.* [Author's italics]
2630-1

We see, then, that protection is ever available to us, if we are seeking to do His Will. This does not mean, of course, that we should not work toward the establishment and implementation of more effective laws, where necessary, to reduce the ravages of unchecked crime and rebelliousness, or to seek out and eliminate their root causes. Our duty to God does not erase our civic responsibilities in any way, but the former does indeed set the pattern for the fulfilling of the latter. Here are a couple of boldly instructive social concepts from the readings, which may point the way, in general, toward establishing a more productive society by legal means:

...in that same principle that he that labors may eat, he that [is able, but] labors not, may not eat.   3976-24

Not that all would be had in common as in the communistic idea, save as to keep that balance, to keep that oneness, to keep that association of ideas, of activity, of the influences throughout the experience of all.   3976-19

Meanwhile, we may be sure that those who engage in harmful or non-productive activities will eventually have to meet same within themselves:

Let us indeed know then that God is not mocked, and that what we sow we must meet in our own selves.   262-114

They that choose some other way become the children of darkness; and they are these: envying, strife, hate; and the children of these are sedition, rebellion, and the like. 262-46

Hence that force which rebelled in the unseen forces (or in spirit), that came into activity, was that influence which has been called Satan, the Devil, the Serpent; they are One. That of *rebellion!* Hence, when man in any activity rebels against the influence of good, he hearkens to the influence of evil. . .

262-52

The use of strife, lording over others, taking advantage of others—these bring doubt, fear, consternation in the mental, and disease, disruption, disorders, in the physical.   **531-1**

As the vital cells of the body—when they have rebelled, and caused sufficient others to do likewise, destruction sets in.

3976-28

For that which has a beginning must have an ending. Hence rebellion and hate and selfishness must be wiped away, and with them will go sorrow and tears and sadness. For *only* good shall rule.   **262-114**

Some of the current strife in our nation has its roots deeply imbedded in unresolved racial injustices, and the white man cannot hope to free himself from racial strife until he accepts and embraces his black brother, or his brown or red or yellow brothers, as souls who are equally loved by God, and justified under the law:

. . .all groups must have their representation and their privileges, that they—too—may have the opportunity. Unless we begin within our own selves and our own household, we are false to ourselves and to the principles that we attempt to declare. By setting classes or masses against other groups—this is *not* brotherly love!   **3976-28**

For know that *God* is not a respecter of persons nor of races, but is as has been given of old, "Know the Lord thy God is *One!*"   **1438-1**

Raise not democracy nor any other name above the brotherhood of man, the Fatherhood of God!   **3976-24**

Yet, what of those minority groups or individuals who feel that they are being victimized by society, and seek to redress the balance according to their own terms? There is a cogent warning for them:

. . .those who attempt to "get even" or who would stand for their rights irrespective of what may be brought for others will find disturbing forces in their experience in the material sojourns.   1539-2

Sexual freedom is probably more discussed today than any other single subject. But here, too, we need to redefine our terms. If we think self-gratification and lust are forms of freedom, we have lost sight of freedom's meaning. From the readings:

Q-6. How should love and the sexual life properly function?
A-6. . . .the relations in sexual life should be the outcome—not the purpose of, but the outcome of the answering of soul to soul in their associations and relations. . .For, in the understandings, know that Love and God are One; that relations in the sexual life are the manifestations in the mental attributes of each as to an expression of that which becomes manifested in the experience of each so concerned.
For, unless such associations become on such a basis, they become vile in the experience of those who join in such relations.   272-7

Q-1. Is sexual intercourse outside of marriage injurious morally and spiritually?
A-1. This must ever be answered from one's own inner self. Those attributes of procreation. . .are from the God-Force Itself. The promptings of the inner man must ever be the guide...In the light of thine own understanding, keep thy body pure, as thou would have others keep their bodies pure. For thy body is the temple of the living God. Do not desecrate same in thine own consciousness.   826-2

Q-1. Are there any sex practices that should be abolished—
A-1. [Interrupting] There are many sex *practices* in the various portions of this land, as in other lands, that should be—*must* be abolished.   5747-3

Q-1. Is monogamy the best form of home relationship?
A-1....monogamy is the best, of course, as indicated from the Scripture itself—*one—ONE!* For the union of one should ever be *One.*   826-6

What of freedom of worship? When we attempt to force our religious convictions upon another, are we observing and remembering the law? We may mean well, but we have forgotten that "truth is a *growing* experience" (281-27), and each individual has a sacred right to seek and choose according to his own emerging needs:

Never force an issue. Never attempt to show individuals, that they may be convinced. There is the necessity for each seeker to realize his need; and unless there is that realization, *how* can such find in that which is spiritual that which is true in his seeking?   254-97

...political and religious views [are] the basis of many of the disputes in the lives of individuals...but [we may] hold to *all*—or that the purpose, yea, the intent of religion is that *peace* may be to body and mind of those who embrace same.
Then the fewer definitions there be of that to which an individual is to subscribe, the greater may be the peace and the harmony in the experience of every soul.   1467-3

...it will ever be found that truth—whether in this or that schism or ism or cult—is of the One source. Are there not trees of oak, of ash, of pine? There are the needs of these for meeting this or that experience...
Then, all will fill their place. Find not fault with *any*, but rather show forth as to just how good a pine, or ash, or oak, or *vine*, thou art!   254-87

The church is in thyself. For, thy body is the temple of the living God...Hence not in an organization, not in a name, not in a title...   2403-1

A particular church organization is well. For it centers the mind. But don't get the idea you have the whole cheese.
3350-1

Correlate not the differences, but where all religions meet—THERE IS ONE GOD! "Know, O Israel, the Lord thy God is ONE!"   991-1

What of patriotism? Remembering what manner of law we keep—loving all as one—we may then be tempted to ask, to what extent can our concept of freedom be hinged to a particular flag, or to conscription under that flag? Here, again, the answer must ever lie within self. But it is not apt to be in the direction of fighting for a flag against the dictates of conscience, merely on the chauvinistic principle of "my country, right or wrong!" At the same time, if the cause for a war is deemed just, and in defense of our vital liberties, the readings suggest that compliance with a higher Law may be involved, and that serving the national interest in such a case may coincide with serving mankind as a whole, and thereby serving God:

One should ever be able and willing even to lay down the life, [that those] principles. . .may live as He indicated; that of freedom not only from the fear of servitude, not only from the dictates as to the manner in which love, sacrifice, obedience may be administered to the faith and hope that lies within him, but that the whole earth may indeed be a better place for an individual, for those that are to come to reside in.   602-7

Thus, our analysis of freedom is concluded. We have remembered the law; love is the fulfilling of the law. The road to freedom, then, is love. "The evasion of a law," Cayce has said quite plainly, "only puts conditions off [that] must eventually be met." (3744-6) The student of that dictum, desiring to be free, will constantly study to analyze self, and he will temper his actions to conform to the law. In this way, he will eventually become a law unto himself.

And ye shall know the Truth, and the Truth shall make you free. (John 8:32)

Gods in the Making

Come, let us ponder a mystery! Are we gods or men?

"I have said, *Ye are gods,*" sang the psalmist, "and all of you are children of the Most High. But ye shall die like men, and fall like one of the princes."[1]

Men or gods? The words of the psalmist are troubling to the soul. They appear to contain a riddle. First, he says we are gods, and the children of God. But can a god "fall like one of the princes"? If we are to die like men, we are surely mortals. Or are we perhaps transitional beings—both men and gods, yet really neither? Men, yes, in the sense of our present state of limited awareness; but gods in the making! Two excerpts from the Cayce readings, containing unfamiliar sayings of Jesus, would appear to corroborate this view:

For, as the Master gave, "Ye *are* gods," if ye will use His force of desire and will in His kingdom, but *not* thine own.

262-64

So are ye gods in the making, saith He that walked among men as the greater teacher of all experiences and ages.

699-1

Marvelous words, those. But what hard evidence do we have that the Master ever actually taught His disciples such a bold doctrine? Nowhere in the New Testament do we find this esoteric teaching openly propounded.

It is alluded to, however, in John 10:34, when Jesus responds to His accusers, saying: "Is it not written in your law, 'I said, Ye are gods'?" He was quoting from the 82nd Psalm, of course. But although the psalmist indeed sang those wondrous words, "Ye are gods," it may have been only a poetic metaphor to match the angelic pluckings of his harp. In fact, the psalm in question was not even composed by David; it is ascribed, instead, to one Asaph, a musician in David's court.

Or was Asaph more than a musician? In II Chronicles 29:30, we find him referred to as "Asaph the Seer." A Levite, he was one of the leaders of David's choir, and also a composer. To this same Asaph are attributed a number of the Psalms, of which several are highly prophetic, and his closeness to David the King is made apparent in this reference from Nehemiah (12:46): "For in the days of David and Asaph of old there were chief of the singers, and songs of praise and thanksgiving unto God."

Did Cayce, in any of his numerous readings that touched upon Biblical characters, have anything to add to our scant knowledge of Asaph? He did. Moreover, if we can accept what he had to say, the revelation is startling. According to Cayce, that same soul-entity who was Adam in the beginning, and who was Jesus in his final projection into the earth-plane, was also (among his more important incarnations) Enoch, Melchizedek, Joseph, Joshua. . .and *Asaph*. (364-7)

In the 82nd Psalm, when Asaph used his prophetic voice to tell the people, "I have said, 'Ye are gods,' " why did he invoke the past tense? If it was a new utterance, not taught or spoken before, surely the present tense would have been more appropriate: "I say ye are gods." We are therefore led to speculate that this cabbalistic teaching (seemingly in contradiction of Mosaic law) may already have been introduced by Asaph in a former time, if only to an initiated few who could comprehend its meaning. The question: Was it some time during his earthly appearance as Asaph? Or had he perhaps spoken thus to the Israelites when he moved among them as Joseph, the interpreter of dreams, or as Joshua, whom Cayce described as the "mouthpiece of Moses"? Or was it as Melchizedek, high priest of Salem, appearing to their father, Abraham? We can only speculate.

While we are speculating, let us ponder another psalm of Asaph's, in which the psalmist makes a sudden and curious transition in his narrative from the third person to the first person singular. He does this when referring to Joseph among the Egyptians, whose language was strange to Joseph's untutored ears: "This he ordained in Joseph for a testimony, when he went out through the land of Egypt: where *I* heard a language that *I* understood not."[2] (italics ours)

Did Asaph, through his great spiritual insight as the reputed seer, have access to the akashic records, even as the entranced

Cayce did, so that it became natural for him to use the pronoun "I" when referring to Joseph, which was one of his own prior incarnations? It would seen probable. Then, as we have already theorized, this might also explain his past-tense expression, *"I have said,* Ye are gods."

But after uttering that saying, what did Asaph mean when he added, cryptically, "Ye shall fall like one of the princes"? We can easily understand his other comment, "Ye shall die like men," for this is a mortal fact we are all conditioned to accept; but it is less easy to comprehend that enigmatic reference to "one of the princes"—unless Asaph was alluding to that fallen Son of God, Lucifer, who had renounced his princely heritage in heaven to become the Prince of Darkness! Are we fallen too, then, like Lucifer? We shall return to examine this idea in detail later on.

Meanwhile, we now come to a cryptic reference from a fourth-century Gnostic source that may shed some light upon that same mystical quotation attributed by Cayce to the Master, and also spoken by Asaph, "Ye are gods." Those words themselves are not used in this particular reference, but they are so plainly implied, in this writer's opinion, that we consider the source worth quoting. It is Logion 13, from *The Gospel According to Thomas.*[3]

"And He [Jesus] took him [Thomas], He withdrew, He spoke *three words* to him. Now when Thomas came to his companions, they asked him: What did Jesus say to thee? Thomas said to them: If I tell you one of the words which He said to me, you will take up stones and throw at me; and fire will come from the stones and burn you up."

What were the three words Jesus spoke, and why did one of the words have such power to shock the ear of an orthodox Jew? If the Master had said to Thomas, "Ye are *gods,"* we can well imagine that such a hard teaching would have sounded blasphemous to some of the disciples, who were probably not spiritually ready at that time to grasp the Master's meaning. After all, as in the days of Asaph of old, these were men who had been brought up in the rigid tradition of the Mosaic laws, whose first commandment was, "Thou shalt have no other gods before Me."[4] The belief in many gods was, of course, sacrilege; it was akin to the heathen profanations of the Roman occupiers. But to claim for oneself, as a Jew, a status seemingly equal to or rivaling Jehovah was an unutterable sin against the Holy One of Israel. Thus, Thomas's reluctance to repeat such a claim to his fellow disciples would be quite understandable. On the other hand, if he had caught the full meaning of the Master's arcane utterance, or even a glimpse of its significance, this would explain his ominous warning in the face of spiritual ignorance: "You will take up stones and throw at me. . .and fire will come from the stones and burn you up!"

However, if the Master taught His disciples, "Ye are *gods*," He also qualified that teaching, according to Cayce, and taught that the demonstration of our divine birthright is dependent upon a gradual process of soul development, or self-realization. For, as given:

So are ye gods in the making, saith He that walked among men as the greater teacher of all experiences and ages.

699-1

Hence the purpose is to grow in grace, knowledge, understanding, for the indwelling in that *Presence*. **1861-4**

Godhood is our destiny, here and now. But we are not there until *we know* we are there, fully conscious of standing in the divine Presence. We are like acorns in a forest. We do not know we are oak trees, really, until we take root and begin to grow. Meister Eckhart, the celebrated 14th-century mystic, has expressed this idea quite beautifully for us:

"The seed of God is in us. Given an intelligent farmer and a diligent fieldhand, it will thrive and grow up to God whose seed it is and, accordingly, its fruit will be God-nature. Pear seeds grow into pear trees; nut seeds into nut trees; and God-seed into God!"[5]

He carries the analogy somewhat further, referring to the divine nature within us as the "inner aristocrat":

"As for this inner aristocrat, stamped with the likeness of God, in whom the divine seed is sown, sometimes this seed and likeness of the divine nature appears, and one is aware of it; and then again it goes into hiding."[6]

It hides from us whenever we *will* it to do so, and not otherwise. For it is only self-will that can separate us from God:

What has been given as the truest of all that has ever been written in Scripture? "God does not will that any soul should perish"! But man, in his headstrongness, harkens oft to that which would separate him from his Maker! **262-56**

One might logically ask: If an all-powerful God truly cares, why then did He create us subject to sin and temptation? Why has He permitted His children to stray, and to suffer the afflictions of the flesh? For the answers, we need to go back to the beginning:

Q-11. Comment upon the following. . .The Creator, in seeking to find or create a being worthy of companionship, realized that such a being would result only from a free will exercising its divine inheritance and through its own efforts find its Maker. Thus, to make the choice really a divine one caused the existence of states of consciousness, that would indeed tax the free will of a soul; thus light and darkness. Truly, only those tried so as by fire can enter in.
A-11. The only variation that we would make is that all souls in the beginning were one with the Father. The separation, or turning away, brought evil. Then there became the necessity of the awareness of self's being out of accord with, or out of the realm of blessedness; and, as given of the Son, "yet learned he obedience through the things which he suffered."   262-56

Yet we know, or find, that the kingdom of heaven is within; and that the awareness, the awakening comes from within.
Not that man is awakened all at once, but here a little, there a little, line upon line, precept upon precept.   262-119

Hence the development is through the planes of experience that an entity may become one *with* the First Cause. . .5749-3

. . .all truth, all knowledge, all light, is at the hand of *every* individual.   333-6

. . .know that within self ye are an individual entity, a universe within self, with all the potential powers and faculties of the Divine—as well as the hellish!   5332-1

Remember, all ye may know of heaven or hell is within your own self.   4035-1

Hence the two influences that are ever before thee: good and evil, life and death; choose thou!   262-119

Now we can begin to comprehend the meaning and magnitude of our divine heritage, and to glimpse the awesome responsibilities attendant upon the decision of the will, uniting with *His* Will, to let the divine seed in us take root and grow. There will be trials and tribulations, to be sure. There will be temptations. But if we are God-seed, we must inevitably grow into God. And He knows His own:

Truly, only those tried so as by fire can enter in.   262-56

In trials, tribulations, temptations even, there may be seen the hand of the Lord—if ye do not blame others for same.
262-116

Count thy hardships, thy troubles, even thy disappointments, rather as stepping-stones to know His way better ...Are ye seeking the easy way? Did He? Come! Be joyous...
262-83

Let the *spirit* be the motivating force in thy desire, rather than the exaltation of the flesh in any individual experience. For God giveth the increase, whether in the flesh or in the mental forces, *as* thou hast purposed or desired from within. For thou *art* gods in the making.   262-67

"The soul grows upon that it is fed," Cayce warned. (262-24) Thus, the danger lies in the misapplication of knowledge, the abuse of spiritual power—seeking power within self, apart from God. This was the sin of the early Atlanteans, we are told:

...in the Atlantean land, during those periods of the early rise in that land of the sons of Belial as oppositions, that became more and more materialized as the powers were applied for self-aggrandizement.   2850-1

Those that look only to the god within may become idol worshippers...   262-83

We are reminded of what the Master said:
"I can of mine own self do nothing."[7] "The Father that dwelleth in me doeth the works."[8]
"I am in the Father, and the Father in me."[9] "I and my Father are One."[10]
In other words, the choice before us—the choice of good or evil—is in choosing to be gods within ourselves, separate from the Father, or in uniting ourselves with Him, as individual parts of the Universal Whole. It is a matter of seeking or rejecting our birthright:

...the soul of each entity is a corpuscle in the body of God.
5367-1

...the gift of God to man is an *individual* soul that may be one *with* Him, and that may know itself to be one with Him and yet individual in itself, with the attributes *of* the whole, yet *not* the whole.   262-11

The soul of each individual is a portion then of the Whole, with the birthright of Creative Forces to become a co-creator with the Father, a co-laborer with Him. As that birthright is then manifested, growth ensues. If it is made selfish, retardments must be the result.   1549-1

Are retardments inevitable? No. If we are truly on the spiritual path, we have now learned the way to avoid them, after many lifetimes of stumbling. Or, if we stumble momentarily, we are quickly up again, making our path straight. But it would appear from the readings that the pattern of development for each soul seeking material expression initially involved a downward trend, as the soul first separated itself from the Maker; then a gradual reversal took place, through a process of suffering and enlightenment, as the soul began its slow ascent back to the primal Source, preparing itself for the ecstasy of true companionship as a co-creator, a co-laborer with Him.

"Since we find God in Oneness," taught Meister Eckhart, "that oneness must be in him who is to find God." Continuing: "Different things will all be parts of that One to you and will no longer stand in your way. The One remains the same One in thousands of thousands of stones as much as in four stones: a thousand times a thousand is just as simple a number as four."[11]

Earlier, we had quoted the psalmist, who prophesied concerning the fall of man: "Ye shall. . .fall like one of the princes!" We identified the fallen prince as Lucifer. And what of the fall of man? Let us go back, once more, to the beginning:

...error or separation began before there appeared what we know as the Earth, the Heavens. . .   262-115

. . .there was the force of attraction and the force that repelled.

In the beginning, celestial beings. We have first the Son, then the other sons or celestial beings that are given their force and power.

Hence that force which rebelled in the unseen forces (or in spirit), that came into activity, was that influence which has been called Satan, the Devil, the Serpent; they are One. That of *rebellion!*   262-52

It has been understood by most of those who have attained to a consciousness of the varied presentations of good and evil in manifested forms, as we have indicated, that the prince of this world, Satan, Lucifer, the Devil—as a soul—made those necessities, as it were, of the consciousness in materiality; that man might—or that the soul might—become aware of its separation from the God-force.   262-89

Q-19. When did the knowledge come to Jesus that He was to be the Savior of the world?
A-19. When He fell in Eden.   2067-7

Q-16. Should Jesus [Adam] be described as the soul who first went through the cycle of earthly lives to attain perfection, including perfection in the planetary lives also?
A-16. He should be. . .   5749-14

Then those so entering *must* continue through the earth until the body-mind is made perfect for the soul, or the body-celestial again.   262-99

All must be lifted up, even as He.   1158-5

. . .He (Jesus) thought it not robbery to be equal with God. . .
                                                                 262-63

Come, then! Let us rejoice! Our heritage has been revealed to us. We ponder a Miracle. We are men in the flesh, but not bound to the flesh. We are bound to the Spirit, from whence we came. We are gods in the making.

Epilogue

Ye, then, are not aliens [but] rather the *Sons* of the Holy One.
                                                                 262-24

Sunspots: Signs of Turmoil

Science, albeit unwittingly, has once again corroborated psychic revelation, and this time on a most unlikely subject: sunspots.*

Before we examine the scientific evidence on the subject, however, let's take a look at the psychic record. At the A.R.E.'s Ninth Annual Congress, on June 21, 1940, Edgar Cayce was asked, while in a trance state, to give a discourse on sunspots, explaining their cause and effect. To any other audience, the explanation that followed would have sounded astonishing and implausible; but to the group assembled on that date, who were already accustomed to a flow of unorthodox answers and information from this same psychic channel before them, Cayce's explanation of sunspots—although undoubtedly unique, as might be expected—was neither implausible nor particularly surprising. It had a spiritual logic of its own,

---

*Author's update: In their recently published book, *The Cycles of Heaven* (St. Martin's Press, N.Y., 1978; pp. 274-6), Playfair and Hill cite the little-known findings of a Russian scientist, Prof. Aleksandr Leonidovich Chizhevsky (1897-1964), who had noted a connection between solar and human activity as early as June 1915, when a large group of sunspots crossed the central meridian of the Sun at a time when the toughest battles of World War I were being fought. Following years of exhaustive research into present and past periods of human turmoil, or "mass excitability," as he termed it, Chizhevsky theorized in 1926, in a strikingly similar but reverse approach to Cayce's explanation of the matter, that "the electrical energy of the Sun is the superterrestrial factor which influences historical processes." Yet—inconsistent with his theory, but not with the Cayce interpretation—Chizhevsky discovered a slight time-lag between peaks of mass excitability (or turmoil) and sunspot indices, with the former peaking first.

transcending presently accepted scientific views of man and the universe, but intuitively "right" to anyone attuned to the concepts presented in the readings. These constantly reiterate the oneness of all force. They demonstrate, over and over, our inseparable relationship with, and individual impact upon, the rest of mankind and all the world around us.

Lines of force at the unconscious level, we discover, connect all life-forms in the universe with one another, and with Spirit, which is their source, so that communications are ever possible to those "tuned in" to the universal forces. The visible universe, we are told, was created to meet the evolving needs for the soul's development upward to the Mind of the Maker, and we are reminded that "the soul of man, thy soul, encompasses *all* in this solar system or in others." (5755-2)

Consequently, it cannot come as a surprise to discover the interaction of the soul's vibration with those vibrations emanating from the various planets, or from the sun, which rules our solar system. And this, in fact, was the gist of Cayce's unconscious discourse on sunspots, in reading 5757-1, from which we quote several key passages.

First, the reading included some prefatory comments on astronomy versus astrology, which are peculiarly appropriate at this time, perhaps, when a group of leading scientists in this country has recently chosen to denounce astrology in a manner that has been more reactionary than objective:

Astronomy is considered a science and astrology as foolishness. Who is correct? One holds that because of the position of the earth, the sun, the planets, they are balanced one with another in some manner, some form; yet that they have nothing to do with man's life or the expanse of life, or the emotions of the physical being in the earth.

Then, why and how do the effects of the sun *so* influence other life in the earth and not affect *man's* life, man's emotions?

As the sun has been set as the ruler of this solar system, does it not appear to be reasonable that it *has* an effect upon the inhabitants of the earth, as well as upon plant and mineral life in the earth?

. . .For, remember, they—the sun, the moon, the planets— have their marching orders from the Divine, and they move in same.

Man alone is given that birthright of free will. He alone may defy his God!

How many of you have questioned that in thine own heart, and know that thy disobedience in the earth reflects unto the heavenly hosts and thus influences that activity of God's command! For *you*—as souls and sons and daughters of God—*defy* the living God!

As the reading proceeded, it became increasingly clear that man himself is responsible for the disruptive activities of solar storms and other phenomena resulting from sunspots, and that he has a relationship with the sun that has never been considered by modern science:

As the sun is made to shed light and heat upon God's children in the earth, it is then of that composition of which man is made, or of that termed the earth; yet, as ye have seen and know, there is solid matter, there is liquid, there is vapor. All are one in their various stages of consciousness or of activity for what? Man—*Godly man!* Yet when these become as in defiance to that light which was commanded to march, to show forth the Lord's glory, His beauty, His mercy, His hope, yea, His patience—do ye wonder then that there becomes reflected upon even the face of the sun those turmoils and strifes that have been and that are the sin of man?

Whence comest this?

All that was made was made to show to the sons, the souls, that God *is* mindful of His children.

How do they affect man? How does a cross word affect thee? How does anger, jealousy, hate, animosity, affect thee *as* a son of God? If thou art the father of same, oft ye cherish same. If thou art the recipient of same from others, thy brethren, how does it affect thee? Much as that confusion which is caused upon the earth by that which appears as a sunspot. The disruption of communications of all natures between men is what? Remember the story, the allegory if ye choose to call it such, of the tower of Babel.

. . .These [sunspots] become, then, as the influences that would show man as to his littleness in even entertaining hate, injustice, or that which would make a lie.

Be honest with thyself, as ye would ask even the ruler of thine earth—the sun—to harken to the voice of that which created it and to give its light *irrespective* of how ye act! For, as given, the sun shineth upon the just and the unjust alike, yet it is oft reflected in what happens to thee in thy journey through same.

The more ye become aware of thy relationships to the universe and those influences that control same, the greater thy ability to help, to aid—the greater thy ability to rely upon the God-force within; but *still* greater thy *responsibility* to thy fellow men. For, as ye do it unto the least, ye do it unto thy Maker—even as to the sun which reflects those turmoils that arise with thee; even as the earthquake, even as wars and hates, even as the influences in thy life day by day.

Finally, in these somber words from his unconscious communion with the universal forces, Mr. Cayce gave a more precise definition of sunspots to his attentive audience, and prescribed a spiritual remedy for this solar "ailment":

Then, what are the sunspots? A natural consequence of that turmoil which the sons of God in the earth reflect upon same...

He has given thee a mind, a body; an earth, a land in which to dwell. He has set the sun, the moon, the planets, the stars about thee to remind thee, even as the psalmist gave, "Day unto day uttereth speech, night unto night sheweth knowledge"...

Know that thy mind—thy *mind*—is the builder! As what does thy soul appear? A spot, a blot upon the sun? or as that which giveth light unto those who sit in darkness, to those who cry aloud for hope?

Now, then, let us examine sunspots through the telescope of science.

A sunspot is a broad, shallow depression lying a few hundred kilometers below the surface of the sun, and for this reason it is seen in photographs as a "black" spot. Yet that adjective is not inappropriate. A big sunspot, when it is directly facing the earth, can literally "black out" our sunlight by as much as four percent! The temperature in these spots, or depressed areas, is significantly lower than the rest of the sun, and it is widely believed that the intense magnetic fields found in association with sunspots are responsible for the reduced temperature in these depressed plains, or umbras, as they are called.

Most frequently, sunspots are found in pairs, one negatively charged and the other positive. There is generally a corresponding pair in reverse placement on the opposite side of the sun's equator, and this phenomenon suggests the passage of magnetic currents directly through the body of the sun, in response to the violent activity generated by these solar hurricanes (sunspots). Sometimes sunspots are located in bipolar clusters of varying magnitude, with the individual spots lasting from just a few days to several months; the bigger spots may be many times the size of the Pacific Ocean. By way of contrast, sunspots in the past were far less numerous than now, and sometimes appeared only singly, for a short duration.

There is a concentrated magnetic field closely allied with each spot, which appears to participate in the growth or the decay of the spot. And it is believed that the entangling of magnetic fields of opposite polarity, which virtually annihilate each other, is the cause of solar flares. The biggest sunspots are also the focal point of the largest flares, some of which rise to extraordinary heights extending for as much as 100,000 kilometers across the solar disk. These flares, in turn, are sometimes accompanied by intense bursts of solar energies, known as proton storms, affecting the earth's ionosphere. The solar wind becomes more gusty, buffeting the earth's magnetic field as it sweeps out through the solar system, and producing geomagnetic storms that disrupt communications, cause magnetic needles to vibrate, and occasionally throw power plants out of kilter. Their less visible and less immediate effects on man and the environment can only be guessed at. But consider this: Radio-astronomy has revealed the existence of ionic "noise storms," with the audible outbursts from sunspots sometimes multiplying in intensity *"by a factor of ten million in a few minutes."*[1] [Author's italics]

Science may one day conclude that the sun is a living organism. As one of the variable stars, it is pulsing regularly. There is also a pulsating rhythm to the sunspot cycles, as we shall discuss presently. In fact, Charles G. Abbot, of the Smithsonian Observatory, claims to have measured as many as 64 different cycles of solar fluctuation. One of these reportedly corresponds to a "212-day cycle noted in some studies of human pulse rate."[2] Others, we are told, "have been correlated with recurrent mental ailments, cholera, meningitis, gestation eclampsia, and even the suicide rate." Such findings imply a meaningful connection between man's vibrations and the sun's. We shall soon reveal yet another.

The history of sunspots can be traced to Chinese observers in the first century B.C., although those early stargazers attributed the dark spots to the passage of birds. However, in 1610 A.D., Galileo made the first scientific observation of sunspots with a telescope. Since that time, there has been a gradual accumulation of scientific data that permits a number of interesting conclusions.

Sunspot activity now occurs in paired cycles of 11 years each, with minimum and maximum phases of activity. The magnetic polarity of the spots is reversed in the second sunspot cycle, as the sun's north and south magnetic poles are exchanged. Despite its consistency, this cyclical pattern was not confirmed until 1843. Its delayed recognition was because of older records, which had shown a more erratic history of sunspot activity prior to that date. Following the discovery of sunspots in 1610, the published records initially suggested a 15-year periodicity; but then the number of sunspots and related solar activity declined to a very low level about 1645, remaining almost entirely absent until 1715.

"After 1715," reports Dr. E.N. Parker, in an article appearing in the September 1975 issue of *Scientific American*,[3] "the sunspot cycle as we know it today appeared and has continued ever since." Yet he cautions against "the prejudice that the 11-year sunspot cycle with its thousands of spots in each cycle is the norm. We can only wait to see what the next few centuries bring." Parker proceeds with this further fascinating observation: "During the 70 years of inactivity observers often had to wait years to see a single sunspot, whereas now there are usually a few spots showing even during the minimum of the sunspot cycle."

Magnetic storms and auroral displays virtually disappeared during the same quiescent period. But the most intriguing aspect of that 70-year interval when sunspots virtually ceased was the astonishing discovery, as late as 1922, that there had been an inexplicable connection between this solar phenomenon and plant growth. This discovery, reports Dr. Parker, came about rather accidentally. A.E. Douglass, whose pioneering work on tree-ring dating was first published in 1920, had noted a cyclical variation in the annual growth-rate of trees, with a tendency for the rings to increase in size through one decade, then decline in the next. (He had not yet linked this phenomenon to the 11-year sunspot cycles, however.) But as his study progressed, and he examined samples of wood several centuries old, Douglass found a remarkable absence of the usual cyclical variation during the last half of the 17th century or so. The annual rings for that period were virtually uniform in width and pattern. Douglass was thoroughly baffled until, in 1922, he learned of the absence of the sunspot cycle and solar activity for the 70-year period covering the last half of the 17th century, and somewhat beyond, coinciding perfectly with the uniform tree-rings he had encountered in older wood samples. His finding was officially reported to the British Astronomical Association; but, as Dr. Parker says, "Why terrestrial weather and plant growth should vary in coincidence with solar activity is a mystery that has been unresolved in the half-century since Douglass' observation." And he concludes: "The problem is difficult and racked by heated controversy, but it is too important to be ignored. The growth of plants, after all, is the basis for life on the earth."

We agree wholeheartedly with that conclusion. However, we feel that the view of science is somewhat too narrow, and we would expand upon it. Quite logically, if plant life followed a more balanced pattern of growth during the 70 years of sunspot inactivity, one should expect that animal life—including man—was similarly affected by a condition of greater equanimity and balanced behavior.

Let the zoologists look to their records. It may prove interesting. As for man, we can seek confirmation in the annals of human history. And what we seek, we shall find.

We find it quite conclusively, in fact, in a record of human warfare, which is that highly aggravated symptom of "turmoils and strifes" mentioned by Edgar Cayce in his reading on the causal factors of sunspots. He has specifically referred to "wars and hates," to "anger" and "jealousy," to "injustice, or that which maketh a lie." War is a manifestation of all of these unworthy qualities, under the guise of self-righteousness and national pride or honor. But the sins of man are not past finding out, and God looks to the heart and the purpose within.

During the period from 1495 B.C. to 1861 A.D., the record shows only 227 years of peace to a staggering total of 3,129 years of war! And from 1861 to the present, mankind has been engaged almost incessantly in warfare somewhere or other on this beleaguered planet of ours.

But what of the 70 years from 1645 to 1715? Years of turmoil, or years of peace? That is the crucial question before us.

The Thirty Years' War, which has been termed the most horrible military episode in Western history prior to the 20th century, was waged from 1618 to 1648. But although it did not officially terminate until the Peace of Westphalia, in 1648, peace overtures had actually begun some few years earlier, and the worst of the carnage came to an end with the conclusion of the Swedish-Danish War, in 1645—*the same year, it will be noted, that marked the beginning of the 70-year hiatus in sunspot activity*. Moreover, was it more than coincidental that astronomical observations for the *preceding* 30 years had indicated two 15-year cycles of sunspot turbulence? The stage for the long and bloody conflict was set with the War of the Jülich Succession, which ended in 1614. And the two 15-year sunspot cycles extended from 1615 to 1645. (Prior to that time, of course, there was no accumulated experience in the limited reporting of sunspots to permit any scientific conclusions about them.)

After the close of the Thirty Years' War, Europe was sick of blood. It is reported in *Collier's Encyclopedia* that "a relatively pleasant interlude in the history of war followed in Europe until the beginning of the Napoleonic wars [1790-1815]." But strife and turmoil of another nature erupted in the affairs of man considerably sooner than that. For one thing, there was the beginning of the Industrial Revolution in the 1750s, which made itself swiftly felt in the military sphere, and also in accelerated colonial expansionism and suppression. But even prior to the birth of the Industrial Revolution, there was the increasing victimization of the African coastal tribes by slave traders in the first half of the 18th century as the development of the Caribbean sugar plantations began to grow more lucrative. In fact, the booming plantation economy of the New World, in general, caused the world slave trade to reach colossal proportions during this period, with Spanish, Portuguese, British, French, and Dutch colonialists all engaged in this cruel and inhuman institution. Asia, too, was being systematically enslaved and plundered by the same selfish European powers. Their insatiable greed seemed to grow apace with the budding new century.

In summary, one might reasonably conclude that it was man's re-emerging injustice and cruelty on a vaster scale, rather than any single historic event, that marked a full-scale resumption of the disruptive sunspot cycles in 1715, after 70 years of relative tranquility.

It is possible that an analysis of sunspot activity from 1715 to the present, which would attempt to find a correlation between the more active periods of solar turbulence and the greater turmoils in human history, might be revealing. But such a study would be complicated by the sunspot pattern of reverse polarity every 11 years, with its alternating effects, and also by a psychological problem: strifes and turmoils have their origin in a complex pattern of attitudes and emotions, which may sometimes precede the recorded actions in human history by many months, or even years.

There will probably be no further opportunity to test our psychic theory on sunspots on a realistic basis until the turn of the century, when the Aquarian Age is ushered in, with its promise of an extended period of peace. Then, if another hiatus in sunspot activity occurs, there will be little room for scientific doubt that Cayce was absolutely right, and that sunspots are signs of strife and turmoil in the terrestrial affairs of men.

Meanwhile, we must observe, with Dr. Parker, that although we have come a long way in understanding the mysteries of the sun, we still have a long way to go.[4] For it is the mystery of man himself that underlies our search.

Age of Glory

An Interpretation of the 70-Year Sunspot Hiatus (1645-1715)

A startling bit of historical evidence has turned up that enables us to enlarge upon our previous interpretation of the 70-year hiatus in sunspot activity, from 1645 to 1715, as reported in the preceding essay.[1] First, however, we must set the stage for our story.

According to the Cayce readings, sunspots are solar disturbances caused by strife and turmoil in the earth. Those dark-looking spots on the sun's surface are actually depressed areas, marked by violent magnetic storms and solar flare-ups that are believed to have far-reaching effects on the entire solar system and probably beyond. If the readings are correct, we may assume that sunspots are triggered by the transmission of discordant vibratory impulses in a collective human pattern. These impulses are then reflected back to us in the form of rhythmic influences generated by the 11-year sunspot cycles. Whether the wave-like movement of the cycles, with their "peaks" and "valleys" of activity, relates to a similar pattern in human behavior is uncertain. The Cayce reading on sunspots failed to specify.[2] We posit the theory that it is more in the nature of a "thrust" effect, comparable to a giant solar pulse-beat, generated by the sun in a cumulative response to the more or less constant flow of discordant human vibrations. These vibrations are regularly building up energy that must subsequently be released as solar "storms," or sunspots. (In any given cycle, of course, the spots will manifest in greater or lesser intensity, depending upon the virulence of the disruptive vibrations, which are continually gathering into eventual "storm" areas on the surface of the sun.) The "pulsation" effect of the periodic sunspot cycles, rotating in reversely charged pairs of 11 years each, would serve to propel the discharge of surplus solar energies vigorously outward on the solar wind and into the earth's magnetic field and the fields of the outermost planets, where many of the speeding particles are "trapped" and stored. It is somewhat akin to the manner of a seed-pod dispersing its contents, which are then carried by the wind for eventual sowing at pre-selected distances. In this particular case, however, the fiery "seeds" are from an abnormal crop that can presage eventual trouble. They consist of a heavy concentration of charged solar particles—primarily protons and electrons.

Science does not yet fully understand the effect of sunspots on terrestrial life, although it is acknowledged that the alternating sunspot cycles have a significant influence upon the weather. In fact, they may even appear at first glance to be beneficial, as we shall discuss later on; but this could be a tragically deceptive conclusion. For opinion is also forming, in less orthodox scientific circles, that the sunspot cycles may adversely affect the earth's spin and play a major role in the occurrence of such catastrophes as earthquakes and floods.[3] Other suspiciously baleful effects of solar flare-ups were mentioned in our previous article. In addition, a French researcher, Michel Gauquelin, has assembled an impressive body of evidence from various scientific sources in support of the view that there is a substantive correlation between the peak periods of solar activity and the increasing incidence of such disruptive phenomena as epidemics, accidents, crime, suicides, and the pathological stimulation of the nervous system, resulting in human migrations and even wars.[4] If these data are proven to be true, it can be said that mankind is constantly witnessing in the reflected activity of sunspots an inescapable application of spiritual law: "As ye sow, so shall ye reap."

However, in the relatively limited period of man's scientific observation of sunspots, dating back to Galileo's invention of the telescope in 1610, there was an unaccountable lapse of 70 years during which sunspots virtually disappeared. Observers sometimes had to wait years to see a single sunspot. This relative absence of solar turbulence, it was discovered as belatedly as 1922, had a curious impact upon plant life in the earth, as shown in the chronicles of tree-ring dating. During those 70 years of quiescent solar behavior, the rings were remarkably uniform; they did not show the variable cycles of widening and narrowing bands, a cycle now considered "normal." From this evidence, we had theorized in our earlier article on the subject, one could expect to find a correlation in the affairs of mankind, which should reveal a similar pattern of relative harmony during the 70-year period of scarcity of sunspots. And, indeed, we found the evidence we sought by examining a history of human warfare—the most blatant testimony of turmoil and strife in earthly affairs, although not the only indicator, of course.

The record shows that this was a period of comparative calm throughout most of the world. Small wars continued to erupt, it is true, at intermittent intervals throughout the 70-year span in question. Yet we must consider the motivation and magnitude of those occasional conflicts in terms of earlier and later wars, comparing the degree of severity or injustice and the amount of human suffering they inflicted on the world. This is the key to understanding their karmic consequences, which underlie the significance of sunspots, according to the Cayce material on the subject. For it is seen that we live in a world of relative values. Man has not yet reached that point of development which enables him to outlaw war as a solution to his disputes and problems, although such a day will surely come. But as our moral awareness advances or recedes, so does our responsibility; and the effects of our actions on the body of mankind, and upon the planet itself, must inevitably reflect the extent to which we are deviating from or conforming to our highest ideals.

The Thirty Years' War, which had seen at least a third of the population of Germany slaughtered and had wrought havoc throughout all of Europe, terminated officially with the Peace of Westphalia in 1648. However, the last big battle ended in 1645—the precise year marking the commencement of the 70-year lull in sunspot activity. From that time forward, with the probable exception of the Battle of Blenheim, in 1704, which cost the French rather dearly, and perhaps the fierce Cossack Rebellion of 1648, which resulted in the large-scale massacre of Polish Catholics and Jews, there were no wars of mass destruction until the dreadful carnage of the Napoleonic Era began. During this relatively tranquil and happy interlude in human affairs, the Christian civilization of the West saw the dawning of an "Age of Glory" as the Classical Era in European history began, replacing the Renaissance and the Reformation. It was an age of significant progress and stability. To the East, however, the Islamic world of the Ottoman Empire had already passed its apogee, and it continued to suffer further eclipse through internal corruption and military setbacks from abroad; while Russia, under Peter the Great, was preparing at the turn of the 18th century to emerge as a military power to be reckoned with. But it is quite accurate to say that, from 1645 to 1715, strife of any gravely disruptive nature was mostly notable for its absence. It was a genuine hiatus. The English Civil War had virtually ended in 1644 with the decisive Battle of Marston Moor (although peace did not become official until 1646); and history has recorded that Cromwell's Protectorate, which followed, gave England "order without despotism," thus marking the commencement of a more enlightened era as the 70-year sunspot hiatus got under way. Similarly, a progressive "new order" was about to be introduced on the Continent with the accession of Louis XIV to the throne of France in 1643. This was a particularly important event, as we shall soon see. In Asia and Africa, the masses were still dormant; while in the New World, the European colonists were much too preoccupied with their immediate problems and opportunities to turn their heads to revolution or major intercolonial strife.

The "Age of Glory" did not last much beyond the life span of most of its key figures. Moreover, the turn of the 18th century saw the growing enslavement and vicious exploitation of the African and Far Eastern populations by all of the major European powers and their increasingly prosperous and greedy colonies abroad. It was this cruel and inhuman activity, we have theorized, which could conceivably have brought about the reactivation, in 1715, of the sunspot cycles as they presently appear.

We now offer surprising, new historical evidence on the subject. It supports our hypothesis and simultaneously expands upon it, thereby strengthening our confirmation of the psychic interpretation of sunspots.

In addressing the 1975 session of the annual meeting of the American Geophysical Union on the subject of sunspots, John A. Eddy, of the High Altitude Observatory in Boulder, Colorado, introduced what may have been intended only as a whimsical observation. Referring to the 70-year lull in sunspot activity, which has continued to puzzle scientists up to this day, he remarked upon the fact that the period in question—1645 to 1715—coincided almost exactly with the reign of King Louis XIV of France, from 1643 to 1715. Moreover, Louis XIV, as students of history will note with a shock of recognition, was called *le Roi Soleil*—"The Sun King." (Another odd coincidence, surely!)[5]

Can there perhaps be a connection of some sort? Is this feasible?* Let us see. We face the task of examining the historical record to see if the influence of this gifted 17th-century ruler of a major European state could conceivably have been so great as to bring about an era of relative harmony and stability in world affairs for the period of his long reign—the longest reign, incidentally, of any king in modern history.

Europe, at the time of Louis XIV's ascendancy, was the undisputed center of civilization. World leadership was in its grasp. Yet, with the tragic Thirty Years' War just drawing to a close, there was great weakness and exhaustion. Faith and virtue were at a low ebb. All of the leading European powers remained distrustful of one another. In short, the situation bordered on chaos. The time was ripe for a strong, central figure to emerge, corresponding to the heliocentric view of the universe that was just then being introduced in Europe as a result of the combined discoveries of Copernicus and his successors, Kepler and Galileo, in what astronomers have termed the Copernican Revolution. Such a figure would be destined to lead the Christian world into an era of glorious scientific and cultural progress and expanding prosperity; and Louis XIV—"The Sun King"—was seemingly picked by the gods to fill this historic role.

Since Louis XIV was only four years old when he became king of France, his mother, Anne of Austria, acted as interim regent on his behalf. But all power was actually placed in the hands of her able minister, Cardinal Mazarin—an Italian. This remarkable man of peace performed triumphantly in his

---

*A stunning correlation is found in the following excerpt from a collection of ancient Chinese manuscripts, compiled circa 1050 B.C., and known as the "Great Law": "It is the duty of the government all the time to watch carefully the phenomena of nature, which reflect in the world of nature the order and disorder in the world of government...When the course of nature runs properly, it is a sign that the government is good, but when there is some disturbance in nature it is a sign that there is something wrong in the government. . .Any disturbance in the sun accuses the emperor."

72

diplomatic efforts, settling international differences and solving domestic troubles with equal skill and patience. In all respects, he appears to have been the perfect forerunner of the young king, and a fitting exemplar. The relationship was a most felicitous one, suggestive of a good karmic pattern being fulfilled. Louis XIV, with appropriate patience and grace, awaited Mazarin's death, in 1661, before wielding full power. He was only 22 at the time, but he was more than ready for the task, having been well prepared by his mentor.

Historians have differed considerably in their assessment of Louis XIV's glorious reign. Nancy Mitford, in her colorful and well-documented biography, *The Sun King,*[6] has perhaps given us one of the most complete pictures currently available. But her focus on court personalities and petty intrigue tends to obscure the spiritual implications of Louis' rule, and we have to look elsewhere for needed facts. Fortunately, they can be pieced together from various qualified sources.

We can start, perhaps, with a psychological interpretation of the period by America's leading humanistic astrologer, Dane Rudhyar:

> Interestingly, the classical society which emerged in Europe during the late sixteenth and seventeenth centuries was modeled, unconsciously no doubt, upon the pattern of the heliocentric system: an autocratic king ruled with absolute power over a country which he theoretically owned and over a people subjected to his personal will; and he was surrounded by ministers, courtiers, and servants of various ranks reflecting his power.[7]

Further, Rudhyar explores the symbolism in "The Sun King" designation:

> A society and its culture are always based upon a set of assumptions which have a metaphysical and/or religious foundation and which find their expression in great symbols and myths. . .
> We should not forget that the new mentality which took form during the Renaissance and became set during the second half of the European seventeenth century was given its basic form by astronomers who were studying

the sky. European man then applied the concept of the universe as a machine to his behavior, and found in a central, all-power-dispensing Sun the symbolic justification of the divine right of kings—*le Roi Soleil*.[8]

Next, we come to the astrological record for the period. It holds a stunning surprise.

In 1650, there occurred a rare conjunction of two of the slower-moving planets, Uranus and Neptune. It lasted through 1653, although its orb of influence extended into the years adjoining both its approach and its departure. This conjunction, which takes place about every 171 years, had been making its measured and somewhat erratic approach (due to a period of retrograde motion) when Louis XIV was born; and Sakoian and Acker report that the conjunction "corresponds to a period of major spiritual and scientific progress,"[9] with many highly developed souls incarnating into the earth to further man's evolution. These souls have a high sense of social responsibility and justice; and if other planetary aspects are favorable, they are called upon to restore order where there was chaos.[10] In its highest expression, the conjunction is said to manifest as "the synthesis of Divine Wisdom and Divine Love."[11] On the available evidence, one might conclude that its key manifestation at that particular period was in the realm of enlightened leadership. This combined with great scientific and cultural achievements to prepare mankind for its next cycle of evolution. (Two great men of science, Sir Isaac Newton and Edmund Halley, were born at the approach and the decline of the 1650-1653 conjunction, respectively, while the Duke of Marlborough—whose star first rose under the military patronage of Louis XIV, but who later became the king's "nemesis"—was born in 1650.)

According to esoteric astrology, the fact that neither Uranus nor Neptune had yet been discovered[12] might account for the absence of any conscious expression in that age of the more revolutionary aspects normally associated with the Uranus/Neptune conjunction. The sign ruling France, however, is Leo—a sign denoting kingship. It favored the rule of Louis XIV at that particular time in history.

"The Sun King" was born on September 5, 1638—preceding the actual conjunction of Neptune and Uranus, of course, but sufficiently close as a result of other planetary aspects to be considered a "New Age" child. When he ascended the throne of

France, at the age of four, Uranus was in the sign of Scorpio. Here it was in its "exaltation." It clearly marked a time of drastic change and regeneration for mankind. (Uranus, in fact, is now [1976] in the same position.) Neptune was over the cusp of the next zodiacal sign, Sagittarius, whose keynote is "wisdom." (Here it would be joined later by Uranus, following the latter's retrograde maneuver into Scorpio.) This Sagittarian placement of Neptune confers "a desire to spiritualize the larger social order."[13] Because his Sun was in Virgo, the sovereignty of the spirit was emphasized for "The Sun King." Yet Louis XIV is essentially regarded by astrologers "as a Leo type," we are told, "owing to the position of the planets in his horoscope."[14] Leo is traditionally the sign of kings and presidents, as already mentioned, and its keynote is "glory." Its ruler is the Sun.

The only subsequent occurrence of the rare conjunction between Uranus and Neptune, incidentally, was during 1821-1824. It produced a phenomenal array of talent extending into all fields of public service, philosophy and the arts. Some of the greater historical figures came in "on the orb," at the conjunction's approach. The years 1821-1824 saw the appearance of such divergent geniuses as Mendel and Pasteur, Ulysses S. Grant (military preserver of the Union) and Mary Baker Eddy. Marx and Engels preceded them by only a year or two. So, in fact, did Queen Victoria, as well as Susan B. Anthony. This raises a natural question: If the 1650-1653 conjunction of Uranus and Neptune produced a more or less "peaceful" generation, coinciding with a 70-year lull in sunspot activity, why didn't the next conjunction, during 1821-1824, produce a similar era in both human and solar behavior?

A number of logical explanations are possible. The most likely explanation takes into account the positioning of the other planetary bodies in our solar system, as well as the sign in which Uranus and Neptune are found. The conjunction took place in the sign Capricorn, which is ruled by Saturn, but with Saturn in Aries, where it is in its "fall." (At the conjunction's approach, Saturn was in Pisces, which is regarded as a "difficult" position because this is a karmic sign.) According to modern astrology, this combination denotes a generation of people who want to effect important changes in society and initiate vital reforms, but—with Saturn in Pisces or Aries—the "timing" is not right to bring about the desired results. Although these people may initiate a new cycle of experience, they cannot reap the benefits of their actions. Thus, the superficial tranquility of the Victorian Era, which ushered in another "Age of Glory," one that seemingly bore many similarities to the reign of Louis XIV, was not sufficient to quell the wave of social unrest rising up in Europe and elsewhere. This undercurrent of strife and turmoil found its most tragic expression, perhaps, in the American Civil War. Disruptive forces remained very much a part of human affairs throughout the era, as the seeds of violent change in the social order took firm root. This would appear to have been the primary difference between the Victorian Age and the Age of Louis XIV: "The Sun King" reigned during a time of general contentment, and the social unrest that ultimately led to the French Revolution did not crystallize until well after his death.

Not too surprisingly, the next Uranus/Neptune conjunction will take place during 1992-1995, as we pass over the cusp of Aquarius and enter more fully into the cycle of the Aquarian Age. Pluto, the outermost planet, will be in Scorpio, and its message in this sign is said to be, "Regenerate or die!" Although Uranus and Neptune will again be in Capricorn (ruled by Saturn, which has been called the "taskmaster"), the successful regeneration of both the spiritual and the social order are clearly indicated by the placement of Saturn in Aquarius, where it is co-ruler with Uranus. Uranus has been called the "awakener." Esoteric astrology suggests that this will be a period in human evolution when Uranus assumes full dominion over Aquarius, and Saturn's future rulership will be restricted to Capricorn. Its present role as the bridge between the lower and the Higher Self will have been fulfilled. The interpretation one finds in most texts on the subject is that it will mark an age of brotherhood and spiritual enlightenment, ruled by neither "kings" nor "presidents," but by individual Man himself, through his inner, spiritual awakening.

We conclude our comments on the Uranus/Neptune conjunction and return to our central subject, the period of Louis XIV. Those who might dispute the placement of "The Sun King" within the orbital influence of this conjunction would at least be obliged to concede that his 72-year rule, corresponding so closely with the 70-year lull in sunspot activity, probably embraced the entire life span of many advanced souls who were born in the precise orbit of the 1650-1653 conjunction. Thus, all of these souls shared in the glory of the era over which "The Sun King" presided, as the central light in a heaven of stellar luminaries.

Finally, some of the more scientifically oriented readers may not be prepared to accept the esoteric teachings of astrology which have just been presented here. While such teachings are, of course, relevant to this article, they are not altogether essential to our case. We have merely introduced, for those who are interested, certain astrological "evidence" to add weight to our testimony. Time will prove or disprove the scientific validity of astrological analyses and predictions. But if these predictions about the Aquarian Age are correct, we should definitely be able to anticipate the commencement of another sunspot hiatus at the approach of the 1992-1995 Uranus/Neptune conjunction.

We shall see. Meanwhile, let us proceed.

Some historians have assumed that Louis XIV's brilliant reign was motivated by a *personal* desire for power and glory. His posthumous appelation, "The Sun King"—actually inspired by the mask of Apollo that adorned the king's chambers at Versailles—is sometimes cited by his detractors as a symbol of his glory-seeking. But an objective analysis of Louis XIV's character, in our opinion, must find him motivated by aims nobler than personal ambition; and we find this view supported by Voltaire's outstanding admiration for France's most powerful and influential ruler. Voltaire was not the sort to admire a self-seeking despot; he admired "philosopher-kings," who advanced the cause of liberty and justice. There is ample evidence that Louis XIV was in this category, despite a number of contradictory acts that might appear to have marred that image temporarily. After all, a king—even one who is endowed by his contemporaries with "divine rights"—is only human. (As the Cayce readings remind us, "It is the 'try' that is the more often counted as righteousness, and *not* the success or failure." [931-1])

Many of Louis XIV's virtues and weaknesses seem to run parallel with those of another king—an ancient Israelite, who ruled his people in much the same manner: Solomon. In fact, one is almost tempted to speculate that they might have been the same soul-entity, filling a given need for kingly qualities in two widely separate periods of history. We do not press the point, however. Let the reader draw his own conclusions.

Louis XIV was always resolute in protecting the Catholic faith from the splintering effect of dissident movements, even when his aims ran contrary to the political expediency of two of the reigning popes. Nor was it personal glory that made the

Sun King aspire to become a Holy Roman Emperor—an aspiration that never materialized. Yet the aspiration undoubtedly reflected his strong allegiance to Church and God, and an underlying sense of holy mission. At the same time, he was by no means a bigot. History has always referred to Louis XIV as "the most Christian king," which he undoubtedly was. It was perhaps appropriate that he sought obedience and unity as the key objectives of his rule.

Unlike his predecessors, Louis XIV built up a thoroughly personal system of government, presiding over the council and many of its committees himself, rather than delegating these duties to a chancellor. In fact, it will be remembered that this was the king who uttered those astonishing words, "L'état, c'est moi!"—*I am the State.* But was it the egoistic voice of a tyrant, or the natural utterance of a ruler of his times—a man, moreover, who seemed to be intuitively aware of his historic role and who accepted his kingly responsibilities as a duty imposed upon him by a Higher Authority? (The readings imply that no national leader, good or bad, is in a position of power except by the grace of God, whether he rules an empire or presides over a democracy.)

Under Louis XIV's rule, at any rate, departmental specialization became firmly established at the outset, and he allowed no single individual to hold a predominant position. In the eyes of the nobility, whose traditional influence on affairs of state was totally eliminated, it was a reign of "low, bourgeois government." In truth, however, the king had surrounded himself with men of enormous wisdom and genius—after Mazarin's death, Colbert and Le Brun come most prominently to mind—men who worked behind the scenes with quiet efficiency and unswerving loyalty, carrying out the king's wishes. Yet Louis XIV was a wise enough monarch to appease the frustrated aristocracy in other ways. During his reign the arts flourished as never before or since in French history. This was the age of Molière, Racine and Saint-Simon, among many others. It is not surprising that the social life at Louis XIV's court became the center of European fashion. As a result, the French language was adopted by many of the courts in Europe, and rulers who came to his elegant palace at Versailles always left in envy, striving to emulate both his court and his castle in their own lands.

Bloodlines connecting him to several of the thrones of Europe gave Louis XIV an ideal opportunity to exercise with generally excellent results his genius for international diplomacy. However, the general peace that prevailed in all of Europe during Louis XIV's reign was due in large measure to his neighbors' respect for his strong and well-disciplined army. Although he used it in a number of military engagements—primarily to enforce his long-standing claim, through marriage, to the Spanish Netherlands—the Sun King was essentially a man of peace. He simply did not have the cruel or unbalanced temperament of a conqueror or a bully. Yet he was capable of tragic misjudgments from time to time. The latter part of his reign saw the rapid depletion of the national treasury through a series of ill-conceived military ventures. The English, uniting with the Dutch and others in common fear of him, tried to bring the French king to his knees. They failed in their combined efforts, for Louis XIV's patriotic subjects rallied to the cause and beat them back. But the king was ultimately forced to the treaty table in 1713.

Based on the Cayce readings, one might reasonably expect that such belligerent activities, occurring from time to time during the 70-year sunspot hiatus, should have triggered a renewal of solar flare-ups. Perhaps they did, on a minor scale. Astronomers of the period saw sunspots from time to time, in restricted numbers. However, the readings make it plain that our human interpretation of history and events is often obscured by our three-dimensional view of the universe. One has to seek the spiritual interpretation of history and look for the esoteric meaning of events underlying the visible record. In the divine plan of things, there may be modifying forces at work that lessen the karmic consequences of certain actions that we can see and interpret only in human terms of "strife and turmoil." Each age has its lessons to learn and its duties to fulfill. The final judgment is not ours. In any case, it is conceivable that, in an age that believed implicitly in the divine right of kings, Louis XIV acted out his role at all times with a sincere conviction that he was serving a Higher Justice. Thus, even when he was wrong the sincerity of his conviction could have lessened the degree of his guilt in the eye of God. Essentially he remained always a bright symbol of unity and progress throughout the dazzling interlude of his long reign.

Louis XIV, like Solomon, had a passion for building. He gave France the Louvre and the Royal Library, which houses one of the greatest collections of books in the world. He also built the Paris Observatory and the Academy of Science. At Versailles he constructed a palace that became the greatest showplace on earth. Even as Solomon brought grandeur and substance to what David had only dreamed of, the king insisted that his architects at Versailles use the classic but simple residence constructed earlier by his father as the cornerstone, as it were, for his airy and sumptuous palace. Yet, quintessentially, it functioned more as a "country home" for a king whose heart was always close to the land.

An admirer of nature with a fondness for riding and hunting, the king spent much time in the surrounding woods and extensive gardens; and perhaps no one was closer to Louis XIV than the royal gardener, Le Nôtre, who would invariably embrace his king as a simple commoner whenever they met after a prolonged absence. If many men feared him—and they did—it was mainly because of the sense of power his presence generated and his uncanny ability to penetrate their thoughts. It certainly was *not* the result of kingly wrath; for it has been said that Louis XIV was "the politest of kings," and his ability to control his temper under stress was phenomenal. These traits served him well. Few men in positions of similar power have been as self-disciplined or as wise.

The king's weaker side, even as Solomon's, was women. He had a succession of mistresses. But his bastard sons were given the unparalleled honor of legitimacy, which further revealed his essentially democratic nature, although it of course infuriated the established aristocracy. At the same time, he was unendingly considerate toward his legitimate queen, the Infanta Maria-Teresa. Since it was not a "love match," and she was said to have had the mind of a child, it must have been trying at times to a man of Louis XIV's broad intelligence and regal temperament.

Firsthand accounts of the king's physical appearance, found in memoirs, unpublished diaries and letters of the period, are surprising in their general agreement. They tend to confirm Bernini's idealized bust of him, rather than some of the less flattering portraits handed down, which show the king in periwig and accentuate his somewhat large nose. He was apparently a tall man, well formed, with dark, flowing locks and noble mien. In the physical summary given by Nancy Mitford it is reported, "All speak of his noble look and extraordinary grace; he never made an ill-considered or meaningless gesture so that he seemed like a deity. . ."[15]

On his deathbed, the king's basic humility was demonstrated

in his touching words to his great-grandson, who would succeed him on the throne of France. Reviewing his own shortcomings and failures as his life ebbed away, the king cautioned the child not to copy him, but to remember his duty and his obligation to God. "See that your subjects honor *Him*," he told the solemn youngster.

With the death of the Sun King, in 1715, it would seem that the sun mourned also. It resumed its cycles of dark sunspots almost at once.

Epilogue

History is full of lessons for those who will seek them out. It is clear that the 70-year hiatus in sunspot activity from 1645 to 1715 did not produce a new Ice Age, nor did it bring on a calamitous drought. Yet these are the currently expressed fears of many of our meteorologists and other "experts" as we approach the nadir of another sunspot cycle, when the number of spots traditionally falls to its "minimum" level.

We do not deny that significant changes in our weather patterns around the globe can be expected if another long-term cessation of sunspots takes place. It is probably true, in fact, that there will be a general cooling of the earth's atmosphere. It reportedly happened once before in the recent past.[16] But is this necessarily "bad"? (There is alarming evidence that our planet has been *overheating* for quite some time!) And what about droughts in some of our present "agricultural belts"? The agronomists shake their heads glumly at that prospect. But even if the rainfall of the future should lessen dramatically in one area of the land, forcing a change of crops or an eventual abandonment of the soil, precipitation elsewhere will almost surely make new areas more fruitful, and do so on a *lasting* basis, in the absence of sunspot cycles. Thus, a temporary tragedy could become a long-range blessing. But the transition, admittedly, would lead to some suffering and hardship.

On the other hand, it is more likely that our modern technology will provide us with an easier solution. Man appears to be on the verge of controlling his environment, and he may soon be able to "create" his own weather. The present techniques of the "rainmakers" are admittedly primitive and often ineffectual: they range from "cloud-seeding" with silver nitrate to exotic experiments with vaporizing wax. But those who doubt the "miracles" born of scientific ingenuity mated to human necessity have only to visit Israel and see how its enterprising citizens have made the desert bloom. If the "rainmakers" fail, we can turn to the sea. It is to be hoped that one day our research efforts will lead to a less costly way to convert salt water to fresh. It will then be possible to irrigate all of the earth's dry plains and deserts while the sun shines down in benevolent splendor, producing unimagined harvests. Hunger will be unheard of and strife unnecessary. Then a true "Age of Glory" will begin.

Such should be the proper fruits of the approaching Aquarian Age, if the Cayce readings can be relied upon, for like begets like: what we sow in strife and turmoil, we reap in kind; but what is sown in a spirit of universal helpfulness and brotherhood, we may expect to reap in universal joy and abundance.

Patterns of Solar and Planetary Influence

The *body* is a pattern, it is an ensample of all the forces of the universe itself.   2153-6

. . .the soul of man, thy soul, encompasses *all* in this solar system or in others.   5755-2

Today we are moving towards a New Astrology.

It is already taking shape, this science of the future. We can see its vague outlines in such far-ranging fields of astral research as cosmobiology, which explores the effects of cosmic forces on terrestrial life, or that Space Age cousin of "aspectology" called gravitational vectoring, which is the scientific term applied by NASA researchers to their work in charting certain planetary configurations that are recognized as harmful to manned space flight. Also, it can be glimpsed in the remarkable "L-fields" of Dr. Harold S. Burr. These "fields" are present everywhere throughout the universe, and are said to contain the "electric patterns of life." Again, its emerging shadow, if not its substance, may be seen in the popular new science of biorhythm, whose multiple waves of energy at criss-crossing levels report; lly follow us in clocked cycles from birth to death, as do the rhythmic cycles of the seasons and the stars.

But these new areas of scientific research, while exciting and important, are only peripheral to astrology. It is the astrologers themselves who must rebuild their own structure, borrowing the tools available to them from other scientific disciplines, in combination with their own intuitive insights and such traditional components of ancient astrological wisdom as can be soundly integrated in a scientifically viable new form. When completed, the New Astrology will represent a powerful synthesis of science, psychology and religion, embodying the holistic principles of cosmic influence clearly intimated in the Edgar Cayce readings. This will include, as well, an understanding of the determinative role of free will in human behavioral responses. The new "astrological science," unlike its predecessor, will be the happily shared domain of scientists and astrologers alike. In fact, the new astrologers will all be hailed as scientists; and, conversely, many of tomorrow's new breed of scientists will eagerly seek to become astrologers. Prodigious research will be necessary in this new discipline.

Astrology, as an interpretive tool for man's understanding of himself and his relationship to the cosmic environment, has evolved from ancient origins. It is an ever changing language. This is due, in part, to the human psyche and its fluid symbols of expression, which are constantly changing form, adapting to a different frame of reference as mankind advances in its evolution from age to age. But that is not all. The cosmic language of astrology is also affected by structural changes within the cosmos itself. We do not live in a static universe, but in a vast, swirling network of celestial organisms whose rhythmic dance in time and space weaves a constantly shifting pattern of intricate harmonics and vibrations.

These giant pulsations in the body of the universe are sometimes so immeasurably slow as to be imperceptible to us, as in the gargantuan frolic that occurs between neighboring galaxies, for instance; yet their remote and ponderous interplay may trigger unguessed-at changes in the force fields surrounding our own Milky Way galaxy. Then there is that kaleidoscopic band of mythical sky-creatures, the twelve constellations forming the familiar signs of the Zodiac. To the ant-like dwellers on Spaceship Earth, these appear as a changeless array of "fixed" stars and symbols, so that we have even established our orientation in space by means of their stable positions. But in reality, there is not a one of them, of course, that isn't altering its position every second at some unthinkable speed! Consider: How do their metered movements affect the music of the spheres? What vibratory note is reaching us now through space from Spica or Aldebaran?

Perhaps it is only in the closer wheeling of Earth and her sister planets around the Sun, in the "inner space" of our own cell-like solar system, that we have some immediate sense of stellar motion, and with it a dim awareness that our lives are somehow being mysteriously affected by this unending ballet in space. Yet, actually, every dancing, pulsating star in the entire universe is an integral part of the one moving Whole, whose subtly shifting vibration continually affects the total orchestration. (Thus, the Edgar Cayce readings refer to "the various influences shed from other solar systems, suns, and so forth." [541-1])

It is typical of the readings that they often conceal unexpected levels of interpretation and usage, which become apparent to us only as we are ready to apply them.

This is presently the case.

In exploring the ancient and discredited "science" of astrology from its vague origins to the present, we have found ourselves turning frequently to the data on astrology in the Edgar Cayce readings. This material has served as a kind of "compass," or reference point, whenever our research bogged down or carried us into questionable territory. One of those dubious areas was the controversial work of a French researcher, Dr. Michel Gauquelin, whose impressive and widely quoted statistical findings[1] would appear to have undermined the basic precepts of astrology, establishing in their stead the sketchy outlines of a new and purely "mathematical" approach to the subject.

According to Gauquelin, there are only four planetary bodies that exert any measurable degree of influence in a birth chart: Mars, Jupiter, Saturn and the Moon. (For convenience's sake, Earth's satellite is commonly referred to by astrologers as a "planet.") His statistical analyses of numerous professional categories showed that one or more of these four planets would tend to "peak" at given angles in a collective horoscope, indicating a distinct relationship between specific planetary patterns of vibration and certain human characteristics. These were identifiable in general terms by analyzing the type of professional group under study. The most "critical" point in the peaking phase occurred as the planet was rising, or had just crossed the Ascendant. (The Ascendant is likened to the "starting point" in a horoscope, and it coincides with the line of the horizon.) Professionals born with this planetary positioning had the highest incidence of success in their respective fields. Next in prominence was a point just past the upper meridian, or zenith (at the vertical apex of the horoscope). Actually, the importance of these two positions in a horoscope has always been recognized by astrologers; and it was not a contradiction of orthodox astrology to learn from Gauquelin's findings, for example, that Mars was prominent on the horizon in the horoscopes of soldiers and athletes, or the Moon among writers.

But the baffling part about Gauquelin's statistics, encompassing the horoscopes of some 25,000 or more Europeans (mostly celebrities), was their peculiarly limited and—to astrologers, at least!—disappointing results. For one thing, the French mathematician and his team of researchers found no overt evidence whatsoever of the Sun's influence in a horoscope. It was a stunning blow to astrology. In fact, the traditional "Sun signs" of astrology appeared to be quite meaningless, based on Gauquelin's exhaustive survey of numerous professional groupings in which a random and nearly equal distribution of natal Sun positions in the twelve signs was the repeated result in virtually every case.[2]

Similar negative findings followed his statistical experiments with the remaining planets—Mercury, Venus, Uranus, Neptune and Pluto—although in subsequent experiments Gauquelin was able to establish some evidence of what he termed "the planetary effect in heredity" for Venus also.[3] But even Gauquelin's discovery of career correlations for Mars, Jupiter, Saturn and the Moon bore no astrological significance beyond the specific planet's angular position in the horoscope as a link to the particular professional category. (Venus did not appear to be influential in the survey of career relationships.) In other words, there was no evidence of a further relationship, identifying individual professions with a pronounced tendency toward certain signs in which Mars, Jupiter, etc., happened to appear, such as "Mars in Gemini" for journalists, and so forth. There were no cresting points; distribution appeared to occur in a totally random pattern, insofar as the twelve familiar signs of the Zodiac were concerned. This was another contradiction of basic astrological principles, of course; and Gauquelin, convinced of the finality of his findings, concluded that he had scientifically disproved traditional astrology's *raison d'être*. He proposed in its stead a scientifically based astrology that would depend solely on statistical findings and their scientific interpretation.

But whatever import could be attached to Gauquelin's admittedly impressive evidence, we somehow felt distrustful of it in the larger context of astrology's accumulated wisdom. It seemed to us that Gauquelin's curiously incomplete "hereditary patterns" were only a small piece of a much larger puzzle; and until the other parts could be fitted into the picture,

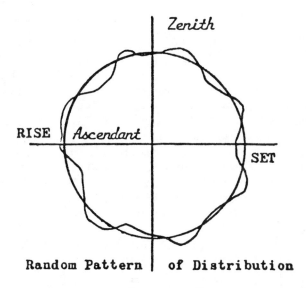

no final scientific conclusions could safely be drawn from them. In this respect, the cavalier dismissal of almost all existing astrological knowledge with a single sweep of the statistical wand struck us as an unfair and premature judgment.

We knew it would be difficult to refute the mathematical evidence compiled by the Sorbonne-trained Dr. Gauquelin, nor was there any desire on our part to discredit the results of his extremely conscientious and professional research efforts. In fact, his contribution to the New Astrology, when finally viewed in its proper perspective, must still remain significant. He has statistically identified specific areas of cosmic influence on human behavior, areas which were not previously known— or, at least, had not been confirmed by science. In other spheres, however, his statistics appeared to be less than logical in a number of respects; this inconsistency caused us to question his methodology.

This was where we now had the support of the Edgar Cayce readings to urge us on in our amateur research and provide the essential clues we needed. In one excerpt, we found a statement we had previously overlooked, which suddenly stood out like a bold, illuminated marker, showing us the way:

The strongest force used in the destiny of man is the Sun first, then the closer planets to the earth, or those that are coming to ascension at the time of the birth of the individual...

3744-3

First, the Sun. That confirmed the obvious. Sun signs surely had to mean *something,* if Cayce were right. But where, in that case, had Gauquelin gone wrong? We would have to find out. (In a number of life readings, we knew that Cayce had referred specifically to the individual's natal Sun sign, which further reassured us in our conclusion.)

"Then the closer planets to the earth. . ." That would include Mercury and Venus, of course, in addition to Mars and the Moon. Yet Mercury, planetary ruler of the mental forces in astrology, had not featured in any of Gauquelin's findings, while Venus had been given only limited recognition in his vast armada of statistics. We clearly surmised that something was amiss.

Finally, what about "those [planets] coming to ascension at the time of the birth of the individual. . ."? This was apparently meant to apply to *any* planet, including even the remote Uranus, or far-flung Neptune and Pluto in their invisible orbits, in addition to Jupiter and Saturn or the "closer planets to the earth." (In Edgar Cayce's horoscope, for example, the planet Uranus—identified with the *psychic* forces—was rising at birth. This was surely significant. And, in fact, reading 5755-1 states that from an astrological aspect "the greater influence at the entrance of this entity that ye call Cayce was from Uranus.") But we knew it would be impossible, unfortunately, in the type of research to which we were restricted, to gather meaningful statistics in most cases on the three outermost planets. This was due to their extremely slow revolution through the twelve signs of the Zodiac, requiring birth statistics dating back through several centuries in order to obtain truly objective results. Also, we were simply not equipped, as Gauquelin and his fellow researchers had been, in Europe, to draw up individual horoscopes based on locally available records of the hour and minute of birth in a lengthy catalog of famous people, past and present! However, using a set of ephemerides and various biographical sources, we could at least establish with relative accuracy the sign positions of the Sun, Moon, and each of the planets at date of birth for famous people born since 1800—omitting from our calculations, of course, the planets Uranus, Neptune and Pluto, for reasons already stated.[4]

The goal of our independent research efforts was to refute or verify, as the case might be, the random patterns of solar and planetary distribution in various professional categories, as reported by Gauquelin. We approached our task objectively. It was certainly a challenging assignment, and we couldn't help wondering at times if it would merit the arduous effort it demanded. As we proceeded to assemble our information, however, our hopes were kindled. It gradually dawned on us where Gauquelin had apparently gone astray. In an obsession with large numbers, which too often underlies the mathematical approach of the trained statistician, he had understandably allowed himself to lose sight of more meaningful factors. We were, of course, thinking of the intuitive and psychological input into the scheme of things. Not that we were disrespectful of the "law of probabilities," mind you; but one could get carried away, perhaps, in search of overwhelming odds to support one's professional findings. This seemed to have been the case.

We carefully rechecked Gauquelin's compilations, group by group: 2,088 sports champions (gathered, it seemed, from virtually every field of sports); 1,409 successful actors (apparently including roles of every type, from romantic lead to comedian); 3,647 successful scientists (doctors, physicists, astronomers, chemists, etc., all lumped unceremoniously together!); 1,352 writers (presumably combining all literary categories); and so forth. In some cases, the selections centered on "secondary" groupings, such as 717 "ordinary" professional sportsmen, or 1,458 scientists who had made "no significant discoveries." This latter approach, of course, was designed as a means of testing the theory of random distribution on mediocre talent. It was a scientifically admirable method in its thoroughness, if not a particularly productive one in a positive sense. However, it at least confirmed the obvious: Ordinary talent produces ordinary results.

So, in fact, does a "mixed bag" of top talent, we decided. Such a broad approach might still permit some of the symbols of a common genius to surface statistically, as in the frequency of Mars' appearance at key angles in certain diagrams, or similar configurations with Jupiter, Saturn and the Moon in others; but we concluded that the professional groupings assembled by Gauquelin were simply too large on the one hand and consequently too indiscriminate on the other to reveal specific patterns of solar, lunar or planetary influence in the accepted terms of orthodox astrology. In short, a preponderance of sheer numbers had proved as much of a downfall as a *paucity* of numbers, the more common cause of unreliable statistics.

It was a useful lesson. We took it to heart. *Specialization* would be our response. We recognized that the important point would be to concentrate on only the most successful figures in any specialized field—an approach that would be more "qualitative" than "quantitative"—and then to hold rigidly to our chosen category of specialization in every case, rather than diluting it for the sake of a "numbers game" with related groupings, however compatible they might appear. As a result, we were able to develop surprising statistical evidence to support our theory that *definite patterns of solar, lunar and planetary influence do indeed exist in the destiny of man.*

The dilemma facing us was this: Before we could present our theory as a scientifically valid conclusion, it was necessary to meet certain scientifically established criteria of "proof." However, our initial compilations—covering about two dozen specialized career categories—were statistically too small, on the whole, to be scientifically tested by the established techniques of statistical evaluation. Those techniques are geared to cope efficiently with relatively large samples only, in which the "expected frequency" range grows proportionately wider as the researcher tries to determine his results with 90% confidence or more. It is a measuring apparatus based on the random nature of observed statistics. This device gains in significance as the statistical input is increased to larger totals, in which the random aspect gradually "levels out" to produce a relatively accurate picture of the odds against chance in any observed sector of a given sample that exceeds, or falls below, the "expected frequency" range for that sector. It is a method of evaluation that works with reasonable success in many areas of statistical research but is less effective where hard-to-measure human variables are involved.

In our particular case, we recognized that we were dealing with a unique set of human factors whose behavior was outside the "norm" of statistical experience, on which the whole theoretical process of formal statistical evaluation is premised. If our theory about the correlation between natal Sun signs and career choices were correct (as it later proved to be), the traditional "random" aspect would be minimal at the outset. Instead, the genius of any class under observation would tend to "peak" rather prominently at a relatively *low* numerical input, whereas it would gradually *lose* its prominence as the statistical input was expanded to include less qualitative factors, even within the same specialized category. In short, the larger numbers that would be essential to the established requirements of statistical evaluation would, in most instances, defeat the very purpose of the survey, for they would introduce a "dilution" factor that would deprive the statistical findings of much, if not all, of their significance.

Because of the difficulty in locating specialized career categories in which the available natal statistics on top talent were in excess of several hundred units (many were less than that!), our solution—at least temporarily—was to rely on the statistics of "repetition" as a measure of success in our findings. Here we repeatedly discovered, without exception, definite cresting points and recessional areas, as opposed to the random patterns of dispersal encountered by Gauquelin. After examining in this manner more than two dozen specialized groupings of top talent, we felt that the statistical odds were certainly piling up in our favor. In several categories, in fact, we extended our survey to include lunar and planetary configurations, as well as solar patterns, and were not too surprised to encounter similar positive results in every case. *In absolutely no instance—either in the solar, lunar, or planetary diagrams of frequency distribution among the twelve signs— did we encounter a random pattern of dispersal.* Invariably there were dominant cresting areas and recessional points in each of our charts, which now totalled fifty or more.

Later on, using an authoritative biographical text on musicians, which will be discussed at the end of this article, we were fortunately able to produce a number of substantially larger compilations of specialized talent in varying qualitative degrees, which fell well within the established test requirements for a formal statistical evaluation. The results were *positive*. This capped our earlier efforts (with which the diagrams in this initial study are mainly concerned) with the aura of "scientific" success. We have included two of those diagrams of larger compilations (see Figures 1 and 2), accompanied by a formal statistical evaluation.

In general, our findings uphold the basic principles of astrology. They also coincide with much of the Cayce data on the subject, while clearly contradicting the negative aspects of Gauquelin's statistics. As a result of their obvious significance,

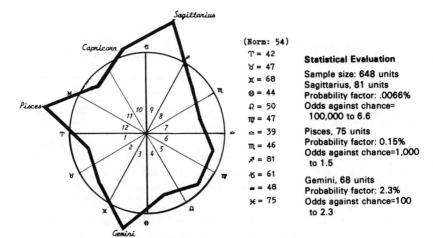

Figure 1. SUN SIGNS
648 Major Classical Composers

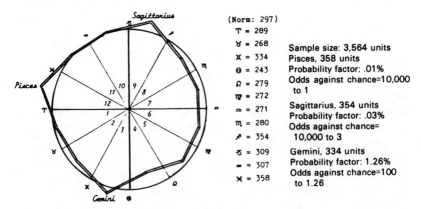

Figure 2. SUN SIGNS
3,564 Classical Composers

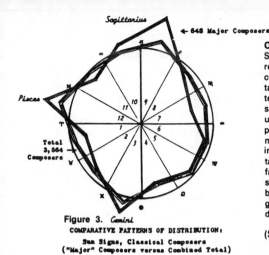

Sagittarius

← 648 Major Composers

Pisces

Total
3,564
Composers →

Figure 3. *Gemini*
COMPARATIVE PATTERNS OF DISTRIBUTION:
Sun Signs, Classical Composers
("Major" Composers versus Combined Total)

Overlay of two Preceding Samples: Smaller sample (648 units) represents only 18.18% of total, but comprises a concentration of major talent. Overlay pattern demonstrates tendency of larger, more random sample of total composers (3,564 units) to follow same general cresting points and recessional areas, but on a modified basis attributable to introduction of mediocre and minor talent. In summary, the qualitative factor declined, but the factor of specialization still perpetuated the basic configuration, where the genius of the class is more dramatically in evidence.

(Statistical evaluation
by Han. Y. Rhyu)

we sincerely hope Gauquelin will be encouraged to repeat his experiments, using our more specialized approach. The New Astrology now in the making, of which he is perhaps the foremost pioneer, can benefit greatly from his vast knowledge and professional experience that would be applied in this more fruitful direction. And if his findings oblige him to reverse his former scientific verdict that traditional astrology is "dead to our way of thinking," they will at the same time reinforce his less hostile, intuitive judgment that "astrology is still to be respected."[5] The latter opinion is much closer to the truth; and it comes from the pen of a life-long researcher in astrology who at heart, we suspect, has always believed intuitively in that which his scientific mind denounces as unbelievable. But now it is time for science and intuition to work *together;* and, together, they can forge the structure of the New Age astrology.

Before we proceed further, let us explain briefly the underlying methodology of our statistics, primarily as applied to the smaller, more rigidly specialized compilations of major talent.

At the outset, our task was to establish a reasonable "total" in each professional category, in which the resulting patterns of solar and, where it could be determined, planetary (including lunar) dispersal among the twelve signs of the Zodiacal wheel could be expected to stabilize sufficiently to give meaningful readings. We naturally recognized the weakness of relying on numbers that were so low as to be subject to wide fluctuation in an expanded grouping of comparable talent. At the same time, our highly specialized approach meant that we could not risk introducing any "dilution" factors that would distort the meaningful patterns we were seeking.

93

It soon became apparent, as we proceeded on an experimental basis, that definite "trends" would begin to manifest themselves in certain groupings even as low as 100, and their reliability as "indicators" appeared to develop in proportion to their initial prominence. As anticipated, the "random" aspect, which would strongly affect a less discriminative grouping, was largely held in check here. Thus, if a given sign, such as Pisces or Virgo, was markedly dominant at the outset, we saw that its above-average influence, although possibly modified later by other developing factors, would still persist in an expanded grouping within the same professional category (viz., "204 Great Composers," Figure 13, versus "648 Major Classical Composers," Figure 1).

In general, we found that the patterns began to stabilize at a point in the neighborhood of 144 sign-factors. We were not sure why; the realm of numbers has its own mystique. But the highly qualitative nature of our statistical compilations, operating in carefully specific areas of talent, had to be regarded as the crucial factor in achieving stabilization at fairly low numerical levels. Beyond 144, the statistical readings grew progressively more "fixed" and reliable, up to a general "holding" pattern in the neighborhood of 200 factors or so. Thus, a statistical determinant of 12 x 17 (totaling 204 sign-factors) was set as the "ideal" quotient for determining a self-regulated dispersal within the twelve different Sun signs. By way of confirmation, it was found that this "204" factor tended to duplicate itself in the dispersal pattern of the next 200-plus birth dates added to any specialized grouping in that larger area of numbers. But where the available biographical data on key talent in any given field (such as "120 Famous Astronomers," Fig. 15) restricted us to a lower statistical input than 144-plus factors, the indicators of its genius were sometimes already "surfacing" in abnormally strong cresting points. Yet they can only be seen as "indicative" in these cases.

Admittedly our statistics have introduced some puzzling contradictions and questions along the way, which will require of modern astrology an updated review of its commonly held opinions and interpretations concerning certain solar or planetary signs and "types" in relation to specific careers or temperaments. But this is not a serious criticism, and at least the remedy is close at hand. In fact, we are sure many professional astrologers have already identified for themselves some of these questionable areas and have applied the necessary adjustments in their own work. Nevertheless, much more research of a statistical nature is needed, and a cooperative effort to codify and standardize the results must follow.

Turning now to our charts and commentary, we shall not concern ourselves overmuch with a technical language. We seek simplification, not complexity. We write primarily for the benefit of other laymen like ourselves, who are sometimes befuddled and misled by too much professional jargon and obfuscation. Therefore, we will not speak of "synchronicity" in lieu of planetary "influences," or the like, eschewing currently popular scientific terms for the common wisdom. The former have their place in other circles. But our frame of reference in this regard remains the Edgar Cayce readings, which have their roots in intuitive perceptions[6] rather than purely intellectual ones! Science can supplement our symbolic language with more precise definitions, but it cannot replace it. We need the symbols, too. They are a part of ourselves.

To interpret the charts on the following pages, all the reader needs is a minimal acquaintance with some of the basic principles of astrology. These are summarized in the next few paragraphs for those who are unfamiliar with them. (A further understanding of the subject can be readily obtained by consulting any standard textbook on astrology.)

Most people are already familiar with their "Sun sign" and its general symbolism. Aries, for example, is the sign of the Ram, and wields its influence from approximately March 21 until April 19. Anyone born in this period is said to be an "Aries," although if he is born with his Sun on the cusp, or margin, of the next sign (Taurus, in this case), he comes under the influence of *both* Sun signs.

The twelve signs of the Zodiac represent the twelve constellations lying in a circular band of sky along the line of the Sun's annual ecliptic. Each sign occupies 30 degrees of arc, thereby constituting the twelve "houses" of the horoscope. Starting at 0° Aries (Υ), which is the point of the vernal equinox on the cusp of the first house, and moving counterclockwise, the signs in the other eleven houses are: Taurus, Gemini, Cancer, Leo, Virgo, Libra, Scorpio, Sagittarius, Capricorn, Aquarius, and Pisces.

We have described the "stationary" Zodiac. However, due to Earth's daily rotation on its axis, the Sun appears to circle Earth every 24 hours in a clockwise direction, carrying the wheel of Sun signs along with it, like a rotating rim superimposed on the fixed wheel of the twelve houses. The wandering planets of our own solar system also move across our sky as minions of the journeying Sun, and the Moon rides swiftly overhead with a face that is constantly changing. On Spaceship Earth, therefore, the moving "map" of the heavens will form a slightly different configuration for every soul-entity arriving on this planet, depending on the exact hour and moment of birth and the precise geographic location. To give an example of how it works: On July 22, 1917, the Sun was in Cancer, on the cusp of Leo. An individual born at two o'clock in the morning on that date, at the precise latitude and longitude occupied by the American town of Evanston, in Illinois, would have found the sign Gemini occupying the cusp of the first house at 25° 01', as the Ascendant sign in his horoscope. The planet Mars would have been rising, while Jupiter would already have moved over the horizon into the twelfth house. Uranus, in the sign of Aquarius, would have occupied a place in the sky just past midheaven, in the ninth house. (The Sun—at 28° 55' Cancer—still lay below the horizon, in the second house.) These and the other planetary positions, as well as the various aspects they formed toward one another, would have constituted this particular individual's unique "orientation in space," as Dane Rudhyar has aptly termed it, setting the cosmic pattern to which he would vibrate in the flesh.

In all our diagrams we have standardized on the basic horoscope for the tropical system of astrology, in which 0° Aries is on the Ascendant, or horizon line. Therefore, the entire first house is occupied by the sign Aries, and so forth, with all the other signs and houses which follow.[7] Our linear patterns in the various charts proceed from the midway point of one sign to the midway point of the next, although this is primarily done as a matter of simplification. The compilation of birth statistics for any given group would normally result in a numerical "peaking" point somewhere off center under each of the signs, particularly, of course, if the cresting curve extends into the neighboring sign. But such demographic precision is not essential to our case.

In astrology, there is at least one "ruling" planet associated with each sign, which lends its influence to any activity occurring within its domain. Thus, in our first diagram, which covers the frequency distribution of Sun signs for 408 Famous Actors and Actresses in leading romantic or dramatic roles only, we have a unique configuration in which the two dominant Sun signs are Taurus and Libra—*both* ruled, oddly enough, by the planet Venus. (See Fig. 4.)

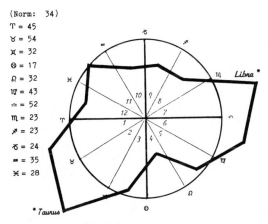

Figure 4. SUN SIGNS
408 Famous Actors & Actresses ("leading roles" only)

* (Ruling planet: Venus)

Taurus and Libra are the dominant Sun signs for actors and actresses in leading romantic or dramatic roles. Aries and Virgo hold secondary prominence. Cancer, it appears, is the least promising Sun sign for anyone aspiring to a career in this sector of the performing arts.

In a statistical evaluation of key cresting points and recessed areas, the prominence of Taurus and Libra rate "highly significant," at odds of 5,000 to 1 and 5,000 to 3.5, respectively. (Among the recessed signs, Cancer falls in a "highly significant" category also.)

The Sun, in whatever sign it appears, reveals the basic personality, although modified by the Ascendant sign and other astrological factors.

In the lunar configuration for actors and actresses, note the Moon's shifting of emphasis from Taurus to Gemini, and the emergence of Scorpio as a lunar influence among thespians.

In this diagram, as well as the five planetary configurations that follow, certain cresting points or recessed areas—although not rated "highly significant"—were found to be statistically meaningful for our purposes, based on a probability factor of 5% or less. (Approximate odds against chance are indicated in each case.)

The Moon influences the emotions.

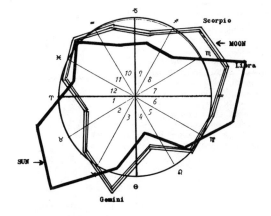

Figure 5. MOON "OVERLAY"
408 Famous Actors & Actresses ("leading roles" only)

97

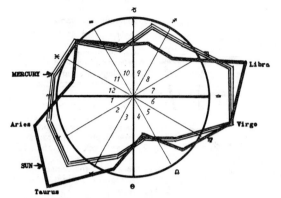

Because of Mercury's relatively narrow orbit, the Mercury overlay of the solar pattern might be expected to duplicate the Sun's points of emphasis rather closely; however, there are some unexpected deviations—most notably at Pisces.

Mercury represents the mental forces.

Figure 6. MERCURY "OVERLAY"

408 Famous Actors & Actresses ("leading roles" only)

Venus offers a surprise: the sharp divergence from the Sun's tracks, at the sign Cancer, whose keynote is, "I feel." Otherwise, as astrological "ruler" of Taurus and Libra, Venus appears to coincide with the Sun's pattern of influence in this professional grouping.

Venus, of course, is the planet symbolizing love and romance.

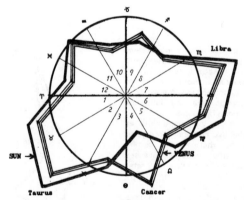

Figure 7. VENUS "OVERLAY"

408 Famous Actors & Actresses ("leading roles" only)

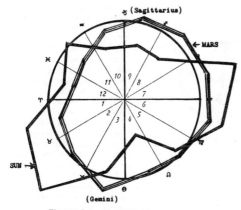

Figure 8. MARS "OVERLAY"

408 Famous Actors & Actresses ("leading roles" only)

In the form of a lopsided wheel, the Mars configuration would reflect a fairly balanced distribution among the signs except for the fact that it is considerably "off-center." All of the signs from Capricorn through Taurus form a *recessed* curve that dips through two quadrants of the Zodiac, while the remainder of the circle displays a "cresting" effect from Gemini through Sagittarius. These opposing curves, although in relatively low profile, are possibly more meaningful indicators than one or two sharply eclipsed or high cresting signs; for they suggest a *sustained* polarity of influence (whether negative or positive), as may also be observed in the diagrams for Jupiter and Saturn.

Mars is called "the energizer." It expresses itself in action and courage—or aggressiveness and anger, if out of control.

Jupiter's pattern, "peaking" only at Virgo and Capricorn, although in a low cresting wave from Taurus to Virgo, has two flanking curves of *recessed* signs on either side of the Capricorn "summit." Yet any attempt to interpret such an arresting phenomenon, which is paralleled by the patterns in both the Mars and Saturn configurations, would be futile on an orthodox statistical basis because the degree of prominence or recession in the *individual* signs is statistically inadequate. Clearly, a new approach must be devised, which takes a "collective" view, wherein the statistical input would have some meaning.

Jupiter's influence is an ennobling one, relating to "universal forces" (2869-1).

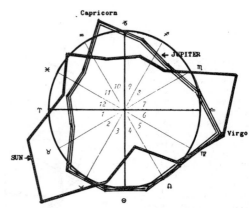

Figure 9. JUPITER "OVERLAY"

408 Famous Actors & Actresses ("leading roles" only)

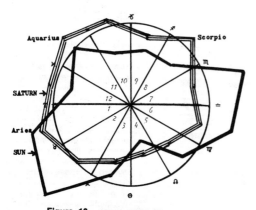

Figure 10. SATURN "OVERLAY"

408 Famous Actors & Actresses ("leading roles" only)

Saturn—called "the taskmaster"—veers away from most of those signs favored by Mars and Jupiter. Its major points of prominence are Aquarius, Aries and Scorpio, while it is most sharply recessed at Cancer.

The Cayce readings refer to Saturn as the planet of changes, which may be "sudden or violent" (1981-1), or simply "the tendency for the starting of new experiences, the starting of new associations in the activities . . ." (361-4).

Saturn's sign and placement in a natal chart appears to be closely linked to the karmic obligations of the individual. (This suggests that one's professional choice may frequently involve a mutual karmic pattern with others in the same profession.)

In traditional astrology, Jupiter represents the expansive and ennobling forces, while Saturn exerts a restrictive and confining influence. In this overlay diagram of the two planets, it is fascinating to note that in precisely those areas where Jupiter is dominant, Saturn tends to withdraw, and vice versa—almost as if choosing opposite sides of the Great Wheel of the Zodiac in which to wield their quite different influences! (Yet such a pattern, while clearly applicable in the acting profession for some reason, has been less noticeable in other career categories we have examined to date.)

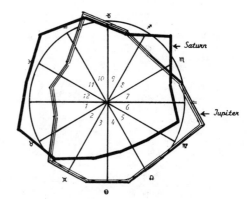

Figure 11. JUPITER/SATURN "OVERLAY"

408 Famous Actors & Actresses ("leading roles" only)

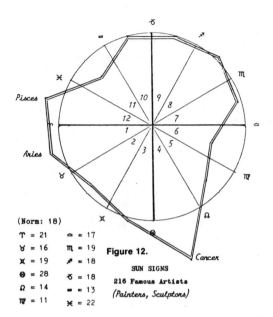

Figures 12, 13, and 14

Moving from the theatrical arts to the creative arts, we find Taurus and Libra replaced by other Sun signs as the prominent cresting points. In terms of traditional astrology, it is not surprising to find the two most "sensitive" signs in the Zodiac—Cancer and Pisces—leading the pack, along with the impulsive Aries, among 216 Famous Artists.

(Norm: 18)

♈	= 21	♎	= 17
♉	= 16	♏	= 19
♊	= 19	♐	= 18
☉	= 28	♑	= 18
♌	= 14	♒	= 13
♍	= 11	♓	= 22

Figure 12.

SUN SIGNS
216 Famous Artists
(Painters, Sculptors)

Among 204 Great Composers, the dominant Sun sign is Sagittarius, whose higher-octave keynote is "wisdom." (Beethoven—perhaps the greatest of composers—not only had his Sun in this sign, but the Moon and Mercury also.) Pisces and Gemini share secondary prominence here.

(Norm: 17)

♈	= 16	♎	= 9
♉	= 15	♏	= 12
♊	= 22	♐	= 25
☉	= 17	♑	= 17
♌	= 16	♒	= 16
♍	= 17	♓	= 22

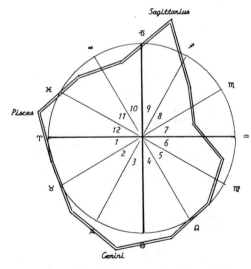

Figure 13. SUN SIGNS
204 Great Composers

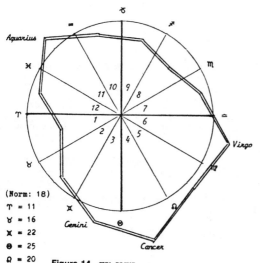

Novelists, as might be expected, are apt to have Gemini as a natal Sun position, since Gemini governs "communications." However, Cancer and Virgo, respectively, are in most frequent evidence in this career category.

The statistical input of the three artistic categories in Figures 12, 13, and 14, if *combined*, would lose its differentiating qualities and assume a "random" pattern, similar to that encountered by Gauquelin in his conglomerate classes.

(Norm: 18)

♈ = 11
♉ = 16
♊ = 22
♋ = 25
♌ = 20
♍ = 23
♎ = 17
♏ = 13
♐ = 15
♑ = 17
♒ = 21
♓ = 16

Figure 14. SUN SIGNS

216 Major Novelists

Among 120 Famous Astronomers (from Tycho Brahe to the present), the Sun sign Cancer is remarkably prominent—90% above the norm. In its higher octave, Cancer relates to the intuitive faculties. Pisces and Aries are also pronounced; but note the large number of recessed areas in this scientific category.

(Norm: 10)

♈ = 13	♎ = 7
♉ = 5	♏ = 12
♊ = 11	♐ = 10
♋ = 19	♑ = 11
♌ = 6	♒ = 7
♍ = 6	♓ = 13

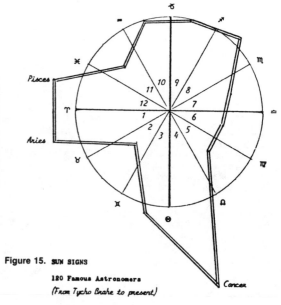

Figure 15. SUN SIGNS

120 Famous Astronomers

(From Tycho Brahe to present)

102

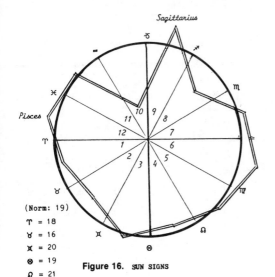

Virgo is often associated with the quest for knowledge, and also with meticulous workmanship. Sagittarians are said to be at home with abstract principles. Is it surprising, then, to find these two Sun signs prominent among 228 of the world's most noted physicists? (Note the sharply recessed Capricorn!)

(Norm: 19)

♈ = 18
♉ = 16
♊ = 20
♋ = 19
♌ = 21
♍ = 24
♎ = 21
♏ = 15
♐ = 24
♑ = 7
♒ = 21
♓ = 22

Figure 16. SUN SIGNS

228 Noted Physicists

Whereas the astronomer is concerned with a cosmic view, the chemist explores the microcosm; and note how opposite, in many ways, is the dispersal of natal Sun positions between the two categories! Still other differences are evident between chemists and physicists. Only Pisces displays a common prominence. Yet, if combined, these three scientific categories would produce a fairly random distribution, devoid of character.

(Norm: 20)

♈ = 22
♉ = 23
♊ = 15
♋ = 12
♌ = 21
♍ = 21
♎ = 21
♏ = 18
♐ = 24
♑ = 22
♒ = 17
♓ = 24

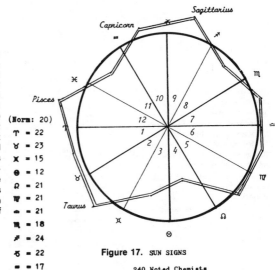

Figure 17. SUN SIGNS

240 Noted Chemists

103

In examining the dispersal patterns of natal Sun signs for two separate and distinctive categories of sports champions—204 Major League Baseball Players and 96 Boxing Champions—we can see at once how sharply contrasting are the temperaments of those athletes who are attracted to widely different sports activities. Merged into a single statistical grouping, however, their almost diametrically opposed natures would give us a totally misleading diagram.

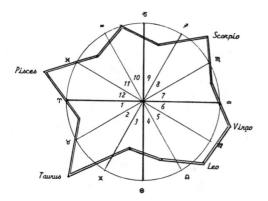

Figure 18. SUN SIGNS
204 Major League Baseball Players
("Hall of Fame," Other Stars)

(Norm: 17)

♈ = 15	♎ = 16
♉ = 23	♏ = 20
♊ = 11	♐ = 13
♋ = 13	♑ = 17
♌ = 19	♒ = 14
♍ = 20	♓ = 23

Of curious note is the prominence of Cancer among boxers. Every sign, of course, has its several octaves of expression; and in the physical type, the sensitive nature of the Cancerian may produce inner hurts in early life that are later manifested in masochistic/sadistic thrill-seeking in the boxing ring. (However, this is only a speculation. We will leave it to the astrologer and the trained psychologist to catalog and evaluate our findings.)

(Norm: 8)

♈ = 6	
♉ = 10	
♊ = 10	
♋ = 11	
♌ = 4	
♍ = 11	
♎ = 4	
♏ = 7	
♐ = 8	
♑ = 10	
♒ = 10	
♓ = 5	

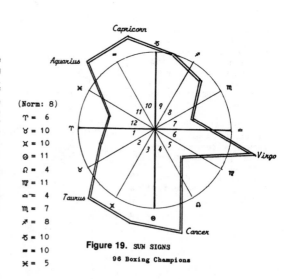

Figure 19. SUN SIGNS
96 Boxing Champions

104

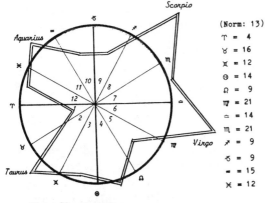

(Norm: 13)

Sign	Count
♈	= 4
♉	= 16
♊	= 12
☉	= 14
♌	= 9
♍	= 21
♎	= 14
♏	= 21
♐	= 9
♑	= 9
♒	= 15
♓	= 12

Our survey of Sun signs for 156 Great Rulers is already detailed elsewhere. It is a significant pattern in many respects. Virgo's emphasis may typify both the higher and lower extremes of "perfectionism" among earthly monarchs, while Scorpio is the sign of the dynamic, forceful ruler, as well as the reformer. (But Leo—the "sign of the king"—is sharply recessed!)

Figure 20. SUN SIGNS
156 Great Rulers
(Kings & Emperors; Ruling Queens; Dictators)

Venus is certainly an appropriate "rulership" for the theatrical arts. Many astrologers link the signs Taurus and Libra to artistic pursuits, although not specifically to the acting profession. Yet the frequency distribution for Sun in Taurus, among our select group of leading thespians, was 58% above the norm, and the incidence of Sun in Libra was 52.9% above average, with odds against chance of 5,000:1 and 5,000:3.5, respectively. This is highly significant. It establishes a definite correlation, in our view, which merits deeper study by astrologers—as do other aspects of the same diagram—plus the lunar and planetary patterns presented in successive diagrams for this specialized career category. (See Figures 5-11.) This professional class provides a nearly perfect example of the sort of frequency distribution revealed by our study of approximately two dozen career classes in our initial research. Therefore, we have chosen it as the focal point of our analysis.

In Figure 4, it will be noted that there is also a strong emphasis on Aries and Virgo, in addition to Taurus and Libra. Cancer, on the other hand, is poorly represented among thespians, as are certain other signs to a lesser degree. One of these is Scorpio, another Pisces. Yet, when we ran a partial check on 78 Famous Comedians for Sun sign indications, we found to our surprise that there were relatively few with their Sun in Taurus or Libra, while two of the "dominant" areas were Scorpio and Pisces. Cancer was "average." This turnabout in natal Sun positions for comedians, as opposed to their fellow thespians in romantic or dramatic roles, clearly told us why Gauquelin's broader-based groupings in the various professional categories he examined had produced only random patterns of solar and planetary distribution. The same theory tested out when we moved from the theatrical arts to the creative arts, where we found distinctly different points of prominence and eclipse in the frequency distribution for 216 Famous Artists, 204 Great Composers, and 216 Major Novelists. (See Figures 12, 13, and 14.) Again, in an individual survey of just three of the categories Gauquelin had included under the common heading, "Scientists," we found surprising divergencies, when examined singly, which would nevertheless tend to "balance out" when bundled together. (See Figures 15, 16, and 17: Sun sign patterns for 120 Famous Astronomers, 228 Noted Physicists, and 240 Noted Chemists.) Finally, turning to the world of sports, we chose two contrasting groups: 204 Major League Baseball Players and 96 Boxing Champions. (See Figures 18 and 19.) Baseball is a "fun" game, and the players are usually of an extrovert nature, whereas prize fighters perhaps use the ring as an outlet for the sadistic/masochistic tendencies inherent in a pugilistic disposition. These contrasts showed up sharply in our two diagrams of natal Sun positions.

The final diagram in our series of solar patterns is, in its way, the most significant. (See Fig. 20.) This survey of 156 Great Rulers, ranging through the royal rosters of emperors, kings, and ruling queens, and moving up to modern dictators, covers a span of several centuries. It holds a definite surprise for those who have always accepted the common verdict of astrologers that Leo is the sign of the king. In our configuration—statistically rather limited, but still sufficient to be "indicative"—Leo is eclipsed by the overwhelming dominance of its neighboring sign, Virgo. (Scorpio looms equally large, while limited prominence is shared by Aquarius and Taurus.)

But why Virgo rather than Leo?

There is a key element to be considered here, that may restore to Leo some of its regal dignity: the precession of the equinoxes.

This will be explored in the following essay, "Towards a New Astrology" which will also include a check-list of biographical source material used in compiling birth statistics for our diagrams so that other researchers may repeat our experiments, if interested. Additionally, it will contain a number of further diagrams, including a statistical evaluation on several larger compilations. An appendix showing percentile readings on the major cresting points in each solar chart will further reinforce our findings and provide useful data for interested students of astrology.

In our closing comments here, we want to refer back briefly to the two statistical evaluations on 648 Major Classical Composers and 3,564 Total Classical Composers, respectively, as well as the solar diagram in Fig. 13 for 204 Great Composers, which actually preceded the other two. For these three charts, among them, do more than any others to substantiate our findings, thus lending important corroboration to the Cayce readings on solar and planetary influence in human destiny.

It will be seen, first of all, that the key cresting points in our smaller, more qualitative diagram for 204 Great Composers were Sagittarius first, followed by Pisces and Gemini in equal influence. According to our theory, this indicates the areas of greatest probability for genius to manifest itself, among those choosing this career category; and it should also show a predilection toward classical composition—if other factors in the birth chart are favorable—on the part of anyone born under one of these three Sun signs. Thus, the useful "counseling" role of scientific astrology is suggested. The 204 components in this initial, smaller compilation of composers were furnished to us by an experienced musicologist, who used as his source *The International Cyclopedia of Music and Musicians*,[8] which is probably the most authoritative text in its field. Its biographical input on literally thousands of musicians extends to every civilized nation in the world, and covers a period of several centuries, so that it occurred to us that this was the ideal compendium for a statistical survey that would meet all of the scientific criteria for an objective statistical evaluation.

To avoid the imprint of personal preference, which may conceivably have colored the choice of 204 Great Composers by our musicologist acquaintance, we simply ran a compilation on the basis of columnar space as the most objective guide to importance; and we came up with 648 Major Classical Composers, as the total number with a biographical input of half a column or more. Here, again, the three major cresting areas were Sagittarius, Pisces and Gemini; but this time, although Sagittarius retained its lead, Gemini had fallen behind Pisces. A fourth factor, Capricorn, had peaked slightly. But in a much larger, and consequently less qualitative, compilation of a total input of 3,564 listed composers (including those whose major career effort often lay in other areas of musical expression, such as conductor, etc., but whose listed compositions reached a minimum of "several," thus meriting inclusion among "composers" as a secondary occupation), Sagittarius lost its leading prominence to Pisces by a marginal factor, and Gemini trailed still further behind the other two. Moreover, the whole configuration showed the "muting" effect of mediocrity, both on its reduced points of prominence and recession, although the continuing impact of "specialization" still prevented the degeneration of the data into a "random" effect, as might have been expected to occur.

In the diagram of 648 Major Classical Composers, where Sagittarius peaked at 50% above the norm, the statistical odds against chance were 100,000 to 6.6, based on a probability factor of .0066%. In the larger configuration of 3,564 Total Classical Composers, the nominal lead by Pisces, at 20.5% above the norm versus 19.19% for Sagittarius, was professionally evaluated at odds of 10,000 to 1 against chance; and Sagittarius rated odds of 10,000 to 3. Conclusion: highly significant.

This single case establishes the validity of astrology on a scientific basis. Numerous other examples are bound to follow, as astrological research pursues this specialized approach. And if the case is proved for astrology, it is simultaneously proved once more for the validity of the psychic data in the Edgar Cayce readings.

APPENDIX

The following statistical tables, showing approximate odds against chance, apply to the diagrams depicted in Figures 5 through 10, for 408 Famous Actors and Actresses ("leading roles" only):

MOON (Norm: 34)	
♈	= 21 *(100 to 1.5)
♉	= 31
♊	= 42
♋	= 24 *(100 to 4)
♌	= 35
♍	= 36
♎	= 44 *(100 to 4)
♏	= 42
♐	= 30
♑	= 35
♒	= 37
♓	= 31

Fig. 5

MERCURY (Norm: 34)	
♈	= 40
♉	= 41
♊	= 27
♋	= 20 *(100 to 1)
♌	= 27
♍	= 45 *(100 to 2.5)
♎	= 46 *(100 to 2)
♏	= 31
♐	= 31
♑	= 27
♒	= 36
♓	= 37

Fig. 6

VENUS (Norm: 34)	
♈	= 40
♉	= 48 *(100 to 1)
♊	= 30
♋	= 40
♌	= 27
♍	= 36
♎	= 46 *(100 to 2)
♏	= 24 *(100 to 4)
♐	= 29
♑	= 27
♒	= 34
♓	= 27

Fig. 7

MARS (Norm: 34)	
♈	= 28
♉	= 31
♊	= 40
♋	= 34
♌	= 35
♍	= 41
♎	= 39
♏	= 40
♐	= 38
♑	= 32
♒	= 26
♓	= 24 *(100 to 4)

Fig. 8

JUPITER (Norm: 34)	
♈	= 27
♉	= 37
♊	= 37
♋	= 37
♌	= 36
♍	= 44 *(100 to 4)
♎	= 34
♏	= 29
♐	= 32
♑	= 40
♒	= 28
♓	= 27

Fig. 9

SATURN (Norm: 34)	
♈	= 41
♉	= 34
♊	= 25
♋	= 22 *(100 to 2)
♌	= 26
♍	= 37
♎	= 29
♏	= 41
♐	= 34
♑	= 38
♒	= 43 *(100 to 5)
♓	= 38

Fig. 10

*Approximate odds against chance.

Towards a New Astrology

Synopsis: In the preceding essay, "Patterns of Solar and Planetary Influence," we presented visual evidence in the form of 20 diagrams to support our conclusion, based on definite patterns of high and low frequency distribution of natal Sun and planetary positions in various professional categories, that the basic principles of astrology are correct. Corroborating excerpts from the Edgar Cayce readings were cited in support of our research efforts. Our findings were presented as statistical confirmation of the concept found in the readings that definite patterns of solar, lunar and planetary influence do indeed exist in the destiny of man.

Our final diagram in the series, pertaining to 156 Great Rulers, had a special significance relating to the precession of the equinoxes. This will now be explained.

Leo, according to common astrological opinion, is "the sign of the king." This Sun sign has traditionally been associated with power and glory, as well as vanity, all apt to be evidenced by kings—at least, such is the historic assumption.

Curiously enough, though, in a statistical survey of natal Sun positions for 156 Great Rulers, ranging through ancient and modern rosters of royalty, and winding up with a number of prominent dictators, we found Leo eclipsed, while its neighboring sign, Virgo, displayed a remarkable prominence. So did Scorpio. Two minor "peaking" points occurred at Taurus and Aquarius. (The diagram is reproduced below.) Our question: Why Virgo, rather than Leo?

This leads us to a consideration of the precession of the equinoxes. Our findings may restore to Leo at least some of its royal dignity.

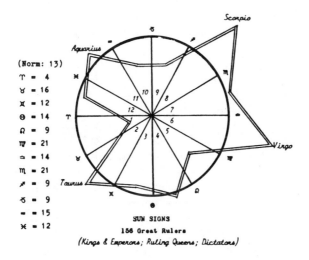

It was Hipparchus, the famous Greek astronomer of the second century B.C., who discovered this phenomenon. Ptolemy later used it as the basis for his geocentric approach to astrology, called the tropical system, which is the "moving" Zodiac still in popular use today among Western astrologers— *moving*, of course, because of the precessional effect. (In practice, however, the tropical system ignores the precession. More on this later.)

The precession was an important discovery for astronomers and astrologers alike. It marks the transit from one age to another, every 2160 years, through a grand cycle of ages totalling some 25,920 years. Due to the earth's slow wobble on its axis, a gradual slip of one degree occurs every 72 years in the lines of the poles, altering the measured positions of the stars at the moving points of intersection between the Sun's ecliptic and the celestial equator. This has pushed the point of the vernal equinox backwards through the constellation Pisces by almost 30° since the time of Hipparchus—by some estimates— so that now, some 2100 years later, 0° Aries approaches the threshold of the constellation Aquarius, where the Aquarian Age commences.

Actually, there are mixed opinions among the experts as to the exact degree the vernal equinox now occupies in Pisces. The Western proponents of sidereal astrology, led by Cyril Fagan,[1] place it in the neighborhood of 6° on the assumption that 0°

Aries did not move into Pisces until the third century. This theory is based on elaborate calculations purporting to show that the vernal equinox passed out of Taurus into Aries about 1963 B.C., ending the Taurean Age and beginning the Arian cycle. If correct, it would mean that the Aquarian Age will not commence until almost A.D. 2400. Esoteric tradition, however, places its commencement several centuries earlier than that. This would imply that 0° Aries was actually moving over the cusp of Pisces—thus marking the opening of the Piscean Age— at about the time of Hipparchus's remarkable discovery of the precession in 130 B.C. or thereabouts. This puts the precession in the likely category of a New Age revelation; for every unfolding age ushers in a new cycle of learning for mankind in its upward evolution and has its appointed precursors. It was the Piscean Age, of course, that brought us the message of the Christ. Moreover, our dating of events in accordance with esoteric tradition coincides with the Cayce readings, which tell us that "the new cycle" will begin in the year 2000 to 2001 A.D., "When there is a shifting of the poles." (826-8) If we calculate backwards 2160 years, this pinpoints the commencement of the Piscean Age at 160 B.C., in the days of Hipparchus.

How does all this affect our statistics on 156 Great Rulers? Very simple. If tropical astrology had remained consistent with its precessional origins, there would have been a visibly changing symbolism over the centuries as the transiting point of the vernal equinox carried the wheel of Sun signs backwards through the constellations until they had moved from their original alignment in the days of Hipparchus to the present overlap of almost 30°. In other words, the sign Aries is presently superimposed on the constellation Pisces, Taurus on Aries, and so forth—until we come to Virgo, superimposed on Leo. And, presto! We now have a tacit and paradoxical basis for astrology's familiar claim that Leo is the "sign of the king." But whence originated the claim? Hardly with our modern tropical practitioners, it seems! For their Sun signs are not in accord with the precessional effect, as already mentioned, but are based on a fixed calendar position (March 21) for 0° Aries, the starting point of the tropical Zodiac.

Let's check with the siderealists, then. In sidereal astrology, which uses a set of celestial coordinates that relate mathematically to a moving vernal point based on precession, we find the sign Leo overlapping tropical Virgo by 24 degrees. This means that most of our "Virgoan" rulers of modern history, born between August 23 and September 22, turn out to be sidereal "Leos," with their Sun in Leo from August 17 to September 16. So the siderealists are "right on," we might say— or relatively so, at any rate—depending on the degree of accuracy in their calculations. But in view of the comparatively few contemporary rulers born with their Sun in *tropical* Leo, as presently measured (from July 23 to August 22), we must still wonder on what basis the practitioners of the tropical system have chosen to assign to their modern-day Leo his regal attributes. It is possible, though not too likely, that they adopted the notion in the fairly recent past from astrologers in India or other parts of the Far East (where the sidereal system has long been practiced) and simply neglected to make the necessary calendar adjustments. (A number of Eastern potentates, incidentally, graces our roster of 156 Great Rulers.) But more probably, the notion originated with the tropical system itself in a bygone age, when court astrologers may have noted the eminence of the Sun sign Leo in the horoscopes of the kings of that era. However, in the checkered flow of history, there are inevitable changes in the character of society and its rulers. Thus, an ancient truism about Leo and kings has been perpetuated beyond its realm of accuracy and meaning, it seems, by the modern heirs of astrological lore.

Whatever the explanation, we do not mean to belittle the tropical system of astrology by pointing out an apparent flaw in one of its present interpretations. We only draw attention to the underlying problems inherent in the continued use of an outdated or simplistic symbolism. In this regard, the siderealists are as prone to err as some of the tropical practitioners. A great king or a powerful dictator should not automatically indicate to the astrologer a symbolic connection with "leonine" traits, even when born under Leo! And it is quite possible, if Virgo and Scorpio were to be recognized in tropical astrology as the current Sun signs under which contemporary rulers are most likely to be born, that the existing astrological insights for those two calendar periods would be found to define more aptly the regal nature, at least insofar as Western rulers are concerned, than the characteristics attributed to tropical Leo.[2]

In any case, the mythic symbolism still in vogue is misleading and needs to be dropped: Virgins and Lions have nothing to do with the astrological facts any more than Crabs or Scorpions! It will be a part of the work of the New Astrology to erase such misrepresentations, however colorful and charming they may appear to us. They do not belong in a scientific lexicon. We can still maintain the imagery, but only as an outer garb, which has no bearing on the wearer; it must *not* be permitted to distort the astrological interpretations, as is too frequently the case at present.

Turning to the Sun signs for several other professions, we now find the tropical practitioners largely vindicated. (See Appendix A.) With pinpoint accuracy, the diagram for 144 Famous Inventors reveals Aquarius as the dominant Sun sign, as any astrologer would be apt to predict. Aquarius is ruled by Uranus, and "originality" is one of the key words here. Because our compilation of inventors dated back to 1706, it gave us a sufficient time-span (200 years plus) from which to draw some meaningful conclusions on the dispersal patterns of the slow-moving outer planets through the signs of the Zodiac. It was not too difficult to plot their respective movements through the Zodiac for a century prior to 1800, the point at which the published ephemerides stop. Therefore, charts showing the configurations for Uranus, Neptune and Pluto are included in Appendix A for this professional category. They are profoundly interesting. While we leave it to the astrologers to ponder and interpret their esoteric significance, brief comments accompanying the charts point to some of the salient features and relate them to insights drawn from the Cayce readings.

Next, the reader will note two charts that are curiously similar in their tendency to "peak" at two fairly equal points, although the prominent signs are sharply divergent—as should be expected of these quite different professions. The first diagram traces the distribution of Sun signs for 144 Outstanding Religious Leaders of America, cresting at Aquarius and Virgo. Virgo, in its higher octave of expression, pertains to service to others and the sovereignty of the spirit, while Aquarius vibrates at the spiritual level to the harmonious tones of humanitarianism and fellowship with God. Quite obviously, in the case of inspired religious leaders, both shoes fit! On the other hand, our diagram for 144 Distinguished Military Leaders peaks at Scorpio and Pisces. The former is not surprising: Scorpio has traditionally been associated with a relentless, driving force amid tactical secrecy, which might readily manifest itself in a successful military career. We suspect that any skilled astrologer would nod in instant comprehension upon learning that three of the greatest generals of World War II—Patton, Montgomery, and Rommel—were Scorpios. Less comprehensible, in our view, is the nearly equal prominence of Pisces. Personally, we would have been more inclined to associate Aries—a sign denoting initiative and enterprise—with military prowess than compassionate Pisces. Pisces, however, is known in astrology as the "karmic" sign; and this could perhaps account for what at first appears to be an inconsistency.

On the subject of Aries, the Cayce readings suggest that this sign denotes "the abilities of a high *mental* development. . ." (406-1) Two career categories in which we found Aries the prominent natal Sun sign were architects and conductors. Whether working with earthly elements or tonal structures, both groups are "builders," and may be described at the mental level as "enterprising," which fits the common astrological interpretation for this pioneering sign. The *mental* demands are well above the ordinary in either of these two professions, requiring an unusual comprehension of the many elements that must be joined together harmoniously in the finished structure, whether shaped from multiple sounds and silences or built of denser materials. Although our solar chart on architects has not been included here, we enclose two diagrams on musical conductors: 156 Major Conductors, in which the overwhelming dominance of Aries was observed at 84.6% above the norm; and a larger grouping of 732 Noteworthy Conductors (incorporating the smaller cluster), in which Aries still maintained its dominance at 22.95% above the norm.

Among performing musicians in several categories, following next in our charts, it can be plainly seen how different in temperament is the violinist from the cellist, or the pianist from the organist; yet it has been traditionally assumed that the musical temperament is of a generally uniform pattern, which is clearly *not* the case.

Further evidence in this direction is found in our compilation of 960 Classical Singers of Distinction, in which Pisces and Capricorn are the dominant cresting areas. Yet, in a separate compilation of Non-Classical Singers (not included here), we found Pisces sharply *recessed,* and the points of major prominence were Taurus and Sagittarius. Lunar configurations for Classical vs. Non-Classical Singers were also markedly dissimilar.

The final set of four charts included in Appendix A introduces an entirely new dimension into astrology. It reveals observed differences of a very pronounced nature between the natal characteristics of the male and female components within two separate career categories, actors and singers. This area of research needs to be explored much further. It holds much potential significance. A "yin/yang" configuration seems to be in evidence, in an alternating pattern of "positive" and "negative" Sun-sign positions, as noted in some of the "peaks" and "valleys" of male talent versus the female demographics. Yet there are also areas of agreement, which do not appear to be coincidental in view of their statistical significance. So it is all quite intriguing, from a psychological perspective, and invites scientific inquiry.

Meanwhile, more needs to be said here about the sidereal system, currently gaining many adherents in the West. It is believed in many quarters to be far more ancient than Ptolemy's tropical method, and probably rooted in the earliest teachings of the Egyptians and the Babylonians. Some impressive evidence has been produced in support of this view. In any event, the sidereal system sets its bearings on several "fixed" star-points in the constellations, as contrasted with the earth-oriented tropical system. Its fiducial, or marking star, is Aldebaran—the "Bull's Eye"—in the mathematical center of the constellation Taurus. This would appear to place it exactly a sign and a half away from 0° Aries, which marks the starting point of the tropical Zodiac; and 0° Taurus, which the siderealists regard as the *true* primogeniture of the Zodiac, dating from ancient times, takes its place one sign removed from Aries. However, in the adjusted reckoning of astrology, where the circle of the Zodiac slips backward along the fixed constellations due to precession, the "Bull's Eye" in 15° Taurus has moved forward some 24 to 30 degrees, depending upon whose calculations are accepted as the most accurate. According to siderealists, who calculate the present precessional effect from the 3rd century A.D.,[3] Aldebaran now lies at about 9° Gemini of the *moving* Zodiac of Sun signs, while esoteric tradition would place it in the vicinity of 15° Gemini. In any case, we find that the tropical vernal point, 0° Aries, now lies approximately two full signs from the constellation Taurus. Is this what Cayce was perhaps referring to in the following reading, with its reference to "some two signs off"?

Hence the entity was born into the earth under what signs? Pisces, ye say. Yet astrologically from the records, these are some two signs off in thy reckoning.   **5755-1**

We cannot be sure, of course, but the underlying intent of the wording may have been to imply that 0° Taurus in the "fixed" sidereal Zodiac was the proper commencement point for all astrological calculations or "reckoning." (In the actual measured difference due to precession, of course, we can only account for a variance of one sign.) Yet there is an important qualification to be made. Reading 5755-1 was given in June 1938, which means that the above-quoted excerpt cannot be construed as an "endorsement" of the current Western version of sidereal astrology, which was not formulated until 1947. In that year, the awesome research efforts of a brilliant Irishman named Cyril Fagan, to whom we referred earlier in this article, established for the sidereal system in the West a very precise set of calendar measurements that does *not*, however, coincide with the Cayce dating for the approaching New Age. Is it possible that Fagan's calculations were somewhat off base because of certain unknown factors or mistaken assumptions?

Two quotations, which bear our scrutiny here, are from the poet Virgil, a near contemporary of Hipparchus. The first quote appears to confirm the constellation Taurus as the commencement point of the ancient Zodiac, prior to the changes introduced later on by Ptolemy:

"When with golden hornes bright Taurus opes
The yeare, and downward the crosse Dog-starre
stoopes. . ."

The second, however—one which is ignored by the Western siderealists—speaks plainly of the Piscean Age already appearing in that 1st century B.C.: "A new great order of centuries is now being born. . ."

We have mentioned that the sidereal system, as practiced today, is rooted in Egyptian and Babylonian origins. This may accentuate the likelihood of some minor miscalculations along the way. For, in one of the readings, Cayce counseled a student of astrology against relying on the Egyptian records, pointing out that "the variations in time have been corrected by the Persians and not by the Egyptians." (2011-3) The entity was told, therefore, to "put the signs" in the Persian calendar. Unfortunately, very little is known today about Persian astrology, except that it appears to have been borrowed from the Babylonians and later modified. So we remain a bit in the dark.

This is precisely where the New Astrology comes in.

A statistical approach to the subject, coordinated with other scientific measures to rectify existing errors of calculation or interpretation, can be combined with the profound intuitive insights of many of our modern astrologers to produce an astrology that is above the reproach or ridicule of science. The starting point, however, must be a spiritual premise: man's oneness with the Soul of the universe. Only then can scientific research proceed on a logical basis from cause to effect.

Meanwhile, we are convinced of the essential validity and value inherent in both the tropical and sidereal systems. These have been compared to two separate lenses through which the same truths are revealed, but in an altered light. And in truth, there may be an intuitive wisdom at work in the stubborn reluctance of tropical practitioners to alter their presently established psychological insights gathered from many centuries of applied astrology under the tropical system, simply on the basis of the often-voiced criticism that their moving Zodiac is "one sign off" and therefore represents an out-distanced symbolism. What we are getting at is this: Although the two systems of astrology—the tropical and the sidereal—now technically stand approximately 24° apart, tropical practitioners have for the most part evolved over the centuries an "adjusted" set of interpretations, which is based on practical application and intuition and which appears to work rather accurately in general, so that both astrological schools are reasonably compatible on a calendar basis. It may be said that they are equally valid in their respective spheres of operation. And precisely for this reason, the Western siderealists—like their counterparts in the East—must evolve their own psychological insights, since it will create grave distortions if they simply "borrow" the tropical interpretations intact, and move them back by 24°, on the assumption that this is a valid "rectification"!

In addition there is some evidence in the readings— particularly in several confirmatory references to the cusps[4]— to suggest that the modern interpretations under the tropical system, though apparently in need of some rectification, are sufficiently close to the mark in major respects. In short, if the signs are "off," it appears to be by approximately 30 degrees today, or a full sign—*not* an odd factor of 24 degrees, which would alter the cusps! The only fly in the ointment, as already mentioned, is the misleading stress by some astrologers on the lingering mythic symbolism attached to the various Sun signs.

In time, it will probably be necessary and desirable for the two systems of astrology to fuse into one, if only to end the general confusion and skepticism their differences have generated in our scientific age.[5] The sidereal system, by hitching its wagon to a fixed star, has automatically bequeathed to itself a sounder basis, perhaps, for becoming the pattern for a New Age Astrology that must be coordinated with other cosmic sciences now evolving. Of course, the accumulated insights of *both* schools will have to be integrated in the new system; and the sidereal system may first need to adjust its chronology.

Finally, any sense of fatalism in connection with the stars must be totally effaced from astrological teachings. This will happen when it is more commonly understood, as already pointed out in the Cayce readings, that we ourselves set the course of our individual destiny and have the power to change it. The astrological aspects in a natal chart are never final. We are told in the readings that they pertain to latent mental urges arising from planetary sojourns at other levels of consciousness during the interim between earthly incarnations, and are only as "signposts along the individual way." (1745-1) Such urges—although an innate part of our self-created heritage, producing definite influences in the flesh for either good or evil—are ever subordinate to the free will:

*. . .but let it be understood here—no action of any planet or the phases of the sun, the moon or any of the heavenly bodies surpass the rule of man's willpower. . .*The inclinations of man are ruled by the planets under which he is born, for the destiny of man lies within the sphere or scope of the planets.

3744-3

Rather, then, than the stars *ruling* the life, the life should rule the stars—for man was created a little bit higher than all the rest of the whole universe, and is capable of harnessing, directing, enforcing, the laws of the universe.   5-2

Astrology, like any other branch of scientific learning, is meant to serve man. Its purpose is to increase his self-awareness. Therefore, its study can, and should, be helpful:

When studied aright, very, very, very much so. How aright then? In that influence as is seen in the influence of the knowledge already obtained by mortal man. Give more of that into the lives, giving the understanding *that the will must be the ever guiding factor to lead man on, ever upward.* 3744-3

It is in this context that we have undertaken the present study of cosmic influences in the life of man. We view such influences as developmental forces in the unfolding pattern of human destiny. These forces, then, when studied aright, not only point the way towards an entirely New Astrology, but towards a higher consciousness of our oneness with the Universal Forces. This is where our real destiny lies.

Man, awakened, finds the Cosmos in himself.

APPENDIX A

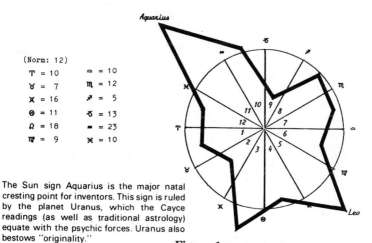

(Norm: 12)

♈ = 10	♎ = 10
♉ = 7	♏ = 12
♊ = 16	♐ = 5
♋ = 11	♑ = 13
♌ = 18	♒ = 23
♍ = 9	♓ = 10

The Sun sign Aquarius is the major natal cresting point for inventors. This sign is ruled by the planet Uranus, which the Cayce readings (as well as traditional astrology) equate with the psychic forces. Uranus also bestows "originality."

Figure 1. NATAL SUN SIGNS
144 Famous Inventors
(Span of 200-plus years from 1706 to 1912)

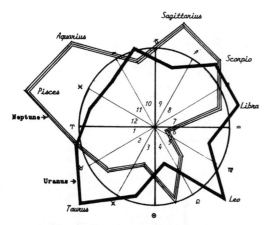

Neptune—"the mystic"—is the ruler of Pisces, which is seen here as the major cresting point among inventors. The Taurean prominence of Uranus—"the psychic"—denotes mastery over matter. This interpretation is uniquely applicable to inventors.

Figure 2. URANUS/NEPTUNE OVERLAY
144 Famous Inventors *(200-yr. span)* *

*NOTE: Our compilation dates from 1706 to 1912, covering 2½ revolutions of Uranus, and more than one full revolution of Neptune through the 12 signs of the Zodiac. (The only signs covered in a partial second revolution of Neptune are Aries, Taurus, Gemini, and 23° Cancer; yet the major influence of Neptune occurs in Sagittarius, Aquarius and Pisces. Pisces is "ruled" by the planet Neptune, and this is the major cresting point for inventors. The third revolution of Uranus, in the above chart, includes only 1° of the sign Aquarius, and omits a third return to the signs Pisces, Aries, Taurus, Gemini and Cancer. Nevertheless, Taurus is one of the cresting points, and Aries slightly, along with Leo, Libra and Scorpio.)

121

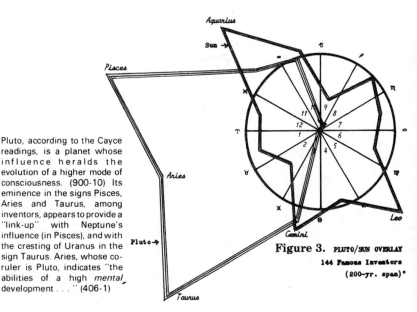

Pluto, according to the Cayce readings, is a planet whose influence heralds the evolution of a higher mode of consciousness. (900-10) Its eminence in the signs Pisces, Aries and Taurus, among inventors, appears to provide a "link-up" with Neptune's influence (in Pisces), and with the cresting of Uranus in the sign Taurus. Aries, whose co-ruler is Pluto, indicates "the abilities of a high *mental* development . . . " (406-1)

Figure 3. PLUTO/SUN OVERLAY
144 Famous Inventors
(200-yr. span)*

*NOTE: During the period from 1706 to 1912—as covered by this chart—Pluto made its rounds from Scorpio through Gemini, but did not reach the other signs of the Zodiac, inasmuch as it takes a total of 248.4 years to complete one revolution. Among inventors, it appears to have wielded its major influence in the signs Pisces, Aries and Taurus, and secondarily in Aquarius and Gemini.

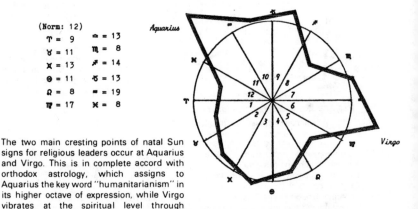

(Norm: 12)

♈ = 9	♎ = 13
♉ = 11	♏ = 8
♊ = 13	♐ = 14
♋ = 11	♑ = 13
♌ = 8	♒ = 19
♍ = 17	♓ = 8

The two main cresting points of natal Sun signs for religious leaders occur at Aquarius and Virgo. This is in complete accord with orthodox astrology, which assigns to Aquarius the key word "humanitarianism" in its higher octave of expression, while Virgo vibrates at the spiritual level through unselfish service to others.

Figure 4. NATAL SUN SIGNS
144 Outstanding Religious Leaders of America
(From 17th Century to Present)

(Norm: 12)
♈	= 11	♎ = 9	
♉	= 9	♏ = 19	
♊	= 13	♐ = 9	
♋	= 10	♑ = 11	
♌	= 12	♒ = 16	
♍	= 8	♓ = 17	

It is hardly surprising to note that military leaders are likely to be born under the sign of Scorpio, with its intensity of purpose and mastery of tactical surprises. The secondary prominence of the sign Pisces, whose key words are "universality" and "compassion," is less easy to explain in this militant career category. (Is it related to the fact that Pisces is also the "karmic" sign?)

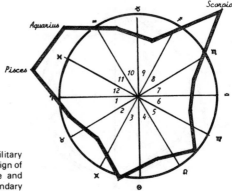

Figure 5. NATAL SUN SIGNS
144 Distinguished Military Leaders *

*NOTE: An international compilation of top achievers in military combat from the 17th century to the present. However, it has been necessary to omit Zhukov and other distinguished Russian generals of World War II fame, inasmuch as specific birth dates are not available from the Soviet Union. Also, naval and air commanders have been excluded. Research indicates that they belong in separate categories.

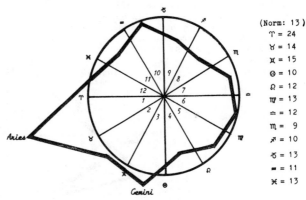

(Norm: 13)
♈	= 24
♉	= 14
♊	= 15
♋	= 10
♌	= 12
♍	= 13
♎	= 12
♏	= 9
♐	= 10
♑	= 13
♒	= 11
♓	= 13

Statistical Evaluation

Sample size: 156 units

Aries, 24 units
Probability factor: .07%
Odds against chance = 10,000 to 7

Figure 6. NATAL SUN SIGNS
156 Major Classical Conductors

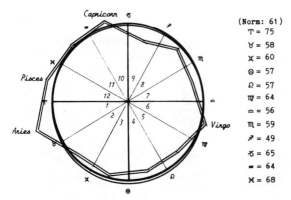

Figure 7. NATAL SUN SIGNS
732 Noteworthy Conductors (Classical)

(Norm: 61)
♈ = 75
♉ = 58
♊ = 60
♋ = 57
♌ = 57
♍ = 64
♎ = 56
♏ = 59
♐ = 49
♑ = 65
♒ = 64
♓ = 68

Sample size: 732 units

Aries, 75 units
Probability factor: 3.1%
Odds against chance = 100 to 3.1

Overlay of Two Preceding Samples:

Whereas the smaller sample (156 units) dramatically demonstrates the genius of its class in the Sun sign Aries, the introduction of lesser talent in the larger compilation (732 units) shows how the qualitative decline in any specialized grouping has a gradual "muting" effect on the key cresting points and recessional areas, producing a more random distribution.

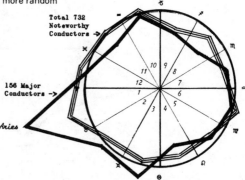

Total 732 Noteworthy Conductors →

156 Major Conductors →

Figure 8. COMPARATIVE PATTERNS OF DISTRIBUTION:
Sun Signs, "Major" Conductors versus Combined Total

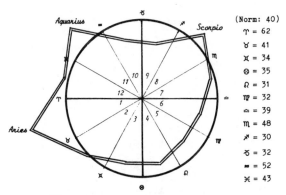

Figure 9. NATAL SUN SIGNS
480 Famous Violinists

(Norm: 40)

♈	= 62
♉	= 41
♊	= 34
☉	= 35
♌	= 31
♍	= 32
♎	= 39
♏	= 48
♐	= 30
♑	= 32
♒	= 52
♓	= 43

Aries, 62 units
Probability factor: .01%
Odds against chance = 10,000 to 1

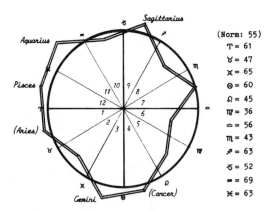

Figure 10. NATAL SUN SIGNS
660 Famous Pianists

(Norm: 55)

♈	= 61
♉	= 47
♊	= 65
☉	= 60
♌	= 45
♍	= 36
♎	= 56
♏	= 43
♐	= 63
♑	= 52
♒	= 69
♓	= 63

Aquarius, 69 units
Probability factor: 2.4%
Odds against chance = 100 to 2.4

125

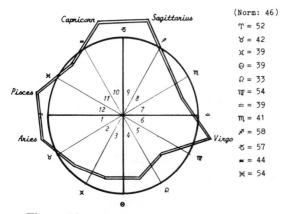

Figure 11. NATAL SUN SIGNS
552 Famous Organists

Sagittarius, 58 units
Probability factor: 3.2%
Odds against chance = 100 to 3.2

Statistical input in relation to prominence of
cresting areas "indicative" only; insufficient
to be meaningful in professionally
established terms of statistical evaluation.

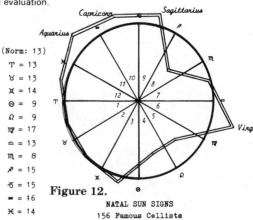

(Norm: 13)
♈ = 13
♉ = 13
♊ = 14
♋ = 9
♌ = 9
♍ = 17
♎ = 13
♏ = 8
♐ = 15
♑ = 15
♒ = 16
♓ = 14

Figure 12.

NATAL SUN SIGNS
156 Famous Cellists

126

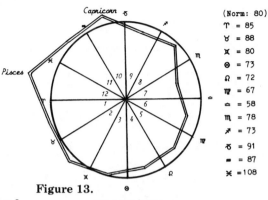

(Norm: 80)
♈ = 85
♉ = 88
♊ = 80
♋ = 73
♌ = 72
♍ = 67
♎ = 58
♏ = 78
♐ = 73
♑ = 91
♒ = 87
♓ = 108

Statistical Evaluation:

Pisces, 108 units

Probability factor .06%

Odds against chance = 10,000 to 6

Figure 13.

NATAL SUN SIGNS
960 Classical Singers of Distinction

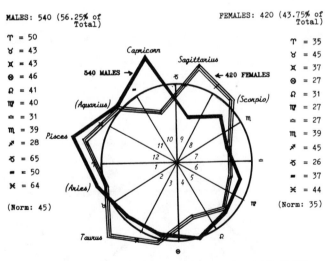

MALES: 540 (56.25% of Total)

♈ = 50
♉ = 43
♊ = 43
♋ = 46
♌ = 41
♍ = 40
♎ = 31
♏ = 39
♐ = 28
♑ = 65
♒ = 50
♓ = 64

(Norm: 45)

FEMALES: 420 (43.75% of Total)

♈ = 35
♉ = 45
♊ = 37
♋ = 27
♌ = 31
♍ = 27
♎ = 27
♏ = 39
♐ = 45
♑ = 26
♒ = 37
♓ = 44

(Norm: 35)

Figure 14. FREQUENCY DISTRIBUTION OF NATAL SUN SIGNS ON BASIS OF SEX
(960 Classical Singers of Distinction)

Probability factors, key cresting areas:

Males:
Capricorn 0.09% (10,000 to 9)
Pisces 0.16% (1,000 to 1.6)

Females:
Sagittarius and Taurus, each 3.9% (100 to 3.9)

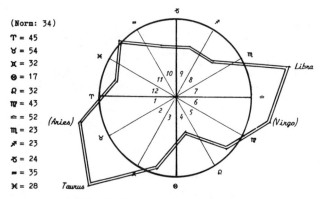

Figure 15. NATAL SUN SIGNS
408 Famous Actors & Actresses ("leading roles" only!)

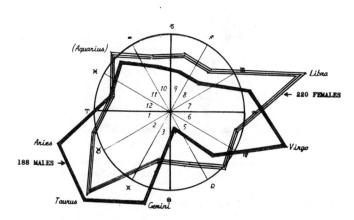

Figure 16. FREQUENCY DISTRIBUTION OF NATAL SUN SIGNS ON BASIS OF SEX
(408 Famous Actors & Actresses)

Fig. 16, continued

Probability factors, major cresting areas:

Females:
Libra .007% (100,000 to 7 odds)
Taurus 0.93% (1,000 to 9.3 odds)

Males:
Taurus and Virgo, each 0.33% (1,000 to 3.3 odds)

(Statistical evaluation by Han Y. Rhyu)

APPENDIX B

Our previous essay, "Patterns of Solar and Planetary Influence," contained diagrams of natal Sun positions for ten professional categories. For those researchers who may be interested in duplicating our efforts, here is a listing of biographical source material used in our compilation of birth statistics:

1. 408 Famous Actors and Actresses. *An Astrological Index to to the World's Famous People,* by Michael Cooper and Andrew Weaver; Doubleday & Co., N.Y., 1975. We chose only actors and actresses noted for romantic or dramatic leads, ignoring comedians in general, as well as character actors.

2. 216 Famous Artists. This category posed a special problem because none of the biographical compendia on artists gave specific birth dates. Consequently we jotted down the names of a total of 216 of the most noted artists, living and dead, and checked out their birth dates in the *Encyclopaedia Britannica* and *Collier's Encyclopedia.*

3. 204, 648, and 3,564 Composers. *The International Cyclopedia of Music and Musicians,* edited by Oscar Thompson; Dodd, Mead & Co., N.Y., 10th ed., 1975.

4. 216 Major Novelists. *Authors Today and Yesterday,* edited by Stanley J. Kunitz; The H.W. Wilson Co., N.Y., 1933 (and later supplements). To avoid any misleading results, we

ignored those novelists who were identified as "poet and novelist," on the assumption that the first-listed category was the "major" one.

5. 120 Famous Astronomers. *Asimov's Biographical Encyclopedia of Science and Technology,* by Isaac Asimov; Doubleday & Co., N.Y., rev. ed., 1972. Where more than one profession was indicated, such as "physicist and astronomer," we assumed that the first-named category was the primary profession and ignored the secondary one, with one or two notable exceptions.

6. 228 Noted Physicists. *Ibid.*

7. 240 Noted Chemists. *Ibid.*

8. 204 Major League Baseball Players. *The Baseball Encyclopedia,* Macmillan Publishing Co., N.Y., bicentennial ed., 1976. "Hall of Fame" players and pitchers led our list, followed by players ranked according to performance rating, up to a total of 204, representing our "ideal" quotient of 12 x 17.

9. 96 Boxing Champions. *The Encyclopedia of World Boxing Champions,* by John D. McCallum; Chilton Book Co., Radnor, Pa., 1975. Unfortunately, birth dates were not shown for all of the boxers listed, which accounts for our relatively low count in this professional category.

10. 156 Great Rulers. *Encyclopaedia Britannica* was our principal source of information. For this category, we were obliged to do extensive research. First we checked under different historic epochs for the names of ruling dynasties, and checked specific countries in Europe, the Middle East and Asia. Then we looked up the individual rulers for birth dates—often, alas, unknown! In general, we ignored smaller countries, unless a ruler from one of these lands had left a significant mark on history. This specialized approach explains why our list was necessarily restricted to only 156 Great Rulers. (*Note:* It is always necessary to consult an ephemeris for the Sun sign of any individual born on the cusp between two signs. For this purpose, we recommend *Die Deutsche Ephemeride.*)

Diagrams of natal Sun positions included in the present essay, "Towards a New Astrology," were drawn from the following biographical sources:

1. 144 Famous Inventors. *Asimov's Biographical Encyclopedia of Science and Technology,* by Isaac Asimov; Doubleday & Co., N.Y., rev. ed., 1972; and *Dictionary of American Biography,* edited by Allen Johnson; Charles Scribner's Sons, N.Y., rev. ed., 1957.

2. 144 Outstanding Religious Leaders of America. *Webster's American Biographies,* edited by Charles Van Doren; G.& C. Merriam Co., Springfield, Mass., 1974; and *Dictionary of American Biography* (cited above).
3. 144 Distinguished Military Leaders. *Encyclopaedia Britannica* and *Webster's American Biographies* (cited above).
4. 156 Major Conductors. *The International Cyclopedia of Music and Musicians.*
5. 732 Noteworthy Conductors. *Ibid.*
6. 480 Famous Violinists. *Ibid.*
7. 660 Famous Pianists. *Ibid.*
8. 552 Famous Organists. *Ibid.*
9. 156 Famous Cellists. *Ibid.*
10. 960 Classical Singers of Distinction. *Ibid.*

APPENDIX C

Percentile ratings of major cresting areas are shown below for each of the Sun sign diagrams included in our two articles, "Patterns of Solar and Planetary Influence" and "Towards a New Astrology":
1. 408 Famous Actors & Actresses (Norm: 34 units per sign)
    Taurus: 54 units—58.82% above norm
    Libra: 52 units—52.94% above norm
2. 216 Famous Artists (Norm: 18)
    Cancer: 28 units—55.55% above norm
    Pisces: 22 units—22.22% above norm
3. 204 Great Composers (Norm: 17)
    Sagittarius: 25 units—47.05% above norm
    Pisces, Gemini: 22 units each—29.41% above norm
4. 648 Major Classical Composers (Norm: 54)
    Sagittarius: 81 units—50% above norm
    Pisces: 75 units—38.88% above norm
    Gemini: 68 units—25.92% above norm
5. 3,564 "Total" Classical Composers (Norm: 297)
    Pisces: 358 units—20.5% above norm
    Sagittarius: 354 units—19.19% above norm
    Gemini: 334 units—12.45% above norm
6. 216 Major Novelists (Norm: 18)
    Cancer: 25 units—38.88% above norm
    Virgo: 23 units—27.77% above norm
    Gemini: 22 units—22.22% above norm
7. 120 Famous Astronomers (Norm: 10)
    Cancer: 19 units—90% above norm
    Aries, Pisces: 13 units each—30% above norm
8. 228 Noted Physicists (Norm: 19)
    Virgo, Sagittarius: 24 units each—26.31% above norm

9. 240 Noted Chemists (Norm: 20)
   Sagittarius, Pisces: 24 units each—20% above norm
10. 204 Major League Baseball Players (Norm: 17)
   Taurus, Pisces: 23 units each—35.29% above norm
11. 96 Boxing Champions (Norm: 8) ("Indicative" only!)
   Cancer, Virgo: 11 units each—37.5% above norm
12. 156 Great Rulers (Norm: 13)
   Virgo, Scorpio: 21 units each—61.53% above norm
13. 144 Famous Inventors (Norm: 12)
   Aquarius: 23 units—91.66% above norm
   Leo: 18 units—50% above norm
14. 144 Outstanding Religious Leaders of America (Norm: 12)
   Aquarius: 19 units—58.33% above norm
   Virgo: 17 units—41.66% above norm
15. 156 Major Conductors (Norm: 13)
   Aries: 24 units—84.6% above norm
16. 732 Noteworthy Conductors (Norm: 61)
   Aries: 75 units—22.95% above norm
17. 480 Famous Violinists (Norm: 40)
   Aries: 62 units—55% above norm
   Aquarius: 52 units—30% above norm
   Scorpio: 48 units—20% above norm
18. 660 Famous Pianists (Norm: 55)
   Aquarius: 69 units—25.45% above norm
   Sagittarius, Pisces: 63 units each—14.54% above norm
19. 552 Famous Organists (Norm: 46)
   Sagittarius: 58 units—26% above norm
   Pisces, Virgo: 54 units each—17.39% above norm
20. 156 Famous Cellists (Norm: 13)
   Virgo: 17 units—30.76% above norm
   Aquarius: 16 units—23% above norm
21. 960 Classical Singers of Distinction (Norm: 80)
   Pisces: 108 units—35% above norm
   Capricorn: 91 units—13.75% above norm

Era of the Big Quake

A Prophecy Updated

I

If you live in California, as I did until recently, you will find most people uneasy about discussing earthquakes, although they are apt to have a private hunch that the "Big One" is overdue. And, indeed, an increasing number of scientists are not only calling a California superquake "inevitable," but they are even daring to risk predictions based on an accumulating bank of scientific evidence.

As a case in point, Drs. John Gribbin and Stephen Plagemann, in 1974, combined the arcana of astrophysics with the latest seismological findings to conclude that a "grand alignment" of planetary bodies, as they termed it,* which was scheduled to reach its culmination in late 1982, could conceivably be expected to act as a cosmic "trigger" to set off many quakes, large and small, around the globe. But tensions already building along the San Andreas Fault on the West Coast, they theorized, would make Southern California the

---

*Technically, the phenomenon is not an "alignment," but a rare conjunction of planetary bodies that occurs about every 179 years. The conjunction, in its final phase in November 1982, finds the planets coming together in a 64° segment of sky, possibly coincidental with maximum solar activity, according to Gribbin's and Plagemann's theory. Such a combination of energies, bombarding planet Earth in unison, as it were, might indeed have a delayed-action effect if not an immediate one. Its consequences could be cumulative and catastrophic. (March of '82, the timing of a less critical conjunction, was marked by a new eruption of Mount St. Helens, a 7.3 quake offshore Hokkaido, Japan, and a 4.5 quake in Borrego Springs, California. There was the worst flood of the century in Ft. Wayne, Indiana, and the Transglobe Expedition reported abnormal melting at the North Pole from a heat wave.)

most likely target for a major quake, with San Francisco next in line.

Their highly original hypothesis earned them the prestigious support of no less a scientific figure than Isaac Asimov,[1] although Gribbin—a Londoner, and under harsh attack from some of his colleagues in the scientific community—was later to repudiate any predictive statements he had made. Plagemann, a resident of California, has not followed suit to our knowledge.

Yet, interestingly enough, the Edgar Cayce readings confirm the role of cosmic influences in quake activity:

The causes of these [quakes], of course, are the movements about the earth; that is, internally—and the cosmic activity or influence of other planetary forces and stars and their relationships produce or bring about the activities of the elementals of the earth. . .   **270-35**

We come, next, to the case of the Palmdale Bulge.

In 1976, when a mysteriously rising hump of earth in Southern California began to generate a lot of scientific curiosity, the carefully chosen words of H. Roger Pulley, State Officer of Emergency Services, were unequivocal. "This section of land," said Pulley, specifically naming the Palmdale Uplift, "is in exactly the same place as the 1857 earthquake and is where another great earthquake is inevitable, possibly within the next decade."[2]

That decade, of course, is now upon us.

As for the 1857 quake in reference, it is believed to have been equivalent to a magnitude of 8.2 on the present Richter scale; and only the relative scarcity of population at that time prevented it from having disastrous consequences. Meanwhile, the Palmdale Bulge remains as baffling and controversial as ever. It sits directly astride the notorious San Andreas Fault, at a point some 80 miles east of Los Angeles, while the great fault-line itself extends in a jagged series of fractures across the whole state. It snakes upward from Baja California, in Mexico, inching all the way north to offshore western Canada, where it finally links up with a series of faults that loop across the whole Pacific Basin, from Alaska to Japan, and across the China Sea to Indonesia and the Indian Ocean. Referred to as the "ring of fire," this awesome girdle of periodically active fault zones and volcanoes is the apparent result of inexorable pressures from the action of huge, drifting plates of the earth's crust, which blindly bump and slide past each other over the aeons, as relentless in their cataclysmic movement as the ice floes in an Arctic sea. Mountains in their pathway slowly crumble. Whole continents are transformed or submerged. And sometimes the accumulating pressure will mount to a peak of such intolerable stress that there is a sudden, violent wrench that rips open the very bowels of the earth.

Such is the genesis of a superquake.

Or *is* it?

If our rather frightening scenario seems to suggest that we are but helpless pawns in the implacable grip of Nature, the Edgar Cayce readings offer a surprisingly different view of things. It is a view that takes us right back to the Book of Genesis.

Man was commanded in the beginning to exercise dominion over the earth; and by attuning himself to the Divine within, he has the potential to move mountains, quite literally, if he wills it, or to still the tempest with a word. Even the heavenly bodies will be responsive to his rule, and obey. For it is given to man to rule the stars, rather than to be controlled by them. However, first he must exercise *self*-mastery, through full compliance with spiritual law. Love is Law, said Cayce, and God is Love. (3574-2) When man is disobedient to his God, chaos results. And then man must indeed tremble in the grip of those very elements he was commanded to subdue. According to the readings, even solar flares and sunspots, as well as other cosmic influences adversely affecting life on earth, are simply a stellar "play-back" of the negative vibrations man is continually projecting outward into the universe.[3]

Earthquakes, it can be concluded, are among the resultant phenomena. And the geological factors that appear to cause these upheavals are merely the response of our planet to the spiritual disorder in man himself:

Tendencies in the hearts and souls of men are such that these upheavals may be brought about. For as often indicated through these channels: man is not ruled by the world, the earth, the environs about it, nor the planetary influences with their associations and activities. Rather it is true that man brings order out of chaos by his compliance with Divine Law. Or by his disregard of the laws of Divine influence, man brings chaos and destructive forces into his experience.   417-7

The readings repeatedly assert that man is ever reaping what he has sown, whether on an individual or a collective basis. On this premise many of the Cayce readings on impending earth changes appear to be purposefully vague as to a specific timetable, as if allowing for an "adjustment factor" based on mankind's future performance in the exercise of free will and choice; while certain other predictions, such as the shifting of the poles in A.D. 2000 to 2001, seem to be irrevocably "set" by a locking pattern of events already past, thus precluding any delay or change in the cosmic schedule. Nor can *any* of the predicted earth changes be *indefinitely* postponed, apparently, inasmuch as a reading given on December 31, 1943, unequivocally stated that these upheavals "*must* in the next generation come," as they did in Atlantis. (3209-2, author's italics) I think this does not reflect any contradiction of what has been said about the ameliorating influence of free will and choice, constructively applied. Rather, it suggests a world situation in which repeated choices of a destructive nature by the majority of mankind have already brought about conditions that were prophesied of old, so that only here and there can the prayers of the righteous be heard at this late stage, perhaps delaying or deflecting the destructive blow to a household or a city, or even a nation, but not preventing the body of mankind from meeting the destiny it has builded for itself through countless generations. For:

These changes in the earth will come to pass, for *the time and times and half times are at an end* and there begin those periods for the readjustments. For how hath He given? "The righteous shall inherit the earth." 294-185

Clearly, the Creator's hand is intervening as an "act of grace" in any cataclysmic changes, despite their essentially karmic nature. Such major planetary readjustments not only serve to chastise and heal His wayward sons in the earth, but they presumably play a cosmic role in the shifting alignment of planetary bodies within our solar system and the galaxy, as one Star Age succeeds another.

A similar situation undoubtedly prevailed in Noah's day, when no action on Noah's part could have reversed the inevitable, nor even have slowed down the timetable, in all probability, although Noah's righteousness did result in a warning to him from the Lord, which he wisely chose to heed.

He built the ark, and he and his family survived the Great Flood.

I think the Cayce prophecies on catastrophic earth changes may be viewed in somewhat the same light as Noah's warning from the Lord. An initial time frame from 1958 to 1998 was indicated in one of the readings on the subject (3976-15), and we are now moving into the final two decades of that period. A New Age is almost upon us, and we are told that a new root race is due to make its appearance out of the loins of the old. (5748-6) Meanwhile, rather sadly, the true peacemakers among us have been few, and their efforts to restore harmony to the planet have gone largely unheeded. Strife and warfare are the worldwide norm, rather than the exception. Among the rich nations materialism is rampant, with extreme hunger and suffering among the poor. Would it not be wise to conclude that the hour is now at hand for "those with ears to hear" to take heed, and start "building their arks," so to speak? (We may pray while we proceed with our planning; but plan we must, as well as pray!)

First, of course, we must study the earth changes prophecies at our disposal to see what hints they contain for our guidance. Since the "Big Quake" in California appears to be the pivotal earth change, marking the commencement of a worldwide cycle of adjustments, this essay will focus primarily on that catastrophic event, examining the most pertinent extracts from the Edgar Cayce readings on the subject, as well as related material from two other psychic sources that offer astonishing confirmation of the Cayce data. (There are still other prognostications than those chosen, although I found them less impressive; but the interested reader can examine them for himself by referring to the bibliography at the end of this essay.)

As early as 1934, one of the Edgar Cayce readings sounded the first clear alert of major earth changes in the offing, with a focus on the west coast of America:

The earth will be broken up in many places. The early portion will see a change in the physical aspect of the west coast of America.   **3976-15, Jan. 19, 1934**

A number of subsequent readings were more specific as to the details. I will quote from two key ones:

If there are the greater activities in the Vesuvius, or Pelée, then the southern coast of California—and the areas between Salt Lake and the southern portions of Nevada—may expect, within the three months following same, an inundation by the earthquakes.   270-35, Jan. 21, 1936

Q-3. Will Los Angeles be safe?
A-3. Los Angeles, San Francisco, most all of these will be among those that will be destroyed before New York even.
1152-11, Aug. 13, 1941

Japan, too, is mentioned in the readings as an early target for destruction, probably following closely on the heels of the California cataclysm. (This is deduced from the sequence of events envisioned by another psychic, whose prophetic account of the "Big Quake" will be examined next. There is nothing given in the Cayce readings from which the relative "timing" for the destruction of Japan can be determined, although the fate of that island nation is apparently similar to that of the southern coast of California. Specifically, the reading states: "The greater portion of Japan must go into the sea." [3976-15])

Meanwhile, in the three Cayce excerpts we have just cited in reference to California and the west coast, it is intriguing to note that a clear "warning" clause appears in each: "The early portion. . ." (3976-15); "If there are the greater activities in the Vesuvius, or Pelée. . .within the three months following. . ." (270-35); and ". . .before New York even." (1152-11) These warning signals can do little to ease the minds of west coast residents, except to provide them with a definite time frame of three months or less to evacuate, following any unusual volcanic eruptions at Mt. Vesuvius, in Italy, or Pelée (a reference, presumably, to the dormant volcano on Martinique, in the Windward Islands). However, for the rest of the nation— that portion, at least, which lies east of the Rockies—it pinpoints the west coast as the first real disaster area. Finally, it can be expected that the "Big Quake," when it hits, will galvanize all America into a state of preparedness. But more important, people everywhere will begin to wake up. There will be a growing realization that what is happening to our stricken planet is related, somehow, to man's gradual drift from the true center of his being. He has wandered far afield. Now he must turn back and find the God within. Then the God without will restore balance and harmony to the planet. For the inner and the outer, the above and the below, are One.

In 1937—only a year after Cayce's prediction of a catastrophic earthquake and inundation affecting Southern California and parts of Utah and Nevada, but some 30 years before his prophecies were to receive public attention through Jess Stearn's best seller *The Sleeping Prophet,* in 1967—a 17-year-old farm boy named Joe Brandt lay in a semicoma in a Fresno hospital. He had fallen from his horse, and the resultant brain concussion lasted several days, during which time Brandt experienced a series of startling psychic visions. He copied them down on note paper during intervals of consciousness, and the sheaf of his unpublished notes came to the attention of Jessica Madigan many years later. She incorporated them in Book Three of her epic work, *World Prophecy* (Mei Ling Publications, Los Angeles, 1967).

The extraordinary thing about young Joe Brandt's untutored revelations, written in simple but impressive prose, was that they so closely paralleled what Cayce had "seen" and reported in his psychic trance-state.

One interesting difference, however, was that the young man's sudden revelatory powers were of a temporary nature only, apparently triggered by his head injury. And the motivative force, it seems, was an inexplicable empathy he felt towards an unhappy young mother he saw in his vision, who was wandering aimlessly through the amorphous crowd on Hollywood Boulevard, just before the earthquake struck. Twin boys walked alongside her, each holding a hand; and it was as if Brandt sensed a "psychic alliance" of some sort with this trio. Were they a part of his future family? Perhaps. And did the vision serve to let him know of a personal tragedy slated to befall someone dear to him in a later period of his life, which could possibly be averted through his temporary gift of precognition? Brandt did not imply as much in his simple notes; but his obvious concern for the safety of the threatened trio surfaced two or three times throughout his hair-raising narrative of the great quake and its aftermath, making it evident that a deep psychic bond existed with a girl who, in all probability, was yet unborn. . .

In brief, then: Joe Brandt's 1937 vision began with "pictures that began to form" in his mind.[4] Then slowly the images took on color, smell, sound and movement. The scene was Los Angeles. "It was Los Angeles—but I swear that it was bigger, much bigger, and buses and odd-shaped cars crowded the city streets."

Just by thinking about Hollywood Boulevard, he was able to project himself there. And he wondered what year it was. "It certainly was not 1937," he writes, taking in the curious scene around him, including "a lot of guys about my age with beards and wearing, some of them, earrings. All the girls, some of them keen-o, wore real short skirts..." (The scene he describes is more reminiscent in some respects of the '60s or '70s than the present, surely. But perhaps mini-skirts will stage a comeback sometime in the '80s?)

The people have "a crazy kind of walk," he notes with fascination, and there is a "funny glow about them. It is like a shine around their heads—something shining." Something big, he senses, is about to happen. Looking at a clock on the boulevard, he sees that it is ten minutes to four. The sunny afternoon weather is "like early spring."

A further clue is a newspaper he sees on a street corner, carrying a picture of the president. And although Brandt can't make out the date because his eyes "weren't working just right," he observes that "It surely wasn't Mr. Roosevelt. He was bigger, heavier, big ears."

It is now five minutes to four. Brandt notes: "There was a funny smell. I don't know where it came from. I didn't like it. A smell like sulphur. . .For a minute, I thought I was back in chem." It is "a smell like death," he further records his impression, and it seems to be "coming like from the ocean." (But since Hollywood is inland, the sulphuric fumes were more probably rising from molten lava, seeping upward through sudden fissures in the trembling earth.)

Then the earthquake struck. What Brandt describes is bedlam.

"The concrete looked as if it were being pushed straight up by some giant shovel. It was breaking in two. . .*And then a loud sound again, like I've never heard before. . .Then hundreds of sounds. . .All kinds of sounds*. . .children, and women, and those crazy guys with earrings. . .I can't describe it. They were *lifted up,* and the waters kept oozing. . .oozing. The cries. God, it was awful."

The earth began to tilt. "It was tilting toward the ocean—like tilting a picnic table." Suddenly, Brandt finds himself transported to a higher level, as if moving into a fourth dimensional plane. "I kept wanting to get higher. I kept willing myself to go higher. Then I seemed to be out of it all, but I could see. I seemed to be up on Big Bear near San Bernardino, but the funny thing was that I could see everywhere. I knew what was happening."

In this altered state, he sees "everything between the San Bernardino mountains and Los Angeles" slide into the sea. Then his vision shifts to San Francisco, which seems to flip over like a pancake, through the interaction of the San Andreas Fault with an intersecting fault line that is probably the Hayward Fault, although Brandt inadvertently confuses it with the Garlock Fault, which is actually down near the Palmdale Bulge in Southern California. In his all-encompassing vista of the cataclysmic nightmare, he sees the Grand Canyon closing in, and Boulder Dam breaking up.

Another sequence: In Mexico, a volcano is erupting violently. Also in Colombia. In Venezuela. But in a striking parallel with Cayce's reference to the greater volcanic activity *preceding* the "Great Quake" within a three-month period, Brandt now comments, in respect to the volcanic eruptions, "I seem to be seeing a movie of *three months before*—BEFORE the Hollywood earthquake." (Author's italics)

Japan comes next in his scenario of destruction.

"I could see Japan, on a fault, too. It is so far off—not easy to see, because I was still on Big Bear Mountain, but she started to go into the sea. . .In a minute or two it seemed over. Everybody was gone. There was nobody left."

How shall we read the event? Simultaneous with California? Or a later catastrophe, perhaps? Hard to say. For, Brandt observes: "I didn't know time now. I couldn't see a clock." Apparently it was not vouchsafed to him to know the precise correlation of the Japanese tragedy and subsequent events. But among these latter was the breaking up of Sicily, as Mt. Etna erupted. "A lot of this area seemed to go," Brandt remarks, "but *it seemed to be earlier or later*. I wasn't sure of time, now."

One of the most touching aspects of Brandt's boyish narrative was his account of the reaction in the United Kingdom to news of the American disaster: "Some places they fell in the streets on their knees and started to pray for the world. I didn't know the English were emotional. Ireland, Scotland—all kinds of churches were crowded—it seemed night and day. People were carrying candles and everybody was crying for California, Nevada, parts of Colorado—maybe all of it, even Utah. Everybody was crying—most of them didn't even know anybody in California, Nevada, Utah, but they were crying as if they were blood kin. Like one family. Like it happened to them."

He did not see them weeping for Japan, for Sicily. Yet these are places and peoples beloved of many, in the United Kingdom and elsewhere. This omission may just possibly suggest that the destruction of these lovely isles, so far apart geographically, yet so similar in the intensity of their beauty, will fall into a somewhat later time frame than the "Big Quake."

III

More than 400 years ago the famous French seer, Nostradamus, predicted an awesome earthquake, which he indicated would rock the world in a future age. That age, we think, is now upon us.

What Nostradamus foresaw, most interpreters agree, was a California superquake followed by large-scale inundation. There are valid reasons for reaching this conclusion, as we shall see. However, there is little concurrence among the experts as to the "timing" of the catastrophe. This is because the 16th-century prophet chose to conceal his prediction in riddle-like verses, called quatrains; and the task of penetrating the underlying meaning of certain abstruse words or phrases in the most crucial of those quatrains, which contains precise clues to the exact date, has confounded even the most astute scholars and linguists. None of their conflicting interpretations appears to be wholly reliable, in fact, based on a close analysis. This has led me to experiment with a totally new approach in deciphering the disputed passages. You may be the judge as to whether or not I have successfully unraveled an enigma.

Meanwhile, there is one more difficulty posed by Nostradamus. In the numbering of his quatrains, which were issued in "books" of one hundred each, there is no sequential order discernible, so that a later quatrain may pertain to the prediction of an earlier or a simultaneous event, or vice versa. In the present case, we are dealing with several noncontiguous verses, which nevertheless appear to be related as to time and event. It is as if Nostradamus may have received his vision of the coming superquake and inundation in progressive stages, some periods apart, and set them down as they occurred, interspersed among other, unrelated prognostications. This is the common interpretation, to which we readily subscribe.

The first significant quatrain in reference to what appears to be a New World superquake (I.87)[5] tells of "volcanic fire from the center of the earth," which "shall cause an earthquake of the New City" (Los Angeles?). But the great magnitude of the quake, and its far-reaching consequences, is made apparent in the next line—"Two great rocks shall have long warred against each other"—which has an all-too-obvious parallel with the two great tectonic plates in subterranean conflict up and down the length of the San Andreas Fault. The quatrain concludes: "Then Arethusa shall redden a new river" (an allusion to the legend of the pursued nymph, Arethusa, who was transformed by the goddess Diana into an underground stream which was eventually to emerge in a distant land). This passage in the prophecy seems to hint at wandering subterranean currents of molten lava suddenly arising. . .

The next quatrain (IX.83) gives a month and day, but no hint as to the year when the awful cataclysm will occur nor the place. It refers to the Sun being in the "20th (degree) of Taurus," which astrologers readily interpret as a reference to May 10th, or possibly the 11th. However, a later allusion to the "ninth hour," or 3:00 p.m., in a subsequent quatrain clearly establishes the date as the 10th, inasmuch as the Sun will already have moved into 21° Taurus by mid-afternoon on the 11th of May.

The following quatrain (X.49) provides some alarming details on the devastating nature of the quake and gives several clues to its location. Nostradamus caught a glimpse of a future cataclysm in which the "Garden of the World" (believed to be a reference to the string of fertile valleys extending from southern to central California) "near the New City" (Los Angeles, presumably) "in the path of the hollow mountains" (a 16th-century view of skyscrapers?) is "plunged into a ferment" and "forced to drink sulphurous, poisoned waters."

Yet another of Nostradamus' quatrains (I.69) hits the mark with rather chilling corroboration of Cayce's prediction that major volcanic activity, involving either Vesuvius or Pelée, would be a signal of coming earthquake activity on the west coast of the United States in a mysterious geological pattern of interrelated global events. (Shades of Arethusa!) For, Nostradamus speaks of "The Great Round Mountain of seven stadia" (recognizable as a reference to Vesuvius, which is known as the "Round Mountain," measuring roughly seven stadia, or 4200 feet, in height); and the quatrain continues: "On the wake of peace, war, famine, and inundation,/It will roll a long way, sinking many countries,/Even ancient kingdoms and their great foundations." (This coincides with Cayce's broader scenario, in fact.)

War and peace seem to be ever with us, in an alternating pattern, while famine and inundation have been occurring in many places, but on a more aggravated scale of late than formerly! Is the time close at hand for major earth changes to commence, beginning in the western portion of America? Or do those dread events still lie dimly in the offing? Will the passage of Halley's Comet through our skies in early 1986 play the "trigger" role, as some suggest? In any case, it is hard to avoid the conclusion that Nostradamus, some four centuries ago, was crystal-balling a California "superscript" similar to the more recent prognostications of Edgar Cayce and Joe Brandt, including the linkage to major volcanic activity as a precursor. But the most vexing question still remains: When?

In his final vision of the event, Nostradamus actually provided us with an answer, although he chose to hide it, like some precious jewel, in a baffling maze of linguistic camouflage. (Perhaps he knew that the time was not yet at hand for an openly dated revelation of this magnitude?)

In the opening line of this final quatrain (X.67), Nostradamus speaks with uncommon plainness: "The earthquake shall be so great in the month of May," he begins. But then he reverts to the symbols of astrology: "Saturn, Caper (Capricorn), Jupiter, Mercury in Taurus;/Venus also Cancer, Mars in 'Non-nay'..." The answer we seek lies hidden in those two middle lines of the quatrain; the closing line, "Then shall hail fall bigger than an egg," should be taken quite literally, I believe, like the first, and involves no fanciful interpretations.

First, then: "Saturn, Caper (meaning *he-goat,* or Capricorn)..." Saturn passes through the sign of Capricorn only once in a cycle of about 30 years. It will be in that sign in the month of May, 1988. This provides us with the initial clue.

Next, "Jupiter, Mercury in Taurus..."

Sure enough, both Jupiter and Mercury will be found in Taurus as the month of May opens, in 1988. So far, this fulfills the stated terms of the quatrain perfectly. And although Mercury later moves into Gemini, this transit is inevitable, of course, since Mercury travels much too swiftly in its orbit around the Sun to remain in any one sector of the Zodiac throughout a full month, as Nostradamus obviously understood.

And now: "Venus also Cancer. . ."

Looking at a planetary ephemeris for May 1988, the explanation becomes crystal clear. Starting out the month in Gemini, Venus also takes up an unusual stationary position in zero degree of Cancer, where it remains for a space of ten days before reverting to its original cycle through the sign of Gemini. This odd maneuver offers a startling confirmation of the prophet's words.

Finally, we come to "Mars in Non-nay," which rhymes with "month of May" *(mois de Mai),* in the first line of the quatrain.

Yet there is no such word as "Non-nay" in the French language. Was it just a case of poetic license, perhaps, to achieve a rhyming effect? One well-known interpreter of this quatrain has apparently concluded that Nostradamus really meant *non,* which translates as "no" or "not"—*ergo,* "nothing"—and on this rather shaky premise has rendered the disputed phrase as "Mars in Zero." Such a conclusion is farfetched, however, particularly in the face of two alternatives that are substantially better. These are the French words *none* and *nonne.* (And although neither word carries an acute accent mark on the "e" to signify a second syllable in the pronunciation, as in Nostradamus's "Non-nay," we can nevertheless speculate that the seer was trying to give us a hint in the direction of one or the other of the two choices with an "e" ending, as opposed to the shorter *non!)*

Nonne is the French word for a nun. So one popular English version interprets this cryptic passage of the quatrain as "Mars in Virgo," since Virgo is the astrological sign of the virgin, as symbolized by a nun. It is a clever bit of reasoning. But such a choice outwits itself. One must now look for a "month of May" in which Saturn is in Capricorn; Jupiter and Mercury in Taurus; Venus partially in Cancer; and—Mars in Virgo! Such an incredibly complex combination of planetary positions will not occur until A.D. 3755. Are we to accept such an unlikely interpretation for the year of the "Great Quake," when so many factors seem to suggest a coming California superquake within our present generation? Moreover, it is commonly believed that the prophecies of Nostradamus extend no farther into the future than the year A.D. 2000.

Let's take a look, then, at our one remaining choice. Surprisingly enough, it is a choice that has been overlooked until now.

The French word *none* means the ninth hour, or 3:00 p.m., by traditional calculation. In astrological terms, this could also be interpreted to mean the descendant position in a horoscope, marked by the setting of the Sun. But in either case, Nostradamus appears to have been giving us an amazingly detailed prediction of the quake, enabling us to compute the very hour of its occurrence. Joe Brandt, you will remember, in his 1937 vision of the superquake, "saw" the hands of a Hollywood Boulevard clock at approximately 4:00 p.m. as the first ominous rumblings began on a spring afternoon (year undetermined). But on May 10, 1988, when Daylight Saving Time would already be in effect, 4:00 p.m. would technically be 3:00 p.m. Standard Time—coinciding precisely with Nostradamus's "ninth hour"! Yet, is "coincidence" the explanation? If so, strange indeed are the roots thereof.

In astrology, Mars is called the energizer. It triggers action. It is also the god of war, of course, governing turmoil and destruction. Nostradamus may have intended his reference to the red planet in this symbolic sense, thereby fixing the precise hour of the disaster at midafternoon on May 10, 1988.

But was Nostradamus right? Only time will tell. He once declared that he could pinpoint the date on any of his prophecies. Yet he blundered in predicting the date of his own death, although the details were accurately foretold. History, however, has already confirmed an impressive number of Nostradamus's prophecies, and certainly his fame as a seer is well established. It would be unwise not to heed his warning in this case.

Above all, let us heed the still, small voice within, knowing that "the day of the Lord is near at hand," and those who choose to walk in the light of His promises are already saved. For true salvation is not of the body, but of the soul.

BIBLIOGRAPHY

Cayce, Hugh Lynn, and a geologist. *Earth Changes Update*. Virginia Beach, Va.: A.R.E. Press, 1980.

Goodman, Jeffrey. *We Are the Earthquake Generation*. New York: Seaview Books, 1978.

Gribbin, John, and Plagemann, Stephen. *The Jupiter Effect*. New York: Walker & Co., 1974.

Iacopi, Robert. *Earthquake Country*. Menlo Park, Cal.: A Sunset Book (Lane Books), 1976.

James, Paul. *California Superquake 1975-77?* 2nd ed. Hicksville, N.Y.: Exposition Press, 1975.

Nostradamus. *The Complete Prophecies of Nostradamus.* Translated, edited and interpreted by Henry C. Roberts. Jericho, N.Y.: Nostradamus, Inc., 1978.

Nostradamus. *Nostradamus: His Prophecies for the Future.* Edited by Frank J. MacHovec. Mt. Vernon, N.Y.: Peter Pauper Press, 1972.

Nostradamus. *Prophecies on World Events by Nostradamus.* Translated and interpreted by Stewart Robb. New York: Liveright Publishing Corp., 1961.

"His Name Shall Be John"

An Objective Look at the John Peniel Controversy

Probably the most oft-disputed prophecy to be found in the entire body of psychic readings given by Edgar Cayce is the one concerning John Peniel. Yet it is also among the most hopeful and inspiring. Its message quickens the heart, for it holds a wondrous promise.

Then, why the controversy?

That astonishing prophecy, which will be examined here in all of its ramifications, has been the subject of unending inquiries and rumors, hosting a spate of ill-founded speculations. There have even appeared in print a couple of flawed quotations from the reading itself (which was admittedly somewhat nebulous and confusing), leading to misinterpretations that have further complicated the controversy. Finally, over the years, a quite astonishing parade of false claimants has turned up, announcing in impressively hushed and solemn tones that *they* are John Peniel (a man, it would seem, of many faces!). Some of these usurpers would deceive the very elect, for purposes of self-aggrandizement, while others—though sincere enough, perhaps—are simply suffering from self-delusion. In one unusual case, there was a medical doctor, and former A.R.E. member, who actually changed his professional name to John Peniel (his given name was not at all similar). Whether he was convinced that this was his true identity we cannot say, but quite obviously he chose to persuade others that it was. So you can see why we are particularly concerned at this time to clarify the record on the John Peniel prophecy.

Actually, the probable lineage of the *real* John "Peniel"

148

(whose surname, like that prophetic reference to "Immanuel," in Isaiah 7:14, may be more symbolic than literal) has already been intimated, if not precisely pinpointed, in other Cayce readings touching on the subject—readings that are generally unknown, or else ignored, by most of those embroiled in the John Peniel dispute. Thus, it is our intention in this article to present all of the available data relating to the matter and let the reader reach his own conclusions. From the perspective of this broader-based evidence, further speculation regarding this important prophecy can at least be minimized, while current misunderstandings should fall away in the light of the added information we are offering.

If the reading that tells of him can be literally interpreted,[1] John Peniel was to be the name of an incoming entity on the "Other Side" at that time (January 19, 1934), who would be a reincarnation of John the Beloved. His unusual mission in the earth was to be as a messenger who would proclaim the long-awaited Second Coming of the Lord. A date of 1998, according to another reading, was set for that epochal event. This was based on Cayce's interpretation of an esoteric chronology in stone, which is an interior aspect of the carefully laid-out architecture within the Great Pyramid at Gizeh:

> In this same pyramid did the Great Initiate, the Master, take those last of the Brotherhood degrees with John [the Baptist], the forerunner of Him, at that place. As is indicated in the period where the entrance is shown to be in that land that was set apart [Israel], as that promised to that peculiar peoples, as were rejected—as is shown in that portion when there is the turning back from the raising up of Xerxes as the deliverer [of the Israelites] from an unknown tongue or land, and again is there seen that this occurs in the entrance of the Messiah in this period—1998. 5748-5, 6/30/32

In excerpts from yet another reading about a year later, further information on the prophesied reappearance of the risen Savior seems to have been communicated through the sleeping Cayce by the Beloved Disciple himself, apparently, for the reading began: "I, John, would speak with thee concerning the Lord, the Master, as He walked among men." The following excerpts are from a question-and-answer sequence:

Q-4. Is Jesus the Christ on any particular sphere or is He manifesting on the earth plane in another body?
A-4. As just given, all power in heaven, in earth, is given to

Him who overcame. Hence He is of Himself in space, in the force that impels through faith, through belief, in the individual entity. As a Spirit Entity. Hence not in a body in the earth, but may come at will to him who *wills* to be one with, and acts in love to make same possible.

For, He shall come as ye have seen Him go, in the *body* He occupied in Galilee. The body that He formed, that was crucified on the Cross, that rose from the tomb, that walked by the sea, that appeared to Simon, that appeared to Philip, that appeared to "I, even John." [John 21:2; Rev. 22:8]

Q-7. When Jesus the Christ comes the second time, will He set up His kingdom on earth and will it be an everlasting kingdom?

A-7. Read His promises in that ye have written of His words, even as "I gave." [Rev. 1:1, 2] He shall rule for a thousand years. Then shall Satan be loosed again for a season. [Rev. 20:1-6]   5749-4, 8/6/33

It would seem evident from the above that John the Beloved, using as his spokesman the sleeping Cayce—termed the "forerunner,"[2] in the readings—was already functioning from the Other Side as one proclaiming the Second Coming! Yet it was not until the next year, actually, in early 1934, that the prophecy about John Peniel was given, announcing John's intended return and his destined role as a messenger.

Here is our initial excerpt from that reading:

First, then: There is soon to come into the world a body; one of our own number here that to many has been a representative of a sect, of a thought, of a philosophy, of a group, yet one beloved of all men in all places where the universality of God in the earth has been proclaimed, where the oneness of the Father as God is known and is consciously magnified in the activities of individuals that proclaim the acceptable day of the Lord. Hence that one John, the beloved in the earth—his name shall be John, and also at the place where he met face to face.
                                                    3976-15, 1/19/34

At this juncture, we are obliged to pause. We must make a few cogent observations. As Gladys Davis's notes point out, "the place where he met face to face" is an apparent allusion to Peniel (or Penuel), mentioned in Genesis 32:30. Originally, it was an obscure encampment—probably nameless—on the River Jabbok, in Eastern Palestine, where Jacob (an earlier incarnation of John, as the reading seems to be telling us) wrestled all night with an angel of the Lord in the form of a man. In the morning, the angel agreed to bless his worthy opponent, giving to the persevering Jacob a new name: Israel. It signified one who has prevailed "as a prince" and has "power with God and with men." (Gen. 32:28) Jacob, in turn, "called the name of the place Pĕn-i-ĕl: for I have seen God face to face, and my life is preserved." (Gen. 32:30)

Peniel. What significance are we to attach to that word in relation to John's proposed re-entry? The reading says that "his name shall be John, *and also at the place where he met face to face.*" (3976-15) (italics ours) Does this mean that John will appear in East Palestine? or are we being told that his surname shall be Peniel? Perhaps both—or neither. While that biblical place-name occurs once again in reading 3976-15, and this time more openly as John's apparent surname rather than as a possible "place" where he might be born or first proclaim his message, we have already suggested the likelihood that the reference to "Peniel" may be of a symbolic character only, signifying "one who has seen God face to face." That would epitomize John's spiritual nature, as well as his mission. There may also be an esoteric correspondence with the pineal gland, seat of the Christed Consciousness. In the same way, the prophet Isaiah referred to the coming Savior as "Immanuel" (Is. 7:14), although He was actually to be known in the flesh as Jesus of Nazareth by his contemporaries; yet Immanuel was a *spiritual* name for Him, meaning "God with us." Peniel, then, may be the same sort of designation for John, regardless of his earthly surname, thus differentiating the human from the Divine, the interior reality from the external image.

Meanwhile, a broader meaning can be ascribed to Jacob's spiritual name, Israel, according to one of the readings:

For those who seek are indeed Israel, and Israel indeed is ALL who seek; meaning not those as of the children of Abraham alone, but of every nation, every tribe, every tongue—Israel of the Lord! That is the full meaning of Israel.
2772-1

Finally, in recognizing John as an incarnation of Jacob, we gain a meaningful new insight into the relationship between Jesus and the Beloved Disciple. For the readings tell us that one of the earlier incarnations of Jesus was as Joseph, the favorite son of Jacob (Israel). What more appropriate choice, therefore, than John, to be that messenger of the Lord who will proclaim to all mankind His Second Coming?

And now, here are further excerpts from reading 3976-15, pertaining to John Peniel:

He comes as a messenger, not as a forerunner, but as a messenger; for these are periods when mental, material, are to be so altered in the affairs of men as to be even bringing turmoil to those that have not seen that the *Spirit* is moving in His ways to bring the knowledge of the Father in the hearts and lives of men.

When, where is to be this one? In the hearts and minds of those that have set themselves in that position that they become a channel through which spiritual, mental and material things become one in the purpose and desires of that physical body!

As to the material changes that are to be as an omen, as a sign that this is shortly to come to pass—as has been given of old, the sun will be darkened and the earth shall be broken up in divers places—and *then* shall He be *proclaimed*—through the spiritual interception in the hearts and minds and souls of those that have sought His way—that *His* star has appeared, and will point the way for those that enter into the holy of holies in themselves. For, God the Father, God the teacher, God the director, in the minds and hearts of men, must ever be *in* those that come to know Him as first and foremost in the seeking of those souls; for He is first the *God* to the individual and as He is exemplified, as He is manifested in the heart and in the acts of the body, of the individual, He becomes manifested before men. And those that seek in the latter portion of the year of our Lord (as ye have counted in and among men) '36, He will appear!   **3976-15**

Once more, we pause before continuing. Some comments are in order. This portion of the reading, although it picks up where our previous excerpt left off, has shifted direction somewhat. In that earlier portion, we were plainly told that "There is soon to come into the world a *body*," (italics ours) whose mission would be to "proclaim the acceptable day of the Lord. Hence that one John, the beloved in the earth—his name shall be John. . ." Now, however, although we are still being told that "He comes as a messenger," we are rather cryptically asked: "When, where is to be this one?"

And the equally cryptic answer is given, "In the hearts and minds of those that have set themselves in that position that they become a channel through which spiritual, mental and material things become one in the purpose and desires of that physical body!" The metaphysical nature of this response has led some to conclude that Cayce may have been implying that John's actual appearance in the world as a messenger would not be in the flesh, but in the spirit. But such a conclusion, though conveniently explaining to the doubters why John Peniel has not yet appeared, is basically a cop-out. It is not consistent with the previous assurance that "there is soon to come into the world a body," nor with a subsequent reference in this same reading (which we shall examine shortly) to the effect that others will one day come and say that "John Peniel is giving to the world the new *order* of things." (3976-15)

Moreover, there are a number of readings, dating from as early as 1929 through as late as 1939, making it abundantly clear that John sought to enter and was just awaiting a suitable flesh-body, or channel. We shall have a look at those readings, further along.

Meanwhile, there is no reason for us to be put off the track by "metaphysical asides" spoken by the sleeping Cayce. When he tells us that John's message is to appear in our "hearts and minds," this is surely a language we can comprehend. The Master, too, appeared in a true sense only to those who were spiritually ready to receive Him in their hearts, in their understanding; for although present in the flesh, it was in the Spirit that He made Himself known to them. It will surely be the same with John the Beloved, when he appears as the Lord's messenger, as Cayce was saying; for John is now perfecting that Christ Pattern in himself.

Before proceeding, we need to analyze briefly the last sentence in the final paragraph previously cited: "And those that seek in the latter portion of the year of our Lord (as ye have counted in and among men) '36, He will appear!" (3976-15)

As indicated by the capitalization of "He," as well as by the general context of the entire paragraph from which this sentence is excerpted, the statement is a reference to the appearance of the *Christ* in '36, rather than John Peniel, as was mistakenly assumed in a recently published book, *Is It True What They Say About Edgar Cayce?*,[3] which purported to take a hard, factual look at certain "failed" or questionable prophecies in the readings, but revealed a lack of adequate or up-to-date research.

Nowhere did Cayce pinpoint the year of John's return to the earth plane, nor can we say today that he is not already among us. Those who are impatient for him to make an appearance should reflect upon the fact that the messenger of an event (unlike its forerunner, who makes his appearance some time in advance) is expected to arrive simultaneously with the event itself, or momentarily ahead of it, heralding its imminent presence. In all probability, John will first appear alone, without any need for followers; although the multitudes will soon gather around him, no doubt, as well as a chosen band of attendants. But at present, if John is already in the earth plane, he may require a long period of solitude and spiritual preparation. Those who would clamor for him to make himself known at this time reveal their spiritual ignorance.

Meanwhile, as to the Lord appearing to "those that seek" in the latter portion of '36, that unusual prophecy was fulfilled, I think, in a way that has not been generally understood. It involved, in part, an extraordinary vision of the Lord received by Cayce himself.[4]

Continuing with the reading about John Peniel, we now find allusions to the approaching Armageddon, hinting at its close proximity to the Second Coming:

...the rottenness of those that have ministered in places will be brought to light, and turmoils and strifes shall enter. And, as there is the wavering of those that would enter as emissaries, as teachers, from the throne of life, the throne of light, the throne of immortality, and wage war in the air with those of darkness, then know ye the Armageddon is at hand. For with the great numbers of the gathering of the hosts of those that have hindered and would make for man and his weaknesses stumbling blocks, they shall wage war with the spirits of light that come into the earth for this awakening; that have been and are being called by those of the sons of men into the service of the living God.

Who shall proclaim the acceptable year of the Lord in him [?] [Cayce? John?] that has been born in the earth in America? Those from that land [a reference to Israel??] where there has been the regeneration, not only of the body but the mind and the spirit of men, *they* shall come [to America??] and declare that John Peniel is giving to the world the new *order* of things. Not that these that have been proclaimed [by Cayce, as the forerunner??] have been refused, but that they are made *plain* in the minds of men, that they may know the truth, the life, the light, will make them free.

"*I* have declared this," [John 17:26?] that has been delivered unto me to give unto you, ye that sit here and that hear and that see a light breaking in the east... "I, Halaliel, have spoken."
3976-15, 1/19/34

154

There is admittedly a lot to wonder about, in the nebulous phrasing of the preceding excerpts, particularly in the paragraph beginning, "Who shall proclaim the acceptable year of the Lord in him that has been born in the earth in America?" Is the "him" in reference here Edgar Cayce—or is it John? Although phrased in the past tense ("has been born"), which would put the odds on Cayce, it could conceivably mean John, since it pertains to a future time when he, John, would already have been born. (The bracketed inserts and question marks which have been added to this particular paragraph, by the way, are attributable to the author of this essay, and not to Gladys Davis. It was felt that they would assist the reader in following the line of reasoning I am now presenting.) "Those from that land" may conceivably refer to Israel, since it says of them that "*they* shall come [to America]"; and inasmuch as "they" (Jewish converts to John's message?) will "declare that John Peniel is giving to the world the new *order* of things," John might be in their midst, or proclaiming his message elsewhere—even in Israel. Even, just conceivably, at that place, Peniel, on the banks of the River Jabbok, in East Palestine! In such a case, is John to be born in that land? or merely to emigrate there for the fulfillment of his mission? (In A-3, reading 3976-15, there appears to be a reaffirmation of America as the birthplace, "for, as given, His messenger shall appear there [in America].")

Speculations, we see, become inevitable. Therefore, our aim is to focus them upon related evidence at our disposal, and not upon vain or improbable imaginings.

Finally, the reading states: "Not that these that have been proclaimed have been refused, but that they are made *plain*. . ." I think we can take this to mean that the prophecies already given by Cayce, as the acknowledged forerunner, are to be confirmed and made plain by John.

On May 1, 1934, a special reading was given on the Second Coming, following a dream, or vision, experienced by Cayce, while giving a reading earlier that same day for Mr. [378]. He was on a train, in his visionary dream, in the company of certain deceased evangelists, who were on their way to a place where John the Disciple was going to teach. Cayce, though wishing to join them, was advised to get off the train before it would be too late for him to return to his body in the earth. In his later reading on that day, Cayce sought information for a talk he was expecting to give the following Monday on the Second

Coming. It was in this reading that Cayce's role as a forerunner was plainly stated. The entire reading is worthy of careful study, although space only permits us to include a few extracts here. The reading counseled against using the information in an "open meeting," such as Cayce had originally planned; but a discourse on the subject, which was deemed "well for those present," apparently including many entities on the Other Side (as seen in his earlier vision) who had ministered and preached in the earth concerning the Second Coming, was then delivered by the sleeping Cayce:

Many of these [discarnate entities "crowding in at the present"] have ministered, have preached concerning this Second Coming. Not a one but what has at some time left the record of his contemplations and experiences in those environs, whether made in the heart and mind of his hearers or in the written word; yet here today, in what ye call time, ye find them gathering in a body to *listen* to that as may be given them by one who is to be a forerunner of that influence in the earth known as the Christ Consciousness, the coming of that force or power into the earth that has been spoken of through the ages.

Listen while he speaks!. . .

He, our Lord and our Master, was the first among those that put on immortality that there might be the opportunity for those forces that had erred in spiritual things. . .And in the coming into the influence of those that would open themselves for an understanding might there be the approach to Him. He has come in all ages through those that were the spokesmen to a people in this age, that age, called unto a purpose for the manifestation of that first idea. . .

Then, as there is prepared the way by those that have made and do make the channels for the entering in, there may come into the earth those influences that will save, regenerate, resuscitate, *hold*—if you please—the earth in its continued activity toward the proper understanding and proper relationships to that which is the making for the closer relationships to that which is in Him *alone*. Ye have seen it in Adam; ye have heard it in Enoch, ye have had it made known in Melchizedek; Joshua, Joseph, David, and those that made the preparation then for Him called Jesus. . .

Then again He may come in body to claim His own. Is He abroad today in the earth? Yea, in those that cry unto Him from every corner; for He, the Father, hath not suffered His soul to see corruption. . .And He comes again in the hearts and souls and minds of those that seek to know His ways.

These be hard to be understood by those in the flesh. . .Yet

here ye may hear the golden sceptre ring—ring—in the hearts
of those that seek His face. Ye, too, may minister in those days
when He will come in the flesh, in the earth, to call His own by
name.   5749-5, 5/1/34

"Those that seek His face"! Does this not hark back to the
true meaning of Israel? Also, it hints at the even higher
significance of Peniel—*pineal*—that place where one "meets
God face to face". . .
It is now time for us to examine some of those little-known
readings respecting various channels in the earth plane that
the entity John the Beloved might have chosen as being
spiritually suitable for his return. The first of these, however,
was clearly aborted. Mr. [137], who was told in one of his life
readings that he had been Jude, the youngest son of Mary and
Joseph, who had two sons and a daughter in a natural marital
relationship following the birth of Jesus through an
immaculate conception, asked the first questions about a
possible entry of John the Beloved in a reading in 1929.
Moreover, it was to the Master Himself that Mr. [137] addressed
his questions:

*Q-10. In John, Thou saidest, "After My death, the Comforter
will come." Who is the Comforter today?*
A-10. The Comforter is the gift of the Holy Spirit for it sheds
abroad in dark places, and him that keepeth My counsel is
brought to the full understanding, and is brought to
remembrance of that Walk with Him [Me?].
Q-11. Which of the disciples was the one You loved the best?
A-11. John. Upon this one Jude [earlier incarnation of (137)]
leaned in days when chains and bonds held thee. Freed with
him and then sent into the wilderness for thy tenderness. He
(John) will aid you.
Q-12. Is John now in the flesh?
A-12. John yet abides in Me.
Q-13. Will he again come into the flesh?
A-13. That remains yet to be seen.   137-125, 11/15/29

The next year, in March, Mr. [137] asked for a reading on
behalf of his wife, [140], who was then pregnant:

Q-6. Will it be a boy or girl?
A-6. As desired. John may come, or if you desire, Joseph.
Q-7. When will the event take place?
A-7. Early part December, or latter part of November.

Q-8. Doctor says end of October.

A-8. As we see, it will be end of November, or early December.

Q-9. Is it John's will to reincarnate in this environment?

A-9. Dependent upon those who may be physically responsible for the entering of John into the mundane sphere, for with the desire this becomes as a law.

Q-10. [140]'s dream.

A-10. Fear only. Hold that in mind, that need, that desire.

Q-11. Is this a divine conception?

A-11. A divine conception may be made. 137-129, 3/30/30

As that gently evasive answer to Q-11 indicates, it had *not* been a "divine conception"! In fact, the child was stillborn, and the marriage between [137] and [140] was doomed to end unhappily in a divorce. The great spiritual opportunity that had presented itself to this young Jewish couple was tragically lost, presumably through their own willfulness. Mr. [137], as a matter of fact, was soon to withdraw from his formerly active support of the work of Edgar Cayce. Yet, these cited excerpts from two of the readings for Mr. [137] begin to give us some idea as to the sort of channel John was—or *is*—seeking, essentially based on close spiritual and karmic ties, and linked to the life and work of the Master.

Next, we come to a pertinent extract from a reading for Miss [295], whose life reading had told her that she had been Mary Magdalene, the sister of Martha and Lazarus, and one closely associated with John the Beloved and his household in the years following the Resurrection:

Q-12. What part will I play in the coming of John, the beloved?

A-12. That depends upon the own self, the own impersonal self, as to whether the channel is made in self as the acceptable channel for His blessings to be on thee. 295-9, 4/13/34

However, Miss [295], who at first had been closely involved in the activities surrounding Edgar Cayce and his work at Virginia Beach, later opted to leave for Oklahoma, where she was married in 1938 and gave birth to two daughters. In 1940, she wrote: "So far as I am concerned, the prophecies [about me] seem to have never come to pass. . ." Her own part in their failure to materialize seems not to have been acknowledged.

Mrs. [540] had been Naomi, a daughter of Zebedee and sister of James and John, in the days of the Master. She was a housewife, and a Baptist, aged 32, when she had her fourth reading from Edgar Cayce in 1936—a reading that contained this thrilling and illuminating message:

As to the activities also as we have given and intimated through these channels, that John (the beloved; Naomi's brother) would again join in those activities in the earth, we find:
The entity, then, [540]—by body, by mind, by position, by soul's development—will be joined nigh unto those experiences with those bodies through which and to which the *entity* **John (the brother) may come and be known among men.**
540-4, 2/20/36

A son born to Mrs. [540] on March 2, 1937, had a life reading the day after his birth. While he had not been John, it was revealed that he had been "a follower of those Disciples," and "a nephew of Peter." (1346-1) In an interesting aside, the reading stated that "A guiding influence may ever be that Pope Leo XIII, as this entity's birth date [March 2, 1937] is a corroboration of that entity's birth [March 2, 1810] who rose to the place as the pontiff." It continued: "Hence we will find an influence in the experience that will ever be as a light to many; an influence towards that which is good." (1346-1)

There is no current contact with Mr. [1346], rather regrettably, but it would appear to us that if he fulfilled the high promise of spiritual development indicated in his reading, then John might well have chosen as an earthly vehicle one of this entity's progeny—if, indeed, Mr. [1346] ever married and became a parent in the intervening years.

However, other likely candidates loom, through the offspring of Mrs. [1158], who had been Ruth, the sister of Jesus. Her husband, Mr. [1151], had been the husband then also—one Philoas, a Roman, who had been with Cleopas and others on the road from Emmaus, when the Master appeared to them following His Resurrection. In this life, they had three children—two daughers and a son. The life readings for the two girls indicated close spiritual links with those around the Master, in Palestine, and thus they could be presumed to be acceptable channels today for John's entry, either directly or through their offspring. The son, too, who had been Gamaliel the Elder, defender of the Apostles, might have been such a channel, although he has chosen to remain a bachelor. But both of the daughters have had male children.

In one of the mother's readings, she was told: "John may enter, and will be known—and as one that may be proclaimed by the entity." (1158-9, 3/28/37)

This woman, at 94, is still very much alive today, and a beautiful soul. She may yet fulfill that promise made to her forty-five years ago. Additionally, it was indicated in the same reading that the children born to Ruth and Philoas in their Palestinian incarnation might enter again "as grandchildren." No readings, of course, could be obtained for any of the grandchildren, who arrived in the earth after Cayce had already departed. But today—provided, as we have said, that he is not already among us—one might reasonably look to the *great*-grandchildren of Mrs. [1158] for John's eventual entry.

Fifteen years remain before 1998 is upon us. Why, indeed, could not the coming messenger be a mere stripling or a child? We tend to forget that the voice of a child may be invested with spiritual authority beyond measure. One thinks of the child Jesus in the temple, discoursing with the Elders as He "went about His Father's business"; or the youthful Samuel; or the lad David, who slew Goliath. Joan of Arc was only thirteen when she first heard the voice of God, instructing her; and the children of Fatima, in the very power of their childish innocence and faith, drew throngs to witness a miracle in the skies over Portugal.

One final reading pertaining to John's promised re-entry in the earth merits our attention. Though the woman for whom the reading was given was already fifty-three, and single, so that the "promise" could not very likely have applied to her personally as a physical channel, she was one who had been in close contact with John as Cleopus, the lady to whom one of his last letters was addressed; and he seemed to be seeking a means of communicating with her again—a "plane of expression," as the reading said—which Cayce indirectly provided:

The entity was close to the younger of the disciples, John; and it was to the entity that one of his last letters was addressed—to the lady. For to that entity, John, who should come again soon into material experience, seeks a means, a plane of expression. 1703-3, 3/8/39

In this essay, I think we have quite clearly identified John Peniel as that messenger who will proclaim the Second Coming of the Lord, while Edgar Cayce's role seems firmly established as a forerunner of the event, who was sent to warn the people to make ready the way. This was confirmed very beautifully in an unusual dream Mr. Cayce experienced (indeed, were not *all* of his dreams "unusual"!) in December, 1942.

The dream, in brief, was this: The voice of God was heard "as from out of the cloud and the lightning," addressing an assembled throng of shrouded figures on the Other Side. Twice the voice asks, *"Who will warn My children?"* The Master offers to go, but is told that the time is not yet fulfilled for His return to the earth plane. Then the deceased evangelist, Dwight L. Moody, speaks up: "Why not send Cayce, he is there now." At this juncture, the Master speaks: "Father, Cayce will warn My brethren." The dream, or vision, concludes with the voices of the assembled throng in a grand chorus: "And we will all help!" (12/12/42 or early A.M. 12/13/42) (See 294-196.)

There is a passage in reading 281-38, which is one of twenty-four psychic discourses on The Revelation, which some have interpreted to mean that John's role as messenger may have been made manifest through Edgar Cayce, the forerunner, thus precluding any need for the Beloved Disciple to return in the flesh. The passage is very brief: ". . .you call him Cayce; John would be better!"[5] However, it appears in a context quite unrelated to the subject of the Second Coming, or John's prophesied return, so that I think we must discount the proposed interpretation as too far-fetched. It appears more closely connected to an earlier reading in The Revelation series, 281-31, wherein names and their significance are discussed. (One is reminded, by the way, that Cayce's name in his prior incarnation, as Bainbridge, was John. And this time, as a "forerunner," his role paralleled that of another John—the Baptist.)

Yet, if the Beloved Disciple is indeed to come again as a messenger, as the readings seem to say he will, Cayce himself is also to enter again, in 1998, coming as a New Age "liberator" of the human race. To gain the full significance of the prophecy, which follows, it must be remembered that the Great Pyramid of Gizeh, mentioned in an earlier reference prophesying the entrance of the Messiah in 1998 (5748-5), was actually constructed "under the authority of Ra," according to reading 294-151, "with Hermes [an incarnation of the Master][6] as the guide, or the actual. . .construction architect with the priest or Ra [an early Egyptian incarnation of Edgar Cayce] giving the directions," and that it was "to be the place of initiation of the initiates. . ."

Here, then, is our closing passage from the readings:

Is it not fitting, then, that these [a reference to Ra and his band of exiled followers] must return? as this priest may develop himself to be in that position, to be in that capacity of a *liberator* of the world in its relationships to individuals in those periods to come; for he must enter again at that period, or in 1998.   294-151, 7/29/32

We offer a new prediction: Thousands will be awaiting his return, and literally millions will be blessed.

The Fifth Option

The Theory of Cosmic Resonance Considered in Relation to Certain Disputed Prophecies in the Edgar Cayce Readings (1932-1936)

In his very interesting and timely book, *Visions and Prophecies for a New Age,*[1] Mark A. Thurston has introduced some disputed readings on earth changes that were scheduled to occur in 1936. There was also to have been a heralded appearance of the Lord in the latter portion of that year, which he includes in his handful of "discredited" predictions.

In the absence of any clear evidence that these several prophecies were fulfilled, Dr. Thurston has proposed four options as alternatives for understanding what he has termed "Cayce Prophecies Which Proved Wrong." It is a premise that some might question. However, the case presented by Thurston is a well-reasoned and convincing one. If his basic premise is to be accepted, then we are led to conclude (as he does also) that the fourth option on his list is the most probable explanation; namely, that "something happened" in the realm of human affairs—something of a mitigating nature—between the date of each of the disputed prophecies and the indicated target-date for its fulfillment, which served to modify or annul the prediction.

To those of us who are familiar with an unusual reading Edgar Cayce once gave on sunspots (5755-2), there would seem to be a sound basis for accepting this fourth option, at least tentatively. Sunspots and, by implication, the solar storms with which they are associated, varying in the degree of their cyclical intensity and negative impact upon our planet, were explained by Cayce as a kind of stellar "feedback" of strife and turmoil generated by man, which vibrate outward into the cosmos and return to us in altered form. Simply put, it may be seen as an application of the law of cause and effect at a universal level. The readings reiterate it in many ways. "Tendencies in the hearts and souls of men are such," Cayce said in one reading relating to prophesied earth changes, "that these upheavals may be brought about." (416-7; 10/7/35) Change the tendencies, he seems to be saying, and you will change the results. . .Elsewhere, we are told that *this* may be established as a *theory:* That thrown off will be returned." (195-29)

But if the fourth option on Dr. Thurston's thoughtfully compiled list surpasses in plausibility the other three (which the interested reader may explore for himself), unfortunately it doesn't "prove out" in a couple of important respects.

First, while several of the seemingly "failed" prophecies for 1936 related to events of a destructive nature, one of them, as we have already noted, was of a quite opposite sort and could not be "explained away" on an identical basis: "And [to] those that seek in the latter portion of the year of our Lord (as ye have counted in and among men) '36, He will appear!" (3976-15; 1/19/34)

On the other hand, with respect to the earth changes predicted for 1936, we can find absolutely nothing in the record of national or international events during that ominous year to suggest an ameliorating or spiritual force at work in human affairs, which might have reversed or modified the fateful prophecies. Quite to the contrary, it was a year marked by mounting turmoil, blurred ideals and ruthless ambitions. (We refer the reader to Appendix A for a thumbnail summary of some of the most critical events in world affairs during 1936.) Shameful indifference and vacillation in England and America permitted and even encouraged a militarized Japan, Germany, Italy, and Russia in their brazenly escalating plans for regional conquest and eventual world domination.

Within such a broad and grim scenario of events, could the "prayers of the faithful" somehow have sufficed to offset or delay the sweeping earth changes prophesied for '36? It seems unlikely. For it was a year of fateful transition from an unstable peace towards total war. We find, in fact, that Edgar Cayce accurately foresaw the approach of World War II, back in 1935, in a reading that combined, quite appropriately, earth-change predictions with his prophetic vision of a worldwide conflict soon to come, in which "the whole *world*—as it were—will be set on fire by the militaristic groups and those that are 'for' power and expansion in such associations." (He specifically pinpointed Nazi Germany, Italy and Japan.) As for a last-minute reprieve from the predicted holocaust, the reading made it sadly plain that the die was apparently already cast, and nothing could be done "unless there is interference from what may be called by many the *supernatural* forces and influences..." (416-7; 10/7/35)

In those shadow-ridden days, there was an obvious need for the Christ to appear in the hearts and minds of those seeking peace and brotherhood, if only to offer them reassurance and hope as to the ultimate outcome. Did Cayce make his prediction of just such an appearance in vain? Or is there another explanation of the matter? I think there is. Let me propose a fifth option, as follows: *That most, if not all, of the disputed prophecies were indeed fulfilled, even as predicted, but in a manner not yet understood.* (I am not speaking symbolically here, but am referring to actual events, as I shall later explain.)

We have now arrived at a point where it becomes necessary to introduce the relatively new theory of cosmic resonance, on which my proposition is largely based. The subject is a truly fascinating one. But before I begin, let me make some preliminary observations.

In esoteric astrology, as well as in the Edgar Cayce readings touching on the subject, it is an accepted rule that certain planetary configurations or aspects, sometimes involving the "fixed stars" as well as the various constellations, may wield a profound influence on our lives and on planet Earth itself, for weal or woe. For, as given in the readings, there are "the various influences shed from other solar systems, suns, and so forth." (541-1) And of earth changes, it is plainly stated that these result not only from "the movements about the earth; that is, internally," but are attributable to "the cosmic activity or influence of other planetary forces and stars and their relationships," which "produce or bring about the activities of the elementals of the earth..." (270-35)

In 1650, to consider one of the more favorable examples of planetary influence, a rare conjunction of two of the slower-moving planets—Uranus and Neptune, then in the sign of Sagittarius—which lasted through 1653, marked the entry of many highly developed souls into the earth plane to further man's evolution. This occurred again in 1821-24, under Capricorn, and will once more occur in 1992-95, as mankind is crossing the cusp of the Aquarian Age.[2]

In a less favorable pattern of cosmic events, we have been undergoing for the past few years a rare series of planetary bunchings, called conjunctions, among the celestial bodies in our solar system, which occurs only every 179 years or so because of the length of the outer planets' periods of orbit. The final phase, in November, 1982, brought the planets even closer together in their periodic clustering effect, which occurred in a 64° segment of sky.[3] The cumulative impact of their force fields on the crust and interior of the Earth has been an ongoing subject of speculation and debate in certain scientific and astrological circles devoted to such matters. And while the immediately discernible effects upon planet Earth are still subject to dispute and speculation (Appendix C), we must ask ourselves if such a "grand conjunction" of planetary forces beaming down upon us, as it were, in unison, could indeed have triggered unseen changes in the Earth's interior, capable of resulting in delayed-action catastrophes, akin to "time-bombs"!

Our preliminary evidence, based upon a 90° cluster effect that occurred on March 10, 1982, points in this direction (refer to Appendix C). Yet, the shifting planetary relationships within each cluster formation, the zodiacal signs in which they occur, and the vibratory relationships they may form with certain of the so-called "fixed stars" in their celestial passage overhead, complicate any kind of astrological prediction as to the outcome. But we may assume that certain astral configurations of a minatory nature will produce more profound changes upon our planet than others, and probably with a slower response time; while those producing a relatively quick and violent reaction—such as the series of catastrophes that followed on the heels of the conjunction of the planets in early March of this year—may actually be comparatively superficial, viewed from a cosmic perspective.

At a more personal level of planetary influence, one's natal chart or horoscope in astrology reveals a highly individual "imprint" of cosmic patterns, based on the exact moment and place of birth, which no other entity can quite duplicate. An astrologer is able to trace the positioning of the planets in such a manner as to determine the various "aspects," as they are called. These will be "favorable" or "unfavorable," depending upon the type of aspect (opposition, square, trine, conjunction, and so forth), and other, related factors in the chart, as modified by the free will of the entity. So we can see how man the microcosm has his correspondence with the larger macrocosm. In a very real sense, they are one, and man has been properly called a "universe in miniature."

I bring up these several esoteric matters because they all serve to demonstrate, at varying levels of application, the "cosmic resonance" principle in astrology. This will now be explained.

The operative link in this principle may well be what the Cayce readings refer to as etheronic energies. In reading 553-1, there is a revealing reference to "a bombardment, as it were, of the planetary influence upon any other realm by its proximity of the relative position—or by the influence in the realm of etheronic energies that affect the activity. . ." (These energies are termed "etheronic wave forces" in 440-13.)

But let us proceed to the present-day findings of two astrophysicists, from whose separate but not unrelated efforts we arrive at a unique interpretation of the theory of cosmic resonance.

*   *   *   *   *

The ancient Hermetic doctrine, "As above, so below," is echoed in a present-day hypothesis by the German physicist, Theodor Landscheidt.[4] Landscheidt's hypothesis entails, in his own words, "the pure numbers of physics representing a cosmic principle of order." He has proposed that the macroscopic ordering of the planets can be related to the microscopic ordering within the atom, using the fundamental constants, or fixed values, of modern physics. (This correspondence between the microcosm and the macrocosm has always been a fundamental aspect of all esoteric teachings and enlightened religious thought, so it is good to see science catching up at last!)

However, Landscheidt's hypothesis is complemented by another, and even more important, scientific proposition. This one is put forward by a Soviet astronomer, A.M. Molchanov.[5] And if there are Hermetic overtones to the first hypothesis, this second one has a decidedly Pythagorean quality to it. Molchanov claims to have discovered a resonant structure in the solar system and, by inference, throughout the whole universe, reminding us of Pythagoras's "music of the spheres."

Starting with the frequency of Jupiter as a reference point, because it is the largest planet in our solar system, Molchanov proceeded by means of the quantum system to formulate equations yielding values for each of the planets and its individual satellites, where applicable, that turned out to be amazingly close to the observed frequencies of modern-day radio-astronomy. The odds against chance of his overall findings are stated at 1,000,000,000 to 1.

What it all means to the layman is that the individual celestial bodies apparently resonate with one another, very much as if they were strings on a piano, at octave-spaced intervals, vibrating in response to a tuning fork. But the really important point about resonance, as any piano-tuner would be quick to comprehend, is that *energy is transferred in the process*. It has even been demonstrated that certain planets may have a "locking" resonance between them, as is believed to exist between Earth and Venus. Thus, they can *exchange* energies. Molchanov contends, in fact, that this is not a limited phenomenon. Conceivably, *all* celestial bodies are connected by an invisible web of interlocking resonances throughout the universe. Such is our speculation.

Do you begin to grasp the enormous implications of all of this, if true? We are suddenly presented with a view of the universe as a "heavenly body" of interrelated and interdependent cells, whose individual discords or harmonics are shared by the Whole. It is a concept that coincides perfectly with the spiritual philosophy found in the Edgar Cayce readings. It is also vital to an understanding of astrological principles, which confirm Landscheidt's "cosmic principle of order."

* * * * *

Golden Arcturus, the brightest star in the northern hemisphere, is one of the "fixed stars" most frequently mentioned in the readings. Another is Polaris, also known as the North Star. These two stars lie in neighboring constellations, Boötes and Ursa Minor, respectively.

But are these stars really "fixed" in their positions? The answer, of course, is no. Only relatively so. In 1718, Edmund Halley observed that Arcturus was no longer where

Hipparchus had placed it on his charts two thousand years before; nor is it now exactly where Halley saw it. Polaris is now approximately within a degree of being directly over the earth's north pole, whereas its future passage will bring it within a half of one degree by A.D. 2095, before it starts receding. . .

In relation to Earth's movement, of course, the "fixed stars" and all the constellations appear to be constantly rotating; and in their passage overhead, they form changing aspects with Earth and the other planets in our solar system, including the Sun and the Moon. These varying alignments, in the terms of astrology, determine the nature of their influence, which is presumably linked in some mysterious way to the resonance factor—and, of course, to that all-pervasive etheronic energy field, which Hindu savants refer to as *akasha*.

As previously demonstrated, astrologers know of the rare conjunctions of celestial bodies such as Uranus and Neptune, within our own little solar system, which can cover a span of several years' influence; but exceptionally little is known about similar astral aspects in relation to the fixed stars, whose influence may also be expected to rise and recede on a cyclical basis, as changing patterns of relationship are formed.

The prominent role of both Polaris and Arcturus in the soul's evolution through time and space is made evident in the following excerpt from one of the readings:

As long as the entity is within the confines of that termed the earth's and the sons of the earth's solar system, the developments are within the sojourns of the entity from sphere to sphere; and when completed it begins—throughout the music of the spheres—with Arcturus, Polaris, and through those sojourns to the outer sphere.   **441-1**

Reading 900-10 tells us that "the man called Jesus," who is the Pattern for us all, went on to Arcturus "as of the developing"; while yet another reading, speaking of its "bright and *glorious* light," refers to Arcturus as none other than the star of the Christ-child—"the star that led the entity," [827], as one journeying from Egypt or Persia, apparently, unto Bethlehem—*"Arcturus,* the wonderful, the beautiful!" (827-1) Elsewhere, it is identified as "that which may be termed the center of this universe. . ." (5749-14)

Of Polaris, the readings say little of a specific nature. We may suspect, however, that the contrast between these two fixed stars (which are curiously linked in reading 441-1, previously cited) is possibly somewhat akin to the difference we see between Jupiter and Saturn, which are linked "opposites" within our immediate solar system. The one—Arcturus—is a benevolent force, like Jupiter; while the other—Polaris, on whose penetrating ray Earth's axis takes aim, as it were, for its equilibrium—may fill the sterner role of cosmic "taskmaster," as does Saturn. (In fact, a fellow-researcher, John Shuster, whose knowledge of astrology exceeds my own, has confirmed my intuitively assigned values for Arcturus and Polaris. He cites an obscure astrological textbook, entitled *Fixed Stars and Their Interpretation,* by Ebertin-Hoffman, in which it says of Arcturus that it "has a Jupiter-Mars nature," while Polaris, the Pole Star, "has a Saturn nature"!) Both of these celestial bodies are involved in our soul development, apparently, whatever their specific cosmic role.

But, come. It is time for us to return to Earth.

We are now ready, I think, to look anew at those disputed prophecies for 1936, viewing them in the light of our broadened consciousness of the subject. They are given in the chronological sequence in which they appear on page 21 of *Visions and Prophecies for a New Age:*

. . .the catastrophes of outside forces to the earth in '36, which will come from the shifting of the equilibrium of the earth itself in space. . .   3976-10, 2/8/32

Q-10. What will be the type and extent of the upheavals in '36?

A-10. The wars, the upheavals in the interior of the earth, and the shifting of same by the differentiation in the axis as respecting the positions from the Polaris center [the North Star].   5748-6, 7/1/32

Q-14. Will the earth upheavals during 1936 affect San Francisco as it did in 1906?

A-14. This'll be a baby beside what it'll be in '36!
                    270-30, 2/13/33

And those that seek in the latter portion of the year of our Lord (as ye have counted in and among men) '36, He will appear!. . .

Q-1. What are the world changes to come this year physically?

A-1. The earth will be broken up in many places. The early

portion will see a change in the physical aspect of the west coast of America. . .There will be new lands seen off the Caribbean Sea, and *dry* land will appear. 3976-15, 1/19/34

The first two predictions confirm each other, although the second is of a more detailed nature. The linking of "wars" with "upheavals in the interior of the earth" is significant, and consonant with the Cayce philosophy. (It reminds us of that reading on sunspots!) But there is an ominous new dimension: "the shifting of the equilibrium of the earth itself in space," as it is first expressed in 3976-10, or "the shifting [of the earth] by the differentiation in the axis as respecting the position from the Polaris center," as more fully explained some five months later, in 5748-6.

The present tilt of the Earth's wobbling axis is calculated to be 23.5 degrees, or slightly less. Life on Earth has been compared to a tightrope phenomenon, requiring the most delicate balance to sustain our planetary wellbeing; and it is the prevalent scientific view that any sudden shifting of the Earth's axis would have immediate and disastrous consequences. This remains to be demonstrated, however, despite the classical Newtonian "proofs" that underlie contemporary assumptions in such matters.

Meanwhile, based on our own theory of cosmic resonance, we can see that "the catastrophes of outside forces to the earth in '36," to which Cayce referred in 3976-10, may already have occurred as prophesied, in the form of a possible "energy transfer" from one or more stellar bodies of major magnitude in an unfavorable configuration. It is certainly conceivable that strong vibratory impulses of a negative nature, emanating from the Polaris center alone, or in some ill-starred aspect with other stellar forces at work, could have produced a faint, unrecorded shifting or imbalance in the Earth's axis in '36. While this might result in no immediate surface changes, it could certainly bring about upheavals in the interior of the Earth, with its molten, magnetic core. And these internal disruptions would work, in time, with other factors (such as the slow shifting of the tectonic plates, for example) to produce surface changes on the planet of a truly cataclysmic nature, at some future and unspecified date.

But other than that reference in reading 5748-6 to "the upheavals in the interior of the earth, and the shifting of same by the differentiation in the axis as respecting the positions from the Polaris center," do we find any further hint of trouble afoot in the changing alignment of Polaris with planet Earth, during 1936? We do. Elsewhere in the same reading, in fact, a date of October, 1932, is given as the commencement-point for a gradual variation in the overhead passage of Polaris, which any astrologer would recognize as an approaching change in its pattern of influence:

In October [1932], there will be seen the first variation in the position of the polar star [Polaris] in relation to the [imaginary] lines [drawn] from [the opening of] the Great Pyramid. The Dipper is gradually changing. . .   5748-6

The above reference to "the first variation" in the position of Polaris, as well as the subsequent statement that Ursa Minor, or the Little Dipper, as it is commonly called, "is gradually changing," must bear our special attention.

Any change in the observed position of one of the so-called "fixed stars," or the whole asterism of which it forms a part, must necessarily be of a gradual nature, of course, within the relativity of time and space. Thus, a span of several years would seem to be inevitable before the initial variation in the position of Polaris could reach its secondary phase, where, in the words of the reading, it "becomes noticeable." Was 1936 such a culmination point? It is a logical deduction, in light of the previously cited excerpt (Q&A-10, 5748-6) from the same reading, which ties "the upheavals in '36" to "the differentiation in the earth's axis as respecting the positions from the Polaris center"!

Further, the reading says of the variation in Polaris's position and the Dipper's gradually changing configuration with respect to our solar system that—

. . .when this change becomes noticeable—as might be calculated from the Pyramid—there will be the beginning of the change in the races. There will come a greater influx of souls from the Atlantean, Lemurian, La, Ur or Da civilizations. These conditions are indicated in this turn [or depression in the passageway] in the journey through the Pyramid.   5748-6

So we can see that Polaris, and perhaps the entire asterism with which it appears to be associated, has a profound influence upon our planet and the destiny of its human inhabitants! Yet these cosmic influences seem to be subject to constantly changing aspects, or patterns of relationship, which modify their effects, heightening or lessening them. (Astrology has its roots in this concept, of course.)

But if the transit of Polaris in relation to planet Earth played a largely inimical role during 1936, what of Arcturus's passage during that same critical year? Could it be that our solar system, in its elliptical revolution around that Central Sun, was just then entering upon a spiritual season of change—the dayspring of a New Age consciousness? At any rate, we have already noted that esoteric astrology assigns an antipodal nature to those two fixed stars, Arcturus and Polaris, similar to the oppositional yet complementary influence of Jupiter and Saturn upon human affairs; so that the favorable focus of Arcturus (which is an aspect of our theory) could be producing beneficial results for those in attunement with its rays, even while stern Polaris—that stellar counterpart of Saturn, the "taskmaster"—might be wreaking unguessed-at havoc and change within the same time-frame...a necessary "purge," as it were, preparatory to a New Age!

Now we come to the third disputed prophecy on our list.

The question is asked, "Will the earth upheavals during 1936 affect San Francisco as it did in 1906?" The answer given: "This'll be a baby beside what it'll be in '36!" (270-30) But in the light of our interpretation of the preceding two prophecies, I think there is no reason to regard this as a "failed" prediction. If studied carefully, it will be seen that Cayce is merely drawing a comparison between the predicted upheavals in the interior of the earth in '36, which were to affect the whole globe eventually (including San Francisco!), and the comparatively minor San Francisco quake of '06. But he did indeed foresee the eventual destruction of San Francisco, according to a later reading in 1941:

Q-3. Will Los Angeles be safe?
A-3. Los Angeles, San Francisco, most all of these will be among those that will be destroyed... 1152-11, 8/13/41

Finally, we arrive at the last "discredited" prediction. Actually, it is a two-part prophecy. For the moment, let's skip the first part, which has no relevance to earth changes. (In fact, it is an excerpt taken out of context, since it actually appears in a quite different section of the reading.)

Reading 3976-15, given in 1934, was an awe-inspiring one. It contained advice on spiritual changes to come, as well as physical. Regarding the physical changes, here is what the sleeping Cayce said:

As to the changes physical again: The earth will be broken up in the western portion of America. The greater portion of Japan must go into the sea. The upper portion of Europe will be changed as in the twinkling of an eye. Land will appear off the east coast of America. There will be the upheavals in the Arctic and in the Antarctic that will make for the eruption of volcanoes in the torrid areas, and there will be the shifting then of the poles—so that where there has been those of a frigid or the semi-tropical will become the more tropical, and moss and fern will grow. And these will begin in those periods in '58 to '98, when these will be proclaimed as the periods when His light will be seen again in the clouds. As to times, as to seasons, as to places, *alone* is it given to those who have named the Name—and who bear the mark of those of His calling and His election in their bodies. To them it shall be given. 3976-15, 1/19/34

Now, it strikes me that anyone present who had heard what had just been said was more than a little irreverent to ask that first question (pertaining to 1934, actually, rather than 1936!): "What are the world changes to come this year physically?" If the answer was misleading or inaccurate, one could argue that the questioner[6] got his "come-uppance"! But I incline to the more likely view that Cayce simply chose to ignore the reference to a specific time-frame—"this year"—as obviously impertinent in the light of the reading; and instead, he simply proceeded with typical patience to offer a brief recapitulation of the previously outlined scenario of change for '58 to '98. I may be wrong.

There is no doubt, of course, that some inaccurate information did emerge, from time to time, in the readings. And one of the Work Readings, 254-67, offers a detailed explanation of psychic errors or lapses, which I will not trouble to recap here. Suffice it to say that all of the evidence, which continues to mount as the validation process grows, points to a phenomenally high "batting average" for the Virginia Beach psychic. I think this will turn out to be the case for his predictions on earth changes, as well, despite some occasional "misses" here and there.

We come, now, to that first part of our final, two-part prophecy: "And [to] those that seek in the latter portion of the year of our Lord (as ye have counted in and among men) '36, He

174

will appear!. . ." (3976-15, 1/19/34)

I love this prophecy for a special reason. But I will come to that.

First, returning to our theory of cosmic resonance, let's consider what was said earlier about the role of Arcturus—particularly in the developing of our Elder Brother, Jesus who became the Christ. Contrasting with the dark shadows cast over that fateful year, 1936, was a ray of hope in Cayce's prediction of the Lord's appearance. But why was the promise directed specifically to those who would be seeking Him in the *latter* portion (or what could be construed to mean the second, or latter, half) of the year? Did astrological considerations play a part, as seems likely? We conceive of the possibility that some special cosmic event was in the making, which might have involved the aspectology of Arcturus in its relationship to planet Earth. Perhaps some uniquely favorable cosmic "window" was about to open, in connection with Arcturus's transit through that period, as suggested earlier, which would permit an unusual transfer of energy, with its illuminating results? *His* star, as it were, beaming down on us?. . .We can only speculate.

Yet, in our speculation, let us digress briefly to consider this stunning passage about Arcturus, drawn from an 1893 text, *The Witness of the Stars,* by the renowned biblical scholar and mystic, E.W. Bullinger: *"Arcturus means He cometh."* (We find this same star *twice* mentioned in Job[7]; and, rather significantly, reading 262-55 identifies Melchizedek—an incarnation of the Christ—as the author of the Book of Job.) The ancient Egyptians, says Bullinger, called Arcturus *Smat,* meaning "one who rules," as well as *Bau,* which means "the coming one."

Remembering what the readings had to say of this Central Sun of our Universe, whence "the man called Jesus" went "as of the developing" (900-10), an astonishing new perspective on the Second Coming emerges. Did the ancient Egyptians, perhaps through the wisdom imparted to them by Hermes (an early incarnation of the Master, in the Ra Ta period), have pre-knowledge of the role of Arcturus in connection with the risen Christ-to-be, and of His Second Coming to our earthly sphere of consciousness, some 12,500 years ahead on the curve of Time?. . . Indeed, did there exist from the Beginning a correspondence between that Central Sun, Arcturus—"the Coming One"—and the prefigured Christ, who was first to come as a crucified Savior some 2,000 years before His prophesied Second Coming in our time as "One who rules" for a thousand years?

These are thoughts for us to ponder in our hearts today.

But back to that final disputed prophecy. . .

Was it ever fulfilled? It certainly was, at least insofar as Edgar Cayce himself was concerned. Yet the date was marginally off.

On or about June 30, as 1936 was crossing the midyear cusp into its latter half, Cayce had an astonishing vision of the Lord while in the conscious state. He described his experience in a subsequent letter to Mr. [1196], dated 7/22/36, and an interpretation was sought in reading 294-185:

Q-3. Interpret the conscious experience which Edgar Cayce recently had of seeing a chariot and man in armor.

[Detailed dream (*sic!* conscious-state vision) described 7/22/36 in Edgar Cayce's letter to Mr. [1196]: "I was in the garden here at work when I heard a noise like the noise of a swarm of bees. When I looked to see where they were, I saw that the noise came from a chariot in the air with four white horses and a driver. I did not see the face of the driver. The experience lasted only a few minutes. I was trying to persuade myself that it was not true, that it was only imagination, when I heard a voice saying, 'Look behind you.' I looked and beheld a man in armor, with a shield, a helmet, knee guards, a cape but no weapon of any kind. His countenance was like the light; his armor was as silver or aluminum. He raised his hand in salute and said, 'The chariot of the Lord and the horsemen thereof.' Then he disappeared. I was really weak, not from fright but from awe and wonder. It was a most beautiful experience and I hope I may be worthy of many more."]

A-3. This was a vision. This is the interpretation:

These are as emblems, these are as figures in the experience of the entity, that: As is builded in the conscious mind of those about the entity, as in the conscious entity itself, if there are not those encouragements from thy friend, if there is not a kind word or a smile, thou dost indeed feel that something is amiss, something is awry!

How well, then, those that have named the Name, those that would know the Lord—*smile!* For what else in God's creation can?

In the experience there is shown that there is not only the whole armor of the Lord as a defense, but the chariot of the Lord that would take wings upon time to show—to make thee know—that His promises abide.

Be faithful through those periods of oppression, as well as those periods that would soon come when the *material* things of life would be as plenteous in thine experience. But keep the whole armor of the Lord that ye may stand even as He in that day when temptations of every nature, when trials of every sort, come upon thee and thy fellow man.

For the Lord forgetteth not those to whom He hath given charge, "Feed my sheep, feed my lambs."   294-185

On December 20, 1936, in a special reading that is now 262-103, in the *Search for God* series, the members of the assembled group, including, in addition to Edgar Cayce, his wife Gertrude, Gladys Davis, Hannah Miller, Florence and Edith Edmonds, Frances Y. Morrow, Hugh Lynn Cayce, Helen Storey and Helen Ellington, received an inspiring message. The words, embodying the Christ Spirit, were akin to a visitation of that Consciousness. Some of them are excerpted here:

. . .not only 1900 years ago but *today,* He may be born into thine own consciousness, thine own understanding; He comes unto His own!

Art thou His? Have ye claimed Him? Have ye put on the Christ. . .?

For He is thy Elder Brother. . .

For as ye behold the face of thy friend, of thy neighbor, of thy foe, yea thine enemy, ye behold the image of thy Savior.

For ye are all His. . .

. . ."Peace, it is I! Be not afraid, it is *I,*" thy Savior, thy Christ; yea, thy *self* meeting that *Babe* in thine own inner self that may grow even as He to be a channel of blessings to others!
262-103

How many other seekers in the earth at that time, totally unacquainted with the obscure psychic of Virginia Beach, may have experienced a vision or presentiment of the Christ Presence in their lives, strengthening and girding them against the dark holocaust then rising? I suggest that their number was probably great indeed. I count myself among them.

For me, following an experience which happened to coincide with my nineteenth birthday, on July 22, 1936, the latter half of that year became a period of great spiritual seeking and awakening. I had gone for my usual long walk, with book in hand, and found my way to a familiar hillock. Here I sat under an old apple tree and began to read. The book, a 19th-century autobiography by Richard Jefferies, *The Story of My Heart,* was a "revelation" of sorts to my young, seeking mind. It contained some remarkable and unorthodox ideas. One of these, which I was to use some 34 years later as an introductory quotation to an article entitled "Science and the Future," in the May 1970 issue of *The A.R.E. Journal* (included in this collection), sparked a deep reverie: "A nexus of ideas exists," wrote Jefferies, "of which nothing is known—a vast system of ideas—a cosmos of thought. There is an entity, a Soul-Entity, as yet unrecognized."

Not until I came across the Edgar Cayce readings, some three decades later, was I again to encounter that intriguing reference to a "Soul-Entity"! And I think it was a pivotal factor in drawing me to the Cayce material.

Meanwhile, on that special birthday in my youth, I found myself drifting into a trance-like state. I suddenly experienced a sense of deep, inner peace and spiritual awakening. I was enraptured by an influx of spiritual wisdom, devoid of words. I just seemed to *know* the answers to unformulated questions about the mystery and meaning of life. My little experience, which lasted, I suppose, no longer than a matter of minutes, had a transforming impact upon my life. It did not involve any kind of "vision" or "spiritual presence"; but it was the sort of experience that could only have resulted from a rousing of the Divine within, or the Christed Consciousness.

I think this is what Cayce was talking about, in that prophecy of his about the Christ appearing in '36 to those who were seeking Him.

Epilogue

It is worth noting, in conclusion, that the readings placed a great deal of stress upon 1936 as a year of significant change, even to the recording of same in certain esoteric measurements within the Great Pyramid; and we should not regard the matter lightly.

In the reading immediately prior to 5748-6, wherein Cayce

predicted "the upheavals in the interior of the earth" for that fateful year, 1936, we find these intriguing questions and answers:

Q-1. Are the deductions and conclusions arrived at by D. Davidson and H. Aldersmith in their book on the Great Pyramid correct?

A-1. Many of these that have been taken as deductions are correct. Many are far overdrawn. Only an initiate may understand.

Q-2. What corrections for the period of the 20th century?

A-2. Only those that there will be an upheaval in '36.

Q-3. Do you mean there will be an upheaval in '36 as recorded in the Pyramid?

A-3. As recorded in the Pyramid, though this is set for a correction which, as has been given, is between '32 and '38—the correction would be, for this—as seen—is '36—for it is in many—these run from specific days; for, as has been seen, there are periods when even the hour, day, year, place, country, nation, town, and individuals are pointed out. That's how correct are many of those prophecies as made.   5748-5

Changes in the affairs of men, during 1936, were of a highly ominous character (see Appendix A). Despite their relatively low visibility, they were to have a drastic impact upon the future history of mankind. If there were matching upheavals in the interior of the Earth in that year, as we contend there were, most of their visible effects may still lie ahead of us.

To summarize, then:

In reading 443-5, we find it stated as a theory on cosmic influence "That there is ever being thrown off not only by the sun but the planets or even the stars, an influence upon life in the earth—or in any sphere." But what is the operative principle? Is it the activity in time and space of etheronic energies (*mental* in character, according to Q&A-7, reading 443-5[8])? And if so, are these energies transferred through some incredibly intricate process of attunement, involving an equally complex network of cosmic resonances set into motion throughout the universe, as we have surmised? Finally, is man himself a cosmic resonator? (Surely he is that, and more. For it is given to man to rule the whole universe, as a god in the making!)

APPENDIX A

In support of our contention that 1936 was a critical year in world affairs, marking the prelude to World War II and its consequent turmoils, which are still with us and growing, here is a brief summary of some of the major developments at that time, based on data in the *Encyclopaedia Britannica:*

a) *Germany*—Hitler, who came to power in 1933, marched his troops into the Rhineland in 1936, thus violating the Treaty of Locarno. With the political value of Locarno destroyed, and spurred on by the inaction of the Western democracies and the USSR, Hitler was emboldened to accelerate his plans for world conquest, confident that he could rely on a policy of appeasement where the Allies were concerned.

b) *Italy*—In defiance of the League of Nations, Mussolini began his conquest of Ethiopia in October 1935, consolidating Italian control by 1936.

c) *Spain*—In July 1936, the Spanish peninsula became the scene of violent struggle, marking the deterioration of French and British power. Civil war erupted in a power-play between Communist and Fascist forces.

d) *Japan*—The 1936 military revolt against the leading political faction, which is remembered in Japanese history today as the "February 26 Incident," is generally acknowledged as a milestone in that country's militarization and its road to World War II. The conquest of Asia was already in progress, but was accelerated.

e) *USSR*—Although the Soviet Union did not invade Finland until 1939, there is no doubt that Stalin was observing the lessons he could learn from the successful German and Italian moves toward conquest in 1936 and began mapping out his strategy for Soviet hegemony at that time. In fact, Communist involvement in the Spanish Civil War in 1936 was typical of the evolving Soviet technique of subversion as a means of achieving its expansionist goals.

f) *United States*—Franklin Delano Roosevelt in 1936 made a fateful economic decision. At a time when the international need for stabilized world economic conditions was known to be urgent, he instead raised the prices of American goods as a domestic political gesture. The result was a critical exacerbation of international economic problems and tensions.

g) *France* and *Great Britain,* like the United States, were too engrossed in their own domestic affairs in 1936 to meet their moral obligations properly in respect to the worsening world situation or to ask themselves: "Am I my brother's keeper?"

APPENDIX B

An ancient Chinese text, known as the "Great Law," compiled ca. 1050 B.C. is quoted in *Star Maps,* by William R. Fix, and provides this fascinating correlation with Edgar Cayce's reading on sunspots and the interrelationship between human strife and turmoil and natural calamities:

"It is the duty of the government all the time to watch carefully the phenomena of nature, which reflect in the world of nature the order and disorder in the world of government. . . When the course of nature runs properly, it is a sign that the government is good, but when there is some disturbance in nature it is a sign that there is something wrong in the government. . .Any disturbance in the sun accuses the emperor."

The year 1936, it might be worth adding, was on the rising crest of a prominent sunspot cycle, which peaked in 1941. (The previous cycle had peaked in 1917. Is it only coincidental that these years—1941 and 1917, respectively—marked American entry into the two world wars, and could be labelled a "turning point" in each?)

APPENDIX C

A less significant conjunction of the planets occurred in a 90° quadrant on March 10, 1982. Though scoffed at by scientists and the news media at the time, it is sobering to note that the event was followed by a rather ominous series of cataclysmic events throughout the remainder of the month.

First, there was a renewed eruption of Mount St. Helens on March 20th, following several days in which as many as 35 or 40 small seismic tremors daily set the stage for the event, which far exceeded in violence what the scientists had been predicting. Meanwhile, on the other side of the "ring of fire" that girdles the Pacific Basin, a 7.3 quake struck offshore Hokkaido, Japan, on March 21st; and on the 22nd, a 4.5 quake rumbled through Borrego Springs, California, at the southern end of the San Andreas Fault. Moderate quakes were also recorded in southern Italy, Turkey and Peru. Meanwhile, Ft. Wayne, Indiana, was reeling under the worst flood of the century, and the High Sierras were to suffer from unseasonably heavy snows and avalanche disaster before the month was out. On March 28, the Space Center at Houston reported the appearance of a large solar flare on the surface of the sun. Down in Mexico, as if to rival Mount St. Helens, the volcano El Chichon, which had been dormant for centuries, suddenly erupted, spewing a billion tons of ash and hot volcanic rocks across a large area, forcing the evacuation of 20,000 people and raining death upon at least 50 who did not escape in time. But perhaps the most ominous news of all came from the British Transglobe Expedition on March 18th, reporting that a polar heat wave at the northern polar cap was resulting in an alarming thawing trend—a trend that some theorists have said might ultimately trigger a shifting of the poles.

As for the planetary impact of the November 1982 phase of the "grand conjunction," it is too early to assess its long-range effects, which are apt to have been of a deep-rooted nature that will only become fully manifest on the earth's surface with the gradual passage of time. At this final writing, however (mid-December 1982), it is possible to attribute a number of more immediate and visible phenomena to unusual solar and planetary influence. "Catastrophes everywhere," read a *Washington Post* headline on November 24. Record-breaking tornadoes and hurricanes struck such diverse points as California and Hawaii, France and Spain, Mexico and several Midwestern states. In Japan, an erupting volcano struck a jetliner with high-flying debris, while down in Indonesia, Mt. Galunggung—the most dangerous active volcano, which had been dormant for 64 years, until April 1982 (following the planetary conjunction of March 10!)—experienced several major eruptions, threatening to wipe out 210 villages with cold lahar (a mixture of volcanic ash and monsoon rains). On November 30, the National Weather Service reported unusual sunspot activity. And in mid-December a severe earthquake struck North Yemen, followed by an even more devastating quake in Afghanistan—precursors, possibly, of other earth changes in the making. . .

The Music of the Spheres

Some Philosophical Notes
on a New Age Astrology

. . .become attuned, as it were, to the heavenly song, the
heavenly music, the vibrations as it were of the spheres. . .
1487-1

I

Night. The music of nature swells around us in a vibrant
chorus of insect calls and creature noises. Let us climb the hill
to a higher promontory. Here an ocean of stars surrounds us, as
far as the eye can see in every direction. And suddenly our little
sphere, the earth, is dwarfed by the utter magnitude of this
outer sphere of limitless space, alive with the shimmering
lights of distant constellations—"home" to how many millions
of our brothers in the universe?

It has been estimated that there are a *hundred billion* stars in
our galaxy alone, all interconnected by an invisible network of
nerve-like pulsations and vibrations, forming the individual
notes and collective harmonies that compose the wondrous
music of the spheres. Mind-boggling? To be sure! Yet, consider:
the nearby Andromeda Galaxy is at least twice as large as our
own Milky Way; and deep in space lie perhaps millions—nay,
billions—of other galaxies, each with its unnumbered chorus of
individual stars emitting their signal-like song. . .

The stars within a galaxy, like the cells in our own bodies, are
born, reach maturity, and die, in an unending cycle of spirit
merging into matter and moving out again.[1] Yet the galactic
body itself retains its given shape, though its manifest

substance is constantly fading and reforming. It assumes a pattern, moreover, that is unique in the heavens, distinguishable from all of its sister galaxies throughout the endless reaches of space, so that no two galaxies are quite alike, even as no two blades of grass on our little earth are ever identical. And do we not sense in this fact a profound significance? Do they not, these celestial cells called galaxies, comprise in their individual and collective essence a representation of the Body of God, even as does Man himself, and all of Nature? For all are One. All bear the imprimatur of Mind the Maker, from which they emanate, and of which they are part and parcel:

It should be understood that Life is One...   294-155

...ye are part and parcel of a universal consciousness, or God—and thus [part of] all that is within the universal consciousness, or the universal awareness; as the stars, the planets, the sun, the moon.   2794-3

Then, the destiny of the soul—*as of all creation*—is to be one with Him; continually growing, growing, for that association. [Author's italics]   262-88

...the coming into the earth has been and is for the evolution or the evolving of the soul unto its awareness...5749-5

...in patience we become aware of our souls, of our identity, of our being each a corpuscle, as it were, in the great body, in the heart, of our God.   262-114

In amplification of these very profound concepts, the Edgar Cayce readings make it clear that "each entity is as a universe within its own self." (279-15) We are told that "the soul of man, thy soul, encompasses *all* in this solar system or in others," (5755-2) and that "The *body* is a pattern, it is an ensample of all the forces of the universe itself." (2153-6)

Such utterances have the freshness of revelation about them. And quite rightly so! Yet, two great spiritual figures of the past—Paracelsus and Swedenborg—had a surprisingly similar vision of man and the universe.

"Heaven is man," wrote Paracelsus, in terms reminiscent of the cabbalistic Tree of Life, "and man is heaven, and all men together are the one heaven, and heaven is nothing but one man."[2] Then, in a logical sequel to that esoteric statement, the great 16th-century physician-philosopher added another, which epitomizes the whole of astrology: "Therefore the starry vault imprints itself on the inner heaven of a man."[3]

A couple of centuries later, Emanuel Swedenborg, the famous Swedish scientist who suddenly became a psychic, thus drastically altering the course of his career almost overnight, expressed essentially the same idea. But he put it in novel terms that equate the material universe with a stage or theatre, as it were, corresponding in an altered sense to the Heavenly Kingdom and the Lord Himself, where the incoming soul must act out its evolution under a human form, drawing its pattern from the very universe itself:

> "The visible universe is nothing else than a theatre representative of the Lord's kingdom, and [this kingdom] is a theatre representative of the Lord Himself...And as he thus acts in unity with the angels, [a man] is also an image of heaven...under a human form."[4]

We find the Swedenborgian imagery closely paralleled in a number of further excerpts from the Edgar Cayce readings:

> ...each soul that manifests itself in human form *is* thy brother—and the spirit and soul of same is in the form of thy Maker. 254-91

> And ye must be one—one with another, one with Him—if ye would be, as indeed ye are—corpuscles in the *life flow* of thy Redeemer! 1391-1

> Then those so entering *must* continue through the earth until the body-mind is made perfect for the soul, or the body-celestial again. 262-99

The Swedenborgian concept of a stage, or theatre, in relation to the soul's passage through the visible universe, is conveyed in the following excerpts:

> Though the conditions about you, about any soul, may be as torments...they are only used as puppets, and are as nothing... 256-5

> In *Him* is the understanding, *by* and through those influences that have taken form—in universes—to meet the needs of each soul—that we might find our way to Him.
> 5755-2

For, without passing through each and every stage of development, there is not the correct vibration to become one with the Creator. . .   900-16

Though the earth, though the stars, may pass away; though there may be changes in the universe as to relative position, these are brought about by those combinations of that speck of human activity as relative *to* the soul's expression in any sphere of experience.   1297-1

"In passing through the law," the readings tell us, "we may become perfect, but not in materiality." (5252-1)

Man's development, as given, is of man's understanding and applying the laws of the universe; and as man applies these, man develops, man brings up the whole generation of man.
                                                      900-70

. . .for man was created a little bit higher than all the rest of the whole universe, and is capable of harnessing, directing, enforcing the laws of the universe.   5-2

The first laws, then, partook of that of the study of self, the division of mind, the division of the solar systems, the division of man in the various spheres of existence through the earth plane and through the earth's solar system.   5748-2

"Flesh," according to the readings, "is the testing portion of the universal vibration." (900-16) For this reason, many earthly cycles may be necessary, as well as repeated sojourns elsewhere in the solar system between incarnations. "For, those sojourns are as lessons, as grades. . ." (3226-1) But with the application of the lessons learned, and the gradual mastery of the universal laws, an advanced soul-entity is ready to move on through "those centers about which thine own solar system moves—in Arcturus," (5755-1) to experience higher and higher "dimension[s] of consciousness or awareness" (5755-2):

When an individual incarnates in the earth, he has *possibly* passed through all the various spheres, either once, twice, *many* times. . .   311-2

Not as a physical body as known in the earth, but as a body adaptable to the environs of [for example] Jupiter; for there's life there (not as known in earth), as there is in Saturn, Sun, Moon, Venus, Mercury, Uranus, Neptune, Mars [and Pluto[5]]; all have their form. . .The elements about same are inhabited, if you choose, by those of their own peculiar environment.

630-2

. . .as long as an entity is within the confines of that termed the earth's and the sons of the earth's solar system, the developments are within the sojourns of the entity from sphere to sphere; and when completed it begins—throughout the music of the spheres with Arcturus, Polaris, and through those sojourns in the outer sphere.

441-1

For man is not made for this world alone.

4082-1

. . .all worlds are the work of His hand, are thine to possess, thine to use—as one with Him.

5755-2

"In my Father's house are many mansions," Jesus told His disciples. We may regard His words as a reference to the soul's habitations as it moves through those countless spheres of evolving awareness or consciousness that constitute our experience in the visible universe, each stage corresponding, as it were, to a different and higher rate of vibration. Yet, in a more spiritual sense, Jesus was undoubtedly alluding to a place in the Heavenly Kingdom—the "New Jerusalem"—where the purged and purified soul regains the body-celestial, at last, in that perfect union with its Source—the Universal Consciousness, or God:

In that city, in that place, there is no need of the sun, nor of the moon, nor the stars; for He is the *Light;* He *is* Light, and in Him is no darkness at all!

262-115

Spiritually, there becomes no time or space, for they—like the Father—are one.

2879-1

Do not think it is a different universe. No. It is the same universe you see about you, even now, though dimly perceived and little understood at present. What is changed, then? It is the soul's awareness of its Self.

II

To reach a "New Age" understanding of astrological principles, we must begin from a spiritual premise. What better premise than the Word Itself?

187

Then, in considering those conditions, those experiences as may be a part of the soul's awareness—in the beginning was the Word, and the Word was God, and the word was with God. *That* is the premise.   5755-2

And the Word became flesh.

In the Edgar Cayce readings, we find this stunning summary of the development of that Soul-entity who first came into the earth plane in "thought form" as Amilius, took on fleshly woes as Adam, and went through some thirty incarnations before completing His own development through our solar system as Jesus, the risen Christ, who became One with the Father, and the Pattern for all of us who choose to follow:

In the Creation we find all force relative one with the other, and in the earth's plane that of the flesh. In the developing from plane to plane becomes the ramification, or the condition of the will merited in its existence finding itself through eons of time.

The illustration, or manifestation in this, we find again in the man called Jesus:

When the soul reached that development in which it reached earth's plane, it became in the flesh the model, as it had reached through the developments in those spheres, or planets, known in the earth's plane, obtaining then One in All.

As in Mercury pertaining of Mind.

In Mars of Madness.

In Earth as of Flesh.

In Venus as Love.

In Jupiter as Strength.

In Saturn as the beginning of earthly woes, that to which all insufficient matter is cast for the beginning [over again].

In that of Uranus as of the Psychic.

In that of Neptune as of Mystic.

In Septimus [Pluto?] as of [Cosmic?] Consciousness.

In Arcturus as of the developing. . .

This man called Jesus we find at a Oneness with the Father, the Creator, passing through all the various stages of development; in mental perfect, in wrath perfect, in flesh made perfect, in love become perfect, in death become perfect, in psychic become perfect, in mystic become perfect, in consciousness become perfect, in the greater ruling forces [represented in Arcturus] *becoming* perfect. Thus He is as the model, and through the compliance with such laws made perfect, destiny, the predestined, the forethought, the will, made perfect, the conditions made perfect, He is an ensample

for man, and only as a man, for He lived only as man, He died as
man. [Author's italics]   900-10

The influences ascribed to the various planets, in functioning
as developmental forces for the evolving Christ—He who
became "the Way"—coincide very closely with the teachings of
orthodox astrology (although the reference to Arcturus
certainly introduces an unfamiliar dimension, both literally
and figuratively!). As "schooling centers" for the soul, so to
speak, each of the planets may wield a positive or negative
influence on our soul development in the earth as we come
under its particular vibration, depending upon a host of factors.
Environment and heredity are most often cited. Esoterically
considered, however, these reflect the soul's choice, based on
what each entity has built for itself through its various earthly
and planetary sojourns. We are not the victims of fate, but
creatures of our own designing. And free will is ever paramount
in our choices and decisions. Thus, when passing under the
influence of any planetary aspect, for weal or woe, everything
depends upon our freely determined reactions. Opportunities
may be converted into pitfalls, and vice versa.

Here is a brief summary of the influences associated with
each of the planets.

Mercury pertains to mental development. In the readings, a
great number of corroborative references occur, such as this
one: "In Mercury [we find] the high mental abilities. . ." (1981-1)
From an astrological standpoint, this would appear to suggest
that Mercury may have been rising, or at a mid-heaven
position, at the moment of [1981]'s birth, since either of these
two configurations in a natal chart indicates a particularly
influential role for the planet—or planets—involved, as we
shall see later. Or Mercury may have been "favorably
aspected" in some other manner in the individual's horoscope,
thus aiding its beneficial influence; even as the reverse may be
true of any sign or planet in a birth chart, reflecting what an
incoming entity has meted for itself, to aid its own spiritual
growth and development in a given incarnation. The negative
traits of Mercury, of course, are seen in that tendency to abuse
one's mental gifts to the detriment of self and others; and this
could lead to an "unfavorably aspected" Mercury in one's next
earthly cycle, with the mental powers afflicted in some manner.

Venus symbolizes love, art and beauty, which may turn to the
extremes of lust and decadence in their more material or

negative phases. The spiritual aspects of Venus are evident in the following excerpt from reading 5755-1—but with a qualification added, which suggests the negative traits also: "What is love? Then what is Venus? It is beauty, love, hope, charity—yet all of these have their extremes."

Mars is referred to in astrology as the Energizer, and its characteristics are action and courage, while its negative connotations would be uncontrolled rage and anger. "In Mars of Madness," says reading 900-10. But in another reading, a more positive view is given: "From Mars we find the urges for activity, the intenseness with which the entity gives itself to that it chooses." (3299-1)

Jupiter represents the ennobling forces, according to both astrology and the readings. Magnanimity and benevolence are Jupiterian traits. "In Jupiter we find the abilities in a helpful, universal way and manner," says reading 3299-1. Carried to its negative extreme, however, extravagance and self-indulgence are manifested, as the readings testify.

Saturn is called the Taskmaster; its traditional role in astrology is to promote patience and endurance under stress. The readings call it the planet of "sudden or violent changes... And yet these are testing periods of thy endurance, of thy patience, of thy love of truth, harmony, and the spirit that faileth not." (1981-1)

Uranus, in the terms of orthodox astrology, is equated with the Psychic. This conforms with the interpretation in the readings. In its negative aspect, however, Uranus is associated with eccentricity and the extremes: "From the Uranian influences we find the extremist." (1206-3)

Neptune is the Mystic. It is also associated with water, as might be expected of one who explores the mysterious depths of the universe. Its negative connotations are those tendencies to overdo a love of mystery and the occult forces. "One that should have been guided close in the study of those things pertaining to the mystery and the occult," says reading 2213-1, relevant to the Neptunian influences.

Pluto, which was not discovered by modern astronomers until 1930, is believed to have been the planet sometimes referred to in the Edgar Cayce readings as Septimus or Vulcan (in fact, reading 826-8 confirms the synonymity with Vulcan); and this suggests that the most distant planet in our solar system may once have been known to the ancients—intuitively or otherwise—and was identified by them under different names than now. Modern astrology has little to say concerning this relatively unknown planet, although it is credited as a broadly "regenerative" influence on mankind in its positive aspect, and a calamitous one in its negative forces. This appears to be an accurate assessment, if we may judge by the following excerpts from the readings: "It [Pluto's influence] is gradually *growing,* and thus is one of those influences that are to be as a demonstrative activity in the future affairs or developments of man towards the spiritual-minded influences, or those influences outside of himself." (1100-27) On the negative side, reading 1735-2 contains a cautionary note to "beware of fire, and especially of firearms or explosives," referring to "the influences that bring for warnings, as seen in Mars and Vulcan [Pluto]. . ."

Seven of the planets have a relative correspondence with the seven endocrine glands, as presented in reading 281-29 (Q&A-21). These glands are viewed in the readings as a conjoined system, or "chain," of physical centers directly linked to our *psychic* evolution. (In esoteric literature, it is stated that each of the endocrine centers has its counterpart in the etheric body, and these are called *chakras.*) Here, then, are the given planetary correspondences: Mercury, the pineal gland; Venus, the thymus; Mars, the solar plexus; Jupiter, the pituitary gland; Saturn, the gonads; Uranus, the thyroid; Neptune, the lyden gland. Pluto, as a gradually growing influence, may not be directly associated in any way with the endocrine system itself, although the nature of its evolving influence implies an indirect connection of some kind with the higher centers. (Some might envision a correlation with the "beam of light" associated with the "crown chakra," in mystical literature.)

The individual vibration of each of the various planetary bodies is also expressed in color, as well as sound. For, "music, color, vibration are all a part of the planets, just as the planets are a part—and a pattern—of the whole universe." (5755-1) (The notes and colors of some of the planets are detailed in an essay written by Edgar Cayce, with Thomas Sugrue, and published by the A.R.E. Press under the title, *Auras.*)

And what of that governing luminary of our solar system, the Sun? Esoteric astrology, following the spiritual tradition of the medieval alchemists, assigns a mystical unity between the Sun and "the Son," or the Christ. Elsewhere in the symbolism of alchemy, Sun and Moon are representational of Adam and Eve, and they embody the male/female, yang/yin principles. The

Sun is associated with the heart, and its nature is fire; while the Moon typifies the imaginative forces and intuition, and its nature is water.

Sun and Moon play dominant roles in our earthly lives, of course, and are obviously important in astrology. In fact, the evolving soul-entity may even have experienced indwellings in their environs at one time, between earthly cycles:

> . . .the being translated in materiality as Ra Ta—was from the infinity forces, or from the Sun. . .   **5755-1**

> . . .the dwellers upon the Moon (the satellite of the earth) preceded the abilities for matter. . .And this entity was among those that so dwelt, and is influenced by two sojourns there.   **264-31**

In astrology, the Sun is a "positive" force. Its position in the natal chart, and its governing sign, form a general guide to the basic character of the individual. The Moon, as a passive or "negative" body, whose subtle influence on the tides can also exert a pull on our bodily fluids, as well as altering our moods and feelings, is indicative of the intuitional and emotional forces affecting the soul-entity throughout its earthly sojourns. The nature of its influence depends, as with the Sun and all of the various planets and signs in a horoscope, upon its location and aspects within the twelve divisions or "houses" of the horoscope, as well as upon the individual's exercise of its divine right of free will and choice:

> There is set before thee two ways, ever. . .   **347-2**

> . . .the soul must make its choice; as to whether things are to be viewed from the material angle or from the soul's development—that must live on and on. . .For, will and choice is the gift of the soul [from the Creator]. . .   **556-1**

> The will of a soul, of a body, is supreme. . .   **416-2**

> As to the application of self respecting the astrological forces—these. . .are only urges. As to what one does *with* and about same depends upon choices made.   **1710-3**

Yet the influence of astrological forces cannot be ignored with impunity, since these forces operate within the framework of universal law, representing distinct dimensions of consciousness or awareness that each soul must meet:

...there is the influence of the planets upon an individual, for all must come under such influence... 3744-3

Hence the sun, the moon, the stars, the position in the heavens or in all of the hosts of the solar systems that the earth occupies—all have their influence... 5753-1

Each planetary influence vibrates at a different rate of vibration. An entity entering that influence enters that vibration... 281-55

...it is not so much that an entity is influenced because the Moon is in Aquarius or the Sun in Capricorn or Venus or Mercury in that or the other house, sign, or the Moon and Sun sign, in that one of the planets is in this or that position in the heavens, but rather because those positions in the heaven are from the *entity* having been in that sojourn as a soul! This is how the planets have the greater influence in the earth upon the entity, see? 630-2

Earth, in this solar system, merely represents three dimensions. Then how many dimensions are in this solar system? Eight! What position does the earth occupy? Third! What position do others occupy? That relative relationship one to another. 5755-2

...but there may be as seven [dimensions], in Mercury—or four, in Venus—or five, as in Jupiter. There may be only one as in Mars. There may be many more as in those of Neptune, or they may become even as nil—until purified in Saturn's fires. 311-2

Intriguing indeed is the probability that our space probes into the solar system, bringing back to us glimpses of Uranus and Jupiter and other planetary bodies in the limited terms of our three-dimensional vision, have brought us no closer to the "reality" of these planets than looking at a locked jewel-box can reveal to our eyes the multifaceted beauty of the gems inside... Moving in the psychic realm, however, it is conceivable that one might "shift dimensions," as it were, by raising or lowering the vibratory rate, and thus gain entrance into the reality of these other worlds. In fact, it is primarily at this *psychic* level, apparently, that planetary influences are felt upon our lives in the earth plane.[6]

To an entity in the earth plane, as Cayce explained it, astrological influences arise as "mental urges" only, while one's prior appearances in the earth create "the urges from the emotions" that have been built as influential forces. (633-2) As the readings make clear, there is an exquisite rationale underlying the concept of free will and choice in relation to the urges experienced; and the implications are indeed sobering:

Q-11. Comment upon the following. Is it worthy of expansion; that is, does it carry any light of truth?

The Creator, in seeking to find or create a being worthy of companionship, realized that such a being would result only from a free will exercising its divine inheritance and through its own efforts find its Maker. Thus, to make the choice really a divine one caused the existence of states of consciousness, that would indeed tax the free will of a soul; thus light and darkness. Truly, only those tried so as by fire can enter in.

A-11. The only variation that we would make is that all souls in the beginning were one with the Father. The separation, or turning away, brought evil. Then there became the necessity of the awareness of self's being out of accord with, or out of the realm of blessedness; and, as given of the Son, "yet learned He obedience through the things which He suffered."   262-56

What is meted must be met.   442-3

For, each soul enters [the earth] that it may make its paths straight.   2021-1

Hence, Destiny is: "As ye sow, so shall ye reap." And like begets like!   276-7

The soul is complete only in the law and realm of its Creator.   553-1

III

The astrological influence most noticeably felt by a soul-entity in the earth is its vibratory attunement with the Sun.

This influence bears a corresponding relationship to the Sun's passage through one of the twelve zodiacal constellations at the time of the entity's birth. And we know these zodiacal correspondences, of course, as the twelve familiar Sun signs of traditional astrology. They represent those mythical figures, from the ram in Aries through the two fishes in Pisces, that lie along the path of our Sun in its annual orbit through the heavens.

However, due to the spinning motion of the earth, the twelve signs are encountered once again, in a much faster cycle, so that a different sign of the Zodiac appears on the horizon every two hours within a 24-hour period of the earth's daily rotation; and this introduces yet another phase of zodiacal influence on the entity, as we shall shortly explain.

Additionally, there is a much, much slower, "backward" passage through the twelve constellations of the Zodiac as the slow wobbling of the earth causes its rotating axis to point to different parts of the sky at different times. This cycle takes almost 26,000 years to complete, and each transit through one of the twelve constellations is called an "Age." It lasts about 2160 years. We are now moving out of the Piscean Age, as almost everyone knows, and into the Aquarian Age. Each 2160-year cycle wields a general influence upon the whole body of mankind.

Now, to explain a bit. . .

A soul-entity born into the earth, say, when the Sun is transiting the constellation of Aries (from March 21 to April 19) will come under the direct influence of that particular Sun sign. This "timing" has actually been chosen by the incoming soul, in all likelihood, as the most suitable solar configuration for its current phase of development.[7] And it may have entered as an "Aries" in more than one of its former lives, repeating the soul's patient journey through the twelve different signs or expressions. For example:

Coming under the influence of Pisces, or that making for a spiritual attunement, we find this—with the sojourns of the entity—is a portion of the entity's whole being.
For *more than once* has the entity in its sojourns in the earth come under the influence of this same astrological aspect. [Author's italics]   1007-1

Yet each cycle will be on a higher rung of the ladder, so to speak, as the soul-entity makes its rounds—*unless, of course, it is slipping!*

If a soul-entity enters on the cusp between two Sun signs, so that its birth date is at the "tail-end" of the one sign's influence and the commencement of the other's, the attributes of *both* signs will likely be revealed or expressed in the individual's basic character; but the incoming sign will normally wield the preponderant influence.

Yet, there are other zodiacal influences, too, that come into special focus. Depending upon the hour of birth, and quite regardless of the particular Sun sign in a natal chart, we will find Scorpio, Taurus, or one of the other twelve figures of the Zodiac rising on the horizon, as viewed from the perspective of the earth's daily rotation; and this will be known as the "Ascendant sign" for that entity. Its influence may be felt and recognized as an aspect of the "revealed personality" in varying degree, depending in part upon which planets, if any, may be rising under the same sign to add their influence to the Ascendant's innate force or influence. Additionally, the readings appear to suggest that the zodiacal sign and planetary bodies found in a horoscope at the "mid-heaven" position (more commonly termed the Zenith) are also strongly influential. And this is in accord with traditional astrology, as well.

To ascertain the positions of the Ascendant and Zenith in a natal chart, simply visualize a circle divided into a quaternary by two dissecting lines in the form of a cross. The horizontal line, quite logically, represents the horizon. Its lefthand extremity marks the Ascendant point, or moment of sunrise, while the righthand extremity of the line marks the setting position, called the Descendant. The vertical arm of the cross terminates at an upper point marking the Zenith, or mid-day, while its lower extremity—called the Nadir—represents midnight. Each quadrant of the circle is divided into three sections, or houses, constituting essentially 30 degrees of arc apiece, and running in a counter-clockwise manner from the first house, just below the Ascendant, to the twelfth, in a position just above the Ascendant. Thus, if one is born at midnight, the Sun will be centered at the Nadir, or base of the horoscope, on the cusp between the third and fourth houses. And if, additionally, one is an Arien (Aries), the cusp will bear the zodiacal sign of the ram at whatever "degree" applies in relation to the date and hour, based on the Sun's 30-day transit (approximately) through that constellation.

Not too complicated, really. Any good astrological textbook will serve to familiarize the interested layman with the rudimentals of this fascinating subject. But let us continue.

First, here are the aforementioned excerpts from the readings that suggest the importance of both the natal Sun sign and the Ascendant in a horoscope, as well as the Zenith, and those planets rising or at mid-heaven at the moment of birth:

The strongest force used in the destiny of man is the Sun first, then the closer planets to the earth, or those that are

coming to *ascension* at the time of the birth of the individual...
[Author's italics]   3744-3

Q-38. Are the tendencies of an individual influenced most by the planets nearer the earth at the time of the individual's birth?

A-38. At, or from that one which is at the *zenith* when the individual is in its place or sphere, or as is seen from that sphere or plane [from which] the soul and spirit took its flight in coming to the earth plane. [Author's italics]   3744-3

Most interestingly, Edgar Cayce's natal chart appears to confirm the nearly equal importance of both positions; for he had Uranus ("the Psychic") rising, while Neptune ("the Mystic") was in the ninth house, following the mid-heaven position, or what is termed the Zenith in astrology, although Uranus's is the dominant influence. For, as stated in reading 5755-1, "From an astrological aspect, then, the greater influence at the entrance of this entity that ye call Cayce was from Uranus."

But going back to the two excerpts just cited from reading 3744-3, a contradiction of sorts is apparent, perhaps due to some obscurity in the wording. It raises a question as to whether it is the Ascendant or the Zenith in a horoscope that should actually be regarded as the more dominant planetary position or sign, normally speaking. (In astrology, the Ascendant is typically regarded as the point of greater influence than the Zenith, although both positions are "key" ones. Yet it depends, of course, upon the given configuration of the planets in a horoscope, which may have a modifying effect.)

A solution looms. It is quite conceivable that the sleeping Cayce, when he used the word "zenith," was actually referring (in quite proper, though uncommon, usage!) to the *horizon,* or point of ascension. For although the more common meaning of "zenith" is a vertical or mid-heaven position, we do find a secondary definition of zenith as *"the point of the horizon at which a heavenly body rises."*(!) This is confirmed in *The Complete Edition of the Oxford English Dictionary.* (In fact, reading 254-2 states that Edgar Cayce was born with "Uranus at its zenith," thus corroborating this interpretation. See Cayce's natal chart, with Uranus actually at *Ascendant.*)

To those who remain unconvinced by this explanation, however, all uncertainty can perhaps be resolved by way of an unlikely source.

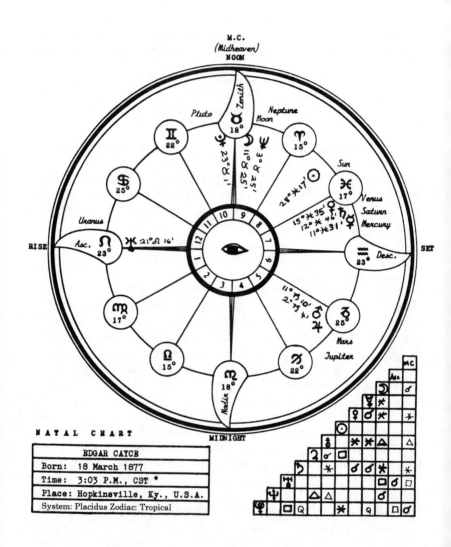

NATAL CHART

EDGAR CAYCE
Born: 18 March 1877
Time: 3:03 P.M., CST *
Place: Hopkinsville, Ky., U.S.A.
System: Placidus Zodiac: Tropical

*Based on Reading 254-2, 3/19/19. (NOTE: Central Standard Time was not in existence in 1877, although it was being used in 1919, of course, when the reading was given. We have applied CST. However, there remains a question as to whether the reading may have referred, instead, to either Local Mean Time—which would have placed the Ascendant at 21° 30′ Leo—or Sun Time, with Leo at 22° on the Ascendant.)

A noted French researcher and statistician, Michel Gauquelin, whose work we have cited in the past with less persuasion, has conducted a detailed scientific study of cosmic rhythms in relation to the career groupings of some 25,000 successful Europeans.[8] We have previously challenged certain of his statistical conclusions[9] because his career categories were not sufficiently specialized to reveal meaningful statistics in respect to natal Sun signs, whose influence his rather broadly based statistical studies refuted. Yet a more specialized approach on our part in a convincing number of career classes yielded consistently positive results. Despite this friendly difference in our respective findings on Sun signs, however, it is worth noting that the frequency distribution of several of the planets observed by Gauquelin (Mars, Jupiter, Saturn and the Moon) in relation to certain of his more generalized career categories—namely, champions, actors, scientists and writers—did indeed manage to yield positive statistical results, despite the lack of specialization. Under a more specialized approach—such as "top achievers" among, say, boxers, comedians, astronomers and novelists, as one set of possible choices in the four fields covered—we believe Gauquelin's findings might have proven even more significant for the four "positive" planets in his survey, as well as yielding similarly positive results for the remaining planets and the Sun, which lost any statistical significance in his too broadly based groupings. But it is not our intention to sound critical, for Gauquelin is an outstandingly fine and innovative researcher, and one who is continuing to contribute much to a more scientific understanding of astrological principles within a statistical format.

Our purpose here is to examine the results of his findings in respect to the four planets mentioned—namely, Mars, Jupiter, Saturn and the Moon (the latter is loosely termed a "planet," in astrology). And those results would appear to indicate a statistical pattern applicable in varying degree to *any* of the planets, we maintain, if observed under a sufficiently specialized approach for career categories likely to be suitable for each planet, such as Uranus for famous psychics, Neptune for well-known mystics, and so on. (In addition to Cayce, by the way, Nostradamus was another famous psychic who had Uranus rising. This points in the direction of our theory, but would require a sufficiently large survey of well-known psychics to be statistically meaningful, of course.)

Gauquelin, in his statistical study of the natal horoscopes of "high achievers" in four different career categories, found Mars, Jupiter, Saturn or the Moon, respectively, cresting in the area of the Ascendant, first, and then the Zenith, followed in sequential significance by the Descendant and the Nadir, although in markedly reduced prominence as compared to the former two areas.

There emerged one curious fact which merits emphasis: The actual "peak" of the four cresting curves occurred at a point "over the line," in each case, falling in what are termed the four cadent houses of a horoscope—namely, the twelfth, ninth, sixth and third, in that order of importance. This contradicts orthodox astrology, which has always taught that the house on the "approaching" side of the quadrant marker (first, tenth, seventh and fourth, respectively) is the more significant. So, based on the implications of Gauquelin's positive statistical results with at least four of the planets, the commonly accepted view about the relative unimportance of the cadent houses is certainly open to question. It will be the role of a "New Age" astrology to explore the implications of such a finding.

We come, now, to two areas of conflicting opinion in the modern practice of astrology.

One relates to whether the sidereal system of astrology, which is heliocentric or "Sun-oriented" in its approach to the casting of a natal horoscope, is more accurate than the earth-oriented geocentric system (called the "tropical") that is in common usage today in the West. Both systems have their ardent adherents, and certain technical justifications can be presented on behalf of each. We formerly leaned toward the sidereal, subject to some modifications in the Western practice of this sytem at the present time. But we have come across a reading[10] that appears to resolve the dispute in favor of the geocentric system:

Q-2. What is the correct system to use in astrology—the heliocentric or the geocentric system?
A-2. ...the Persian—or the geocentric—is the nearer correct.
933-3

This does not leave totally unresolved a number of other perplexing questions of a related nature; but we are confident that the astrologers will ultimately find the answers for themselves as they continue to seek for them.

The second area of debate is whether a natal chart should be based on the time of conception or the moment of birth; most astrologers would agree to the latter, and so do we. But if the latter, should the birth of the body-physical or the soul-body be the decisive factor? Here is what the readings say:

Q-5. *Should an astrological horoscope be based on the time of physical birth or the time of soul birth?*
A-5. On time of physical birth; for these are merely *inclinations,* and because of inclinations are not the influence of will.
826-8

Hence the position or the period of the entrance [birth] is not *ruled* by the position [of Sun and planets] but it may be *judged* by the position as to the influence. . . [Author's italics]1347-1

IV

From the beginning of time, man has sought to read the message of the stars. He has stood between heaven and earth, and has tried to discern in the face of the sky the path for his feet to follow. It has been a natural inclination on his part to gaze upward for guidance: his half-forgotten origins, after all, were celestial.

The predictable outcome of all man's astral ponderings was the creation of a "divining art" which he called astrology. Down through the ages, that "art" has been "reworked" and redefined. Today it is viewed as an emergent science. Unlike astronomy, however, which is only concerned with looking outward for the answers, astrology also looks within. It seeks to decipher the celestial hieroglyphics by tracing the patterns of their influence upon human destiny. The problem, until recently, lay in the absence of a heavenly "Rosetta stone" to aid in deciphering a celestial language that abounds in symbols whose meanings are often interior and concealed. The result has been a veil of mystery and confusion that still lies between man and the stars.

We make bold to suggest that an astrological "Rosetta stone" now exists, although largely ignored and unrecognized. We refer to the voluminous body of the Edgar Cayce readings, with their countless references and insights on the subject of astrology, providing innumerable keys to its interpretation. Indeed, within the readings lie the roots for a whole new approach to the inner self, which might aptly be termed "Akashic Astrology."

Drawing on what are called the akashic records, which constitute that "Book of Life" written on the skein of time and space by each soul-entity throughout its total experience from the dawn of time, Edgar Cayce gave some 2500 "life" readings, as they were termed. In these readings, he included astrological reference points and explanations pertaining to the more influential mental urges brought to bear on the individual in the present as a result of astrological sojourns elsewhere in the solar system between the entity's prior incarnation (or incarnations) in the earth and the present one, as modified by the individual's collective soul development or retrogression during earlier appearances in the earth. (Those previous lives having a direct impact on the present development were given.)

It is obvious that this sort of detailed information on literally hundreds of individuals, whose date and location of birth, sex, and occupation are also included in the transcript of each reading, must necessarily provide the astrological researcher with a highly promising reservoir of material from which a great number of meaningful statistical conclusions may be drawn. (Initial work in this direction, in fact, has already commenced on a limited basis; the preliminary findings, particularly as they relate to planetary aspects, are profoundly interesting.)

The eventual results, as more and more astrological researchers probe the wealth of data in the readings—including, in addition to the "life" readings, special readings touching on such related topics as the use of astrology in vocational guidance (5753-3), or heredity and environment (900-19, 900-23)—are apt to be surprising.

It will not be an easy task to organize and analyze the psychic information on astrology in the readings, but if pursued with patience and persistence it will enable the perceptive researcher to interpret many esoteric aspects of the subject that have heretofore defied a proper understanding. The results will revolutionize astrology as it exists today, setting it on a totally new and more spiritual foundation.

V

The twelve familiar figures of the Zodiac have often had other faces, other names. Not always have they been the ones we know today. Leo the Lion, for example, has been a dog, a cat, and an elephant in its gradual evolution from its Babylonian and Egyptian origins. In Chinese and Hindu astrological lore, moreover, the zodiacal asterisms bear utterly different animal representations than those that are popular in the West. Yet, the Edgar Cayce readings seem to subscribe to the view (although it is not anywhere stated in specific terms, to our knowledge) that certain psychological factors may play a determining role in setting the "right" symbols for us in any given phase of our development in a relative world, a relative universe. Thus, while once pointing out that our present placement of the Sun signs is "some two signs off" today (5755-1), other readings nevertheless did not hesitate to support the current symbolism now in use under the popular geocentric system of astrology. For example, an individual born with the Sun at 26° 58′ Pisces, near the cusp of Aries, was told: "...coming near the cusps, and under the influence of Pisces..." (282-2) In summary, it seems as if mankind, through its own mass beliefs, forming the "Collective Unconscious," is capable of influencing and even reshaping certain of the "stage props"— at least, here in the earth plane! For, "thoughts are things," as the readings repeatedly stress; and mind is indeed the builder of its own little universe, as well as contributing towards the "collective image" of the outer universe—the Macrocosm.

The influence of the signs, or cycles, of the Zodiac is clearly confirmed in the readings:

For various individuals, under various cycles, of course, are subject to changes as they pass through the various periods of the Zodiac. 3688-1

The study of the meaning of Aries, Sagittarius, Pisces, Libra, or any or all of such phases, would indicate the activity of the individual. For, remember, it is body manifestation...

5746-1

According to the readings, twelve is a number relating to "the mystic forces," and is emblematic of "a *finished* product, as is given in all forces in nature," and in those "*twelve* combined forces" that brought into the world "those strengths...as [were] necessary for a replenishing of same." (5751-1) The twelve signs of the Zodiac fit into this category, of course, as do the twelve months of the year, or the twelve tribes of Israel; and we are also reminded of the twelve Apostles.

St. Bede the Venerable, an English monk of the eighth century, who was well known for his scholarly commentaries on the Bible, envisioned a mystical correspondence between the twelve Apostles and the twelve signs of the Zodiac, which he set down in Latin for posterity, although posterity has largely ignored his efforts. But one of the readings, without any reference to the Venerable Bede, of whom Mr. Cayce had almost surely never heard, confirmed the ancient monk's spiritual insight:

> As each of the twelve Apostles represented major centers or regions or realms [constellations] through which consciousness became aware in the body of the earth itself, so did He find—as in thine own self ye find—those twelve stumbling stones. . .These are the price of flesh, of material consciousness, and are only passing.   2823-1

More recently, the well-known psychic, Jeane Dixon, reportedly experienced a beautiful illumination while kneeling in meditation at St. Matthew's Cathedral, in Washington, D.C., followed by a more complete vision at the same spot some few weeks later, in which she saw a circle divided into twelve segments. Each segment contained the figure of an Apostle and one of the twelve signs of the Zodiac. The correlations, which form the basis of her book, *Yesterday, Today, and Forever,*[11] are shown in the following chart. To these we have added our own interpretation—based on astrological teachings, in general, and corroborative data in the readings—of the "twelve stumbling stones" referred to by Edgar Cayce, under the heading, "Negative Trait"; while the column headed "Positive Trait" contains the opposite quality, by means of which each of the twelve stumbling stones to which we are *all* subject, at one phase or another of our earthly development, may be converted into a stepping-stone:

SIGN	APOSTLE	NEGATIVE TRAIT	POSITIVE TRAIT
Aries	Peter	Impulsiveness	Patience; Self-restraint
Taurus	Simon	Obstinacy	Flexibility; Adaptability
Gemini	James (the Less)	Doublemindedness	Singleness of Purpose
Cancer	Andrew	Hypersensitivity	Loving Indifference
Leo	John	Pride; Willfulness	Humility; Love; Gentleness
Virgo	Philip	Fault-finding; Exacting	Grace; Forgiveness
Libra	Bartholomew	Equivocation; Uncertainty	Balance; Judgment
Scorpio	Thomas	Doubt; Scorn; Suspicion	Trust; Faith; Hope
Sagittarius	James	Recklessness; Foolishness	Wisdom
Capricorn	Matthew	Self-aggrandizement	Unselfishness; Purity
Aquarius	Jude (Thaddaeus)	Eccentricity; Alienation	Altruism; Brotherhood
Pisces	Judas/(Jesus)*	Materialism	Spirituality

*According to reading 587-6, Jesus was actually born "on the 19th day of what could now be termed March." The symbolic significance of "the sign of the fish" in relation to the birth of Jesus, at the opening of the Piscean Age, is obvious. And although the Apostles appointed a successor to Judas, in a real sense it was the resurrected Christ Himself who filled the twelfth seat, thus completing the circle, or cycle of signs, as Master of them all.

We conclude our comments in this regard with an interesting excerpt from the readings:

> . . .all entities realize they in themselves are both positive and negative influences, and that the First Cause—or the Spirit—must of necessity within itself be likewise, yet more positive than negative, for it attracts with attraction and repels with rebellion of that same activity of which every entity is a part. 264-31

VI

As we move into the cusp of the Aquarian Age, with its many implications of spiritual change and promise, we may well pay heed to a highly curious astrological note in one of the readings:

> This building [the Great Pyramid]. . .was formed according to that which had been worked out by Ra Ta in the mount as related to the position of the various stars, that acted in the place about which this particular solar system circles in its activity, going towards what? That same name as to which the priest was banished—the constellation of Libra, or to Libya were these people sent. 294-151

This alludes, of course, to Edgar Cayce's incarnation in ancient Egypt as the High Priest Ra, or Ra Ta, who had actually come to that land from the Caucasian hills, near what is now Mount Ararat. But his priesthood in Egypt was interrupted by a nine-year period of exile to one of the high Nubian hills, in what is now the Sudan region and (by name only) an extension of the Libyan Desert. The current rulership in Libya, however, has already once invaded the neighboring state of Chad, and appears to have a covetous eye upon the Sudan, as well. Since our cited excerpt from reading 294-151 makes it clear that the Nubian mount of Ra's temporary exile was under the domain of ancient Libya at that time, we may well be witnessing the beginnings of a cyclical return of certain historical phases. . .At any rate, another reading—one which speaks of things to come—says: "Strifes will arise through the period. . .Watch for them in Libya and in Egypt. . ." (3976-26)

So much for the mundane phase of coming changes. An enigma of a more esoteric nature confronts us with that astrological reference to the apparent movement of our solar system towards the constellation of Libra—symbol of balance! Surely the correlation with Libya, a state presently in the throes of extreme political imbalance, is both implausible and puzzling. . .

The trouble lies in our perspective. We need a larger view, unlimited by the blinding immediacy of current events.

A time of fulfillment approaches, as foretold. A New Age begins. And history tends to repeat itself, although the cycles carry us upward in our evolution. There will be another shifting of the poles, we are told, which may greatly alter astrological foundations. What role, if any, does Libra play in all of this, if we are headed there? Do we have a rendezvous with Destiny at some far-off point in time and space within that minor constellation's realm of influence? And with the acting-out of everything in cycles, as it were, is there to be some inscrutable role ahead for that land so seemingly hostile today towards the West—namely, Libya?

Cogent questions, these. The answers lie ahead of us. And they may lie, to some extent, within the realm of astrological prediction, as our "New Age" astrologers begin to grasp the marvelous workings of their art as it was apparently practiced aeons ago, by Ra and Hermes in the Nubian mount.

Meanwhile, we have some clues at hand for a working hypothesis of sorts.

In a remarkable little book that combines both scholarly and esoteric dimensions, an Anglican clergyman named E.W. Bullinger (a direct descendant of the great Bullinger of the Swiss Reformation) created quite a stir in ecclesiastical circles in the latter part of the 19th century with an exquisitely researched and highly original interpretation of the Zodiac, viewed from a biblical perspective. His book, *The Witness of the Stars,* first published in London in 1893, began with the proposition that the true primogeniture of the Zodiac was apparently at a point somewhere in the constellation of Virgo (sign of the "virgin"). By inference, if we trace the precession of the equinoxes back through the Grand Cycle of the Ages to its last "beginning," in Virgo, using an approximate measuring-stick of 2,160 years for the backward-moving passage of the precession through each of the individual "ages" along the way (starting from the cusp of the Age of Aquarius, where we now stand), we arrive at a period somewhere between 13,119 B.C. and 10,960 B.C., which is the time-span of the Age of Virgo. Somewhere within that frame of reference, according to Bullinger's interpretation of events, Adamic Man must have had his beginnings. Bullinger, however, seems scrupulously to have avoided making such a controversial inference as to the days of Adam and Eve, and the Garden of Eden, instead contenting himself with a more narrow and specialized view: the *forward* progression of the zodiacal signs in the path of the Sun's annual ecliptic, in which he was able to trace a remarkable pattern of the Redeemer's advent and history.

We shall come to that.

First, however, let us further consider the precession of the equinoxes, based upon Virgo as our ancient starting-point. Where does this lead us? Why, to a point somewhere in the Age of Libra—even as Cayce prophesied—as the terminal point for the current Grand Cycle of the Ages, covering a time-span of some 25,920 years! The Age of Libra will take place from A.D. 10,641 to A.D. 12,800. Is this age to mark the "end of time," as we know it? Will all prophecy pertaining to man's evolution and soul development within the earth plane then be fulfilled, as we take flight to other mansions? It is an interesting speculation!

Back to Bullinger. . .

His counter-clockwise view of the zodiacal wheel, based on the Sun's annual passage through the twelve signs, starts with the "virgin," in Virgo, which is the prelude to the coming of a Holy "Seed," or Redeemer, and ends with the constellation of Leo (the Lion of the Tribe of Judah), symbol of His Second Coming, in glorious victory over His enemies. And Bullinger even views the Egyptian Sphinx as a representation, esoterically conceived by early astrologers, of the conjoining of Virgo and Leo. Throughout his book, Bullinger presents his case with scholarly skill and mastery, as he moves from one constellation to the next in revealing what he believes to have been an ancient Teaching of things to come, prophetically given to mankind by Adam or Enoch, in the beginning, but largely corrupted and "lost" as Greek and Roman myth systems were superimposed upon the original zodiacal symbols. A linguist *par excellence,* Bullinger provides the reader with the meanings originally ascribed to various stars, asterisms and constellations by ancient Hebrew, Egyptian and Chaldean star-gazers, as well as probing some of the interpretations found in Sanskrit, and finally showing how the Greek and Latin corruptions—some of which retained certain aspects of the original Teaching, but in a less-than-recognizable disguise—finally gave us the Zodiac we know today, which, alas, is devoid of its sacred origins and meanings.

In summary, then, when we speak of a "New Age" astrology, what are we really talking about but a rebirth of the old? For, in truth, there is nothing new under the Sun.

To conclude these philosophical observations, we revert to our initial premise: the Word.

As the Master gave, "Before Abraham was, I AM—before the worlds were, I AM." 262-57

"Before the worlds were"!

When we are attuned to Him, the Maker of the worlds, we are in touch with Eternity. And if we would but harken, we may hear the heavenly music of the spheres, which lies within us; and we ourselves are the music. Astrology merely interprets for us some of the individual notes of that inner language through signs and symbols.

As given, then:

Attune thine inner man to the harps and the chords of the universe, and harken to the love that brings service—service—to all. 1735-2

NOTES

Before Abraham Was

1. John 8:58.
2. *The Gospel According to Thomas;* Coptic Text Established and Translated by A. Guillaumont, H.C. Puech, G. Quispel, W. Till and Yassah 'Abd Al Masih; Harper & Bros., New York, 1959 (E.J. Brill, Leiden). (Subsequently, an English translation of this same gospel, by Thomas O. Lambdin, has appeared in *The Nag Hammadi Library,* edited by James M. Robinson; Harper & Row, N.Y., 1977.)
3. *Edgar Cayce on Reincarnation,* by Noel Langley; Hugh Lynn Cayce, editor. Hawthorn Books, Inc., New York, 1968.

Science and the Future

1. Teilhard de Chardin, Pierre: *The Phenomenon of Man,* p. 35. Harper & Brothers, N.Y., 1959.
2. Jefferies, Richard: *The Story of My Heart: My Autobiography,* pp. 39-40. Thomas B. Mosher, Portland, Maine, 1909.
3. Los Angeles *Times,* April 6, 1959, quoting Donald Hatch Andrews, professor of chemistry, Johns Hopkins University (article, "Statues That Sing").
4. *Time* magazine, July 4, 1955, quoting Dr. John R. Brobeck, professor of physiology, University of Pennsylvania (article, "Scientist on Miracles").
5. Beckett, L.C.: *Unbounded Worlds,* pp. 80-81. The Ark Press, London, 1959.
6. *Ibid.,* pp. 20-21.
7. Stromberg, Gustaf: *The Soul of the Universe,* p. 221. David McKay Co., Philadelphia, Pa., 1948. (2nd edition)
8. Eckhart, Johannes: *Meister Eckhart,* A Modern Translation by Raymond B. Blakney, p. 233, Harper & Brothers, N.Y., 1941.
9. Thoreau, Henry David: *Walden and Other Writings,* p. 275. The Modern Library, Random House, N.Y., 1950.
10. Einstein, Albert: *Cosmic Religion,* with Other Opinions and Aphorisms, p. 97. Covici Friede, N.Y., 1931.
11. Barnett, Lincoln: *The Universe and Dr. Einstein,* p. 105, William Sloan Associates, N.Y., 1957. (Revised edition.)
12. Op. cit., Einstein, pp. 48 & 52.
13. Bucke, Richard Maurice: *Cosmic Consciousness,* A Study in the Evolution of the Human Mind. E.P. Dutton & Co., N.Y., 1956. (18th edition.)
14. *Stanford Today,* published quarterly by Publications Service of Stanford Univ., Stanford, Calif. Winter 1969 issue. Article, "The New Copernican Revolution," by Willis W. Harman.
15. *The Center Magazine,* published bi-monthly by the Fund for the Republic, Inc., Santa Barbara, Calif. Nov.-Dec. 1969 issue. Article, "The Biological Revolution," by Paul R. Ehrlich.

16. Edgar Cayce reading 3976-18.
17. Ibid, 5749-3.
18. Ibid, 262-32.
19. The value of faith, or belief, has been scientifically demonstrated in biofeedback experimentation. (Refer p. 41, *The Dimensions of Healing: A Symposium,* The Academy of Parapsychology & Medicine, Los Altos, Calif., 1972.)

The Chronicles of Issa

1. *The Unknown Life of Jesus Christ; from an Ancient Manuscript Recently Discovered in a Buddhist Monastery in Thibet,* by Nicholas Notovitch; translated from the French by Virchand R. Gandhi. Indo-American Book Co., Chicago, 1907.
2. *Tibet,* by Thubten Jigme Norbu and Colin M. Turnbull; Simon & Schuster, N.Y., 1968.
3. The answer to this question—"From thirteen to sixteen"—may conceivably have been based upon a literal interpretation of the wording in which the question was posed. In other words, if Jesus had remained in India three years before crossing over into neighboring Nepal or Tibet, later returning to India, Cayce's answer might have ignored the second interval of residence. But this point remains highly speculative.
4. A reference to the Brahmins, a white race of priests and rulers; the highest caste in ancient India.
5. *The Aquarian Gospel of Jesus the Christ,* by Levi. Devorss & Co., Publishers; Los Angeles, 1964. (First published in 1908.)
6. Prince Shakya-Muni, believed by certain Buddhist sects to be the 20th incarnation of Buddha; born in Nepal, 1500 B.C., or perhaps earlier. (Other sects identify Shakya-Muni with Gautama, born circa 560 B.C., as the only Buddha.)
7. Origin of the Pali language is uncertain; generally traced to the 7th century B.C., and identified as the language used by the educated classes in Northern India.

Cycles of Vibration

1. Los Angeles *Times,* 11/22/67; "Science Notebook" column, by George Getze, *Times* science writer.
2. *CBS Evening News* television report from Temple Buell College, Denver, 10/16/70.
3. *The Power of Prayer on Plants,* by The Reverend Franklin Loehr (Presbyterian minister), Doubleday & Co., Inc., Garden City, N.Y., 1959.
4. *Science Digest,* November, 1970. Article, "Five Unexpected New Discoveries About the Moon," by Jeanne Reinhert, pp. 9-14.

The Almond—Symbol of Life

1. *The Secret Books of the Egyptian Gnostics,* by Jean Doresse; The Viking Press, N.Y., 1960; p. 48.

2. *Ibid.,* p. 48.

(*Note A—James:* Cayce reading 5749-7, Q&A-60, confirms the birth of three natural children to Mary and Joseph, beginning ten years after the birth of Jesus, who was immaculately conceived. These three, in succession of birth, were James, Ruth and Jude.)

(*Note B—Mariamne:* In *Hidden Records of the Life of Jesus,* by Jack Finegan (Pilgrim Press, Philadelphia, 1969, p. 261) reference is made to Berlin Papyrus 8502, a fifth-century Coptic codex identified in a colophon as *peuaggelion kata Marihamm,* or "The Gospel According to Mariam." The personal name is written in various forms as Mariham, Mariam, or Mariamme, and the author states that she is "probably to be identified with Mary Magdalene." The text of Berlin Papyrus 8502 is incomplete, but in certain passages this Gnostic manuscript bears some close similarities to *The Gospel According to Thomas.*)

3. "Before Abraham Was," by W.H. Church.
4. Same as (1), p. 92. (See Finegan, pp. 100-101, on the Pleroma.)
5. *Hunza Health Secrets,* by Renee Taylor; Prentice-Hall, Inc., Englewood Cliffs, N.J., 1964.
6. *Composition of Foods,* by B.K. Watt and A.L. Merrill, U.S.D.A. Agriculture Handbook No. 8, 1950.
7. *Almonds for All,* by J. DeWitt Fox, M.D. (An article originally published in *Life and Health* magazine, Washington, D.C., Nov. 1966.)
8. Annual Report for Fiscal Year ending June 30, 1970; California Almond Growers Exchange, Sacramento, California.
9. For an updating on this subject, including an evaluation of the mineral content of the almond, refer to "An Almond a Day," by W.H. Church, which appears in *An Edgar Cayce Health Anthology,* pp. 62-75; A.R.E. Press, Virginia Beach, Va., 1979.

Gods in the Making

1. Psalm 82:6, 7 (KJV).
2. Psalm 81:5 (KJV).
3. Harper & Bros., N.Y., 1959, pp. 9-10.
4. Exodus 20:3.
5. *Meister Eckhart,* trans. by Raymond B. Blakney, Harper & Bros., N.Y., 1941, p. 75.
6. *Ibid.,* p. 76.
7. John 5:30.
8. John 14:10.
9. *Ibid.*
10. John 10:30.
11. *Op. cit., Meister Eckhart,* p. 78.

Sunspots: Signs of Turmoil

1. Page 158, *Music of the Spheres,* by Guy Murchie; Houghton Mifflin Co., Boston, 1961.

2. *Ibid.*
3. "The Sun," pp. 48-50.
4. See the next essay, "Age of Glory," for an expansion of ideas expressed here.

Age of Glory
1. "Sunspots: Signs of Turmoil." *The A.R.E. Journal,* A.R.E. Press: Virginia Beach, Va., January, 1976, pp. 19-26.
2. See reading 5757-1.
3. See *The Jupiter Effect,* by John Gribbin and Stephen Plagemann. New York: Walker & Co., 1974.
4. See *The Scientific Basis of Astrology.* New York: Stein & Day, 1969.
5. "The Time the Sun Lost Its Spots," by Charles Petit. *San Francisco Chronicle,* December 12, 1975.
6. New York: Harper & Row, 1966.
7. From the book *The Sun Is Also a Star,* by Dane Rudhyar. Copyright © 1975 by Dane Rudhyar. Reprinted by permission of the publishers, E.P. Dutton & Co., Inc., pp. 3-4.
8. *Ibid.,* pp. 4, 10.
9. *The Astrologer's Handbook,* by Frances Sakoian and Louis S. Acker. New York: Harper & Row, 1973, p. 313.
10. See pp. 63-64, *Planets in Aspect,* by Robert Pelletier. Gloucester, Mass.: Para Research, Inc., 1974.
11. Sakoian and Acker, *op. cit.,* p. 313.
12. Uranus was discovered in 1781, Neptune in 1846.
13. Sakoian and Acker, *op. cit.,* p. 216.
14. *Astrology,* by Louis MacNeice. New York: Doubleday & Co., 1964, p. 91. (Note: The Sun King's natal chart shows Jupiter rising on the Ascendant. This alone would justify regarding him "as a Leo type," says MacNeice. It is a sign of kingly blessings, which was given special significance in ancient Chaldean astrology.) (However, see our subsequent essay, "Towards a New Astrology," for a rather different conclusion regarding "Leo" and "Kings.")
15. From p. 24 of the book *The Sun King,* by Nancy Mitford. Copyright © 1966 by Nancy Mitford. Reprinted by permission of the publishers, Harper & Row, N.Y.
16. The 420-year period from 1430 to 1850, which not only embraces the 70-year sunspot hiatus but also a hypothetical period of solar minima from 1468 to 1516, is sometimes referred to in rather exaggerated terms as "the Little Ice Age," based on records of cold extrema and glacier advances during those four centuries of generally reduced solar activity, although the evidence is not yet conclusive.

Patterns of Solar and Planetary Influence
1. See *Cosmic Influences on Human Behavior* and *The Scientific Basis of Astrology,* by Michel Gauquelin (Stein and Day, New

York, 1973). Other titles by the same author, which elaborate upon his theory, are also currently available.

2. "The natal distribution of the sun remains in complete conformity with the laws of chance," quoting Gauquelin, in *Cosmic Influences on Human Behavior,* p. 204.

3. Of Gauquelin's hypothetical "planetary effect in heredity," West and Toonder comment: "To call it 'heredity'. . .simply replaces one mystery with another." See *The Case for Astrology* (Coward-McCann, Inc., New York, 1970), p. 214.

4. Some of our charts, on Sun signs only, include birth statistics preceding the year 1800. Where birth statistics were available far enough prior to 1800, in a sufficient ratio to establish meaningful patterns of dispersal, it was fairly easy to compute sign positions for Uranus, Neptune and Pluto, thus providing some limited insights on the three outermost planets.

5. *The Scientific Basis of Astrology,* p. 233.

6. "Intuition is not by any means just a mysterious and unexplained certitude," writes Rupert Gleadow, in *The Origin of the Zodiac* (p. 21). "It was defined by Jung as 'perception by way of the unconscious, or perception of unconscious contents.' "

7. In our tabulations, we are only concerned with the frequency distribution of the Sun and the planets in the twelve signs. We have no way of determining the houses in which the distribution falls, which depends upon the individual horoscope.

8. Edited by Oscar Thompson; Dodd, Mead & Co., N.Y. (10th edition), 1975.

Towards a New Astrology

1. Interested readers may refer to *Astrological Origins,* by Cyril Fagan (Llewellyn Publications, St. Paul, Minn., 1973).

2. A typical example, perhaps, is Louis XIV of France, the "Sun King," who was a Virgo, with Scorpio as the sign on his Ascendant. A perfectionist of the higher order, as well as a dominant and forceful ruler, he stands most accurately revealed to us in the existing "tropical" characterizations for these two signs.

3. The current precession commences at a point where 0° Aries of the moving Zodiac passes across 0° of the constellation Aries, and moves backwards into the constellation Pisces. We place this in the period of Hipparchus, about 160 B.C. (According to reading 5749-8, the signs of the approach of the Piscean Age were observed by the Essenes as early as 300 years before the advent of the Christ, while the world was still technically in the cusp between Aries and Pisces.)

4. See Chapter Five of *Astrology and the Edgar Cayce Readings,* by Margaret H. Gammon, A.R.E. Press, 1973.

5. In the evolution towards a common astrology, the present conflict and confusion inherent in the existing Sun-sign symbols could perhaps be resolved by developing for the constellations a new set

of symbols, borrowing their inspiration from actual human attributes associated with each sign, rather than mythic or "animal" qualities.

Era of the Big Quake

1. *The Jupiter Effect,* by Gribbin and Plagemann (foreword by Isaac Asimov), New York: Walker & Co., 1974.
2. Cited in an article by Tom Emch, "Predicting the Next Great Quake," *San Francisco Sunday Examiner & Chronicle,* March 4, 1979.
3. See "Sunspots: Signs of Turmoil," by W.H. Church, *The A.R.E. Journal,* Vol. XI, No. 1, 1976; and its sequel, "Age of Glory," Vol. XI, No. 5, 1976.
4. All quotations attributed to Joe Brandt in this section have been excerpted from Chapter 10 of Paul James's book, *California Superquake 1975-77?* (2nd ed.), Hicksville, N.Y.: Exposition Press, 1975.
5. See Roberts's *The Complete Prophecies of Nostradamus* (ref. bibliography), which contains both French and English versions of the quatrains.

"His Name Shall Be John"

1. Edgar Cayce reading 3976-15.
2. Edgar Cayce reading 5749-5. (Also see 281-17, Q&A-2.)
3. See pp. 19-20, "Where Is John Peniel?"; by Lytle W. Robinson; Vulcan Books, Inc., Seattle, Wa., 1980.
4. A detailed account is contained in the following essay, entitled "The Fifth Option"; *The A.R.E. Journal,* Vol. XVII, No. 5 (September 1982).
5. The Hebrew meaning of John, or Johanan, is "Jehovah has favored."
6. Ref. article, "As Above, So Below," by W.H. Church; Vol. IX, Nos. 3 & 4 (May & July 1974; two parts), *The A.R.E. Journal.*

The Fifth Option

1. A.R.E. Press, Virginia Beach, Va., 1981.
2. See "Age of Glory: An Interpretation of the 70-Year Sunspot Hiatus (1645-1715)," by W.H. Church, *The A.R.E. Journal,* Vol. XI, No. 5, September 1976.
3. See *The Cycles of Heaven,* by Guy L. Playfair and Scott Hill, St. Martin's Press, N.Y., 1978, p. 152.
4. *Ibid.,* p. 27.
5. *Ibid.,* pp. 27-30.
6. G.D.T. advises us that the questions asked by Mr. T.M.H., in whose home the reading was given, were actually drawn up in advance of the reading. This exonerates the questioner, but it does not alter our supposition that Mr. Cayce chose to overlook that portion of Q-1 pertaining to a specific time-frame, "this year physically," and

simply answered in the broader terms of his prophecy as originally stated, namely, '58 to '98.

7. Job 9:9, 38:32.
8. *Q-7. Is etheronic energy amenable to mental control?*
   A-7. It is mental control.   (443-5)

The Music of the Spheres

1. The galactic core, it is now theorized by astronomers, is a massive black hole in space that alternately accretes and excretes matter. (Ref. article, "The Central Parsec of the Galaxy," by Thomas R. Geballe; June, 1979.)
2. Page 39, *Paracelsus: Selected Writings,* edited by Jolande Jacobi; Bollingen Series XXVIII, Princeton University Press, N.J., 1969.
3. *Ibid.,* p. 40.
4. Pages 3483 & 3634, *Arcana Coelestia.*
5. Ref. 945-1, confirming inclusion of Pluto as one of the spheres of consciousness. Also see 3126-1 and 900-10.
6. In his book, *Earths in the Universe,* Swedenborg describes in startling detail his out-of-body visitations to the various planets within our solar system, including a curious account of the inhabitants and other matters.
7. This raises an important philosophical question. To what extent may "forced labor" or Caesarean section disrupt the plan of a given soul-entity to use a certain channel for its re-entry into the earth? Does a different soul, perhaps, take over in such cases (at least occasionally) with resultant problems for all concerned? In the coming Aquarian Age, the emphasis should focus more and more upon "natural" childbirth, as opposed to the present "forced labor" techniques so frequently practiced by attending physicians for their own convenience.
8. See *Cosmic Influences on Human Behavior,* by Michel Gauquelin; Stein & Day, N.Y., 1973.
9. Ref. "Patterns of Solar and Planetary Influence," *The A.R.E. Journal,* May 1977 (Vol. XII, No. 3).
10. Ref. *The Hidden Laws of Earth: An Edgar Cayce Handbook,* by Juliet Brooke Ballard; A.R.E. Press, Virginia Beach, Va., 1979. (Note: The author is indebted to this excellent "source book" for many of the excerpts from the Edgar Cayce readings that appear in this article.)
11. William Morrow & Co., Inc., N.Y., 1976.

CHRONOLOGY OF PUBLICATION

The essays in this collection were all previously published in the pages of The A.R.E. *Journal (issues as indicated below), with the exception of the final essay, which has not been previously published.*

THE WORK OF EDGAR CAYCE TODAY

The Association for Research and Enlightenment, Inc. (A.R.E.®), is a membership organization founded by Edgar Cayce in 1931.

- 14,256 Cayce readings, the largest body of documented psychic information anywhere in the world, are housed in the A.R.E. Library/Conference Center in Virginia Beach, Virginia. These readings have been indexed under 10,000 different topics and are open to the public.

- An attractive package of membership benefits is available for modest yearly dues. Benefits include: a journal and newsletter; lessons for home study; a lending library through the mail, which offers collections of the actual readings as well as one of the world's best parapsychological book collections, names of doctors or health care professionals in your area.

- As an organization on the leading edge in exciting new fields, A.R.E. presents a selection of publications and seminars by prominent authorities in the fields covered, exploring such areas as parapsychology, dreams, meditation, world religions, holistic health, reincarnation and life after death, and personal growth.

- The unique path to personal growth outlined in the Cayce readings is developed through a worldwide program of study groups. These informal groups meet weekly in private homes.

- A.R.E. maintains a visitors' center where a bookstore, exhibits, classes, a movie, and audiovisual presentations introduce inquirers to concepts from the Cayce readings.

- A.R.E. conducts research into the helpfulness of both the medical and nonmedical readings, often giving members the opportunity to participate in the studies.

For more information and a color brochure, write or phone:

A.R.E., Dept. C., P.O. Box 595
Virginia Beach, VA 23451, (804) 428-3588

**EDGAR CAYCE FOUNDATION and
A.R.E. LIBRARY/VISITORS CENTER**
Virginia Beach, Va.
OVER 50 YEARS OF SERVICE

BUSINESS REPLY CARD
First Class Permit No. 2456, Virginia Beach, Va.

POSTAGE WILL BE PAID BY

A.R.E.®
P.O. Box 595
Virginia Beach, VA 23451